Contents

FOREWORD

Nearly every one of these recipes has a story, and as we make the recipe, we remember the person who gave it to us, and the occasion we met. Often it was in the supermarket, at suppers or at a party. These memories make cooking a pleasure. Many of these recipes have been a long time in the family, and a lot are from "The County"—Aroostook. Most of the ingredients used are readily available at the local grocery store.

Included in this cookbook are some of the recipes from previous editions. They are family standbys that have pleased the guests, gone to potluck and covered dish luncheons and suppers, picnics, wedding receptions, parties, and food sales. They have been requested again and again by cooks of all ages, and will probably prove popular with future cooks.

I started my "cooking career" at ten years of age, using a recipe my mother learned when she was a child. Our measuring cup was a coffee cup without a handle. The food on our farm was home-grown or picked in the wild, cooked on a wood stove and served to a hungry table of seven to eleven at each meal. During summer vacations from college I cooked for a woman and her granddaughter at their summer cottage. The menus and recipes were far different from the food on the farm—a learning experience! Cooking has always been an interesting and exciting way of life. I've enjoyed working with youngsters decorating cookies and making pies, and love to teach cooking classes.

The introduction in the grocery stores of convenience foods, including special dinners, gourmet dishes, ethnic foods and dietary menus, allows the busy homemaker to stop after work and pick up the family meal from the frozen food shelves or the deli, and put them in the microwave for the evening meal. Still, cooking from "scratch" can be an adventure, and we have noted lately that many magazine articles say that "scratch" cooking is on its way back. This cookbook will help the novice as well as the experienced cook.

Brownie Schrumpf

©Copyright 1989, Bangor Publishing Company
ISBN 0-9623890-0-5

CINDY'S GARDEN VEGETABLE DIP

1 green pepper, chopped
1 tomato, chopped
1 bunch scallions, sliced
1 (8 oz.) cream cheese, softened
½ cup sour cream
1 teaspoon dry mustard
1 teaspoon salt
½ teaspoon pepper

Soften cream cheese then mix in the sour cream. Prepare vegetables, chopping quite fine. Mix into the cheese mixture and add seasonings. Chill the dip to allow the flavors to blend.

SHRIMP STUFFED EGGS

12 hard-cooked eggs
1 can shrimp, drained, mashed
   Mayonnaise
   Salt and pepper to taste

Cut the cooked and peeled eggs lengthwise. Mash yolks; add shrimp and mayonnaise with seasonings and fill cavities mounding filling. Chill.

PETER'S KIELBASA SLICES

We still savor, in our mind, the kielbasa served as an hors d'oeuvre at an open house. Speared with a toothpick, this sliced kielbasa, or Polish sausage, competed with other hors d'oeuvres: stuffed mushroom caps, spinach balls and meat balls.

2 or 3 rings of kielbasa sausage
2 cups catsup
⅔ cups vinegar
⅔ cup brown sugar
2 teaspoons Worcestershire sauce
2 teaspoons soy sauce
   Onion salt or finely chopped onion to taste

Cook the sausage rings (as a rule the sausage comes this way) in boiling water for 15 to 20 minutes. Drain and slice in ¼-inch thick slices. Place in a casserole or baking dish. Prepare the sauce with the catsup, vinegar, brown, sugar, Worcestershire sauce, soy sauce and finely chopped onion or onion salt to taste. Pour over the sliced meat and bake for 20 to 25 minutes at 350°. Serve hot.

HORS D'OEUVRES

1

HAM AND CHEESE SNACKS

This recipe can be prepared to serve at your next party. It can be assembled ahead to be ready when the time comes for broiling.

2 tablespoons butter or margarine, softened
1 can (4½ ozs.) deviled ham
2 teaspoons minced onion
½ teaspoon prepared mustard
2 slices white bread, toasted
8 slices Cheddar cheese
   Chopped parsley

Combine butter, deviled ham and mustard in a small bowl; spread on bread. Place on baking sheet. Sprinkle with parsley; top with cheese. Broil 2 to 3 minutes or until cheese starts to melt. Cut in half and serve immediately.

NAVAJO FRY BREAD PIZZA

Fry bread is just what the name implies—a simple flour, salt, baking powder dough which is kneaded and quickly fried in a small amount of sizzling oil. It is a thin, slightly crunchy bread native to the American Southwest. It makes a good base for pizza, which may be cut in wedges for finger food appetizers.

2¼ cups flour
 ½ teaspoon salt
 ½ teaspoon baking powder
 1 cup warm water
   Vegetable oil for frying
 4 cups grated sharp Cheddar cheese
1⅓ cups finely chopped ripe olives
   Bottled or canned green chili salsa

Combine flour, salt and baking powder in a bowl. Stir in water until a dough forms. Turn out onto floured board and knead about 5 minutes, using extra flour to form a smooth dough. Separate dough into quarters. Let dough rest 5 minutes for easier handling. Pat or stretch dough into four (6 or 8-inch) circles. Poke a small hole through center of each. Fry dough rounds one at a time in ¼-inch sizzling oil in skillet for about 1 minute on each side, or until browned. Drain. Top each round with 1 cup cheese and ⅓ cup olives. Place under broiler for 2 to 3 minutes or until cheese is bubbly. Ribbon 2 to 3 tablespoons salsa over each round. Cut into wedges to serve. Makes 24 to 32 wedges.

DILLY BEANS

One of the vegetables on the hors d'oeuvres tray could be dilled green beans. These beans are picked while still small but firm—not quite as large as are used for green beans for dinner.

Green beans, whole, to pack 6 pint jars
1 quart vinegar
1 cup pure bag salt
3 cups cold water
Powdered alum
Dill
Garlic cloves
Horseradish root and leaf

Pick young, tender green beans; wash and remove ends. Sterilize pint jars. To each jar add 1 peeled clove of garlic, a 1-inch piece of horseradish root, 2 heads of fresh dill or 1 teaspoon dill seed. Fit prepared beans lengthwise in jar. Add ⅛ teaspoon powdered alum to each jar. In stainless steel cooking pot combine vinegar, salt and water. Bring to boiling and pour, boiling hot, over the beans in the jar. Add a washed grape leaf or a piece of a horseradish leaf to top of each jar. Leave about ¼ inch of head space in the jar. Seal jars according to manufacturer's directions. Store in a cool place.

JUNE'S SALMON PATE

This salmon pate was a conversation piece at a party. Canned smoked salmon was the base for a spread for small, crisp crackers, followed by a seafood casserole, tossed and jellied salads and hot rolls. A cheesecake with a choice of thawed strawberries or raspberries was the happy touch for dessert.

1 can smoked salmon
1 (8 oz.) package cream cheese
2 tablespoons grated or finely chopped onion
¼ teaspoon salt
1 tablespoon fresh lemon juice
Dash of pepper or Tabasco sauce
1 teaspoon grated horseradish
Chopped pecans, parsley or paprika

Beat the cream cheese until smooth and add the salmon, onion, salt, lemon juice, pepper and horseradish. Mix well. Make into a ball or log and roll, if desired, in chopped nut meats, fresh parsley or paprika. Chill for several hours. Once shaped in desired form, pate may be frozen.

3

PIZZA TREATS

These pizza treats were served at a wedding reception and kept the caterer busy because the supply ran out so fast. The pizza treats were quartered English muffins which make great finger food along with other goodies. The family will enjoy the whole half of a muffin as a quickie lunch.

> 1 can (8 oz.) tomato sauce
> 1 can (4¾ oz.) roast beef spread
> 2 tablespoons grated onion
> ½ teaspoon oregano
>   Dash of garlic powder
> 4 English muffins, split and toasted
> 1 cup (4 oz.) shredded Monterey Jack cheese

In small bowl, mix tomato sauce, roast beef spread, onion, oregano and garlic powder. Spread tomato mixture on toasted muffins and top with cheese. (Mozzarella cheese may be used instead of Monterey Jack.) Place muffins on baking sheet and broil about 4 inches from the broiler until hot and bubbly. Serve at once.

VEGETABLE-STUFFED MUSHROOMS

Mushrooms, stuffed, are wonderful as hors d'oeuvres or as an accompaniment to grilled fish or chicken.

> ½ pound medium-sized fresh mushrooms
> ½ cup diced tomato
> 2 tablespoons chopped celery
> 2 tablespoons garlic salad dressing
> 2 tablespoons chopped cucumber
> 1 tablespoon chopped green pepper
> 1 tablespoon chopped onion
> ⅛ teaspoon instant garlic powder
> 1 tablespoon chopped radish

Bottled low-calorie garlic salad dressing is used in this recipe. Rinse mushrooms, pat dry and remove stems. Set aside. Mix all remaining ingredients thoroughly. Spoon mixture into mushroom caps. Chill until ready to serve. Yields about 18 hors d'oeuvres.

DEVILED EGGS

6 hard-cooked eggs
2 tablespoons bottled lite Italian-style salad dressing
½ teaspoon prepared mustard
1 jar (2 oz.) drained, chopped pimiento
1 tablespoon chopped, fresh mushrooms
1 tablespoon chopped green pepper

Cut hard-cooked and shelled eggs in half lengthwise. Remove yolks and set whites aside. Mash yolks with fork. Stir in dressing and mustard until well-blended. Stir in remaining ingredients. Refill whites, using about 1 tablespoon yolk mixture for each egg half. Chill to blend flavors.

GREEK ISLAND

This recipe is a skinny dip for potato skins, fries and chips and it has a delicious flavor. Try a tablespoonful on a hot, baked potato.

½ cup lowfat cottage cheese
½ cup crumbled feta cheese
½ cup milk
1 teaspoon grated lemon peel
1 teaspoon oregano
 Pepper to taste

In container of electric blender combine all ingredients. Blend smooth, stopping to scrape sides as needed. Makes about 1 cup.

HELEN'S VEGETABLE DIP

The Thursday Club at the University of Maine took an evening trip to Hawaii via music, colored slides and an exhibition of hula dancing, followed by refreshments from Hawaiian recipes. A dip flavored with curry was served in a bowl surrounded with cucumber, green pepper, celery and carrot sticks. You may like to try this recipe.

2 cups mayonnaise
½ cup sour cream
¼ teaspoon turmeric powder
2 cloves garlic, minced
2 tablespoons curry powder
4 teaspoons sugar
½ to 1 teaspoon salt
2 teaspoons fresh lemon juice
¼ cup minced parsley

Combine and blend all ingredients. Chill for 6 hours or overnight.

JOHN'S CHEESE BALL

2 (8 ounces each) packages cream cheese
1 small pimiento, drained, chopped
1 tablespoon finely minced onion
1 lemon juice
1½ tablespoons finely shredded green pepper
1 tablespoon Worcestershire sauce
2 drops hot sauce
1½ cups shredded sharp Cheddar cheese
    Finely chopped nut meats

Mash the cream cheese or beat it in the electric mixer and beat in the shredded Cheddar cheese. Add lemon juice, Worcestershire sauce and hot sauce. Stir in pimiento, green pepper and onion. Chill until you are able to mold the mixture into a ball. Roll the ball in finely chopped nut meats; chill to serve.

CRAB DIP

1 package (3 oz.) cream cheese
1 can crabmeat, drained
1 tablespoon mayonnaise
1 teaspoon horseradish
½ teaspoon Worcestershire sauce
½ teaspoon onion juice
    Dash Tabasco sauce
    Juice of ½ lemon
    Salt and pepper

Beat cream cheese until fluffy; add seasonings and lemon juice. Blend in crabmeat and mayonnaise. Refrigerate for several hours before serving. May be heated and served hot in a chafing dish.

SPINACH BALLS

2 10-oz. packages frozen, chopped spinach, cooked and well-drained
1 cup grated Romano or Parmesan cheese
¾ cup softened margarine
6 eggs, beaten
2 cup Pepperidge Farms stuffing mix, dry

Blend all ingredients together, add salt and pepper to taste. Roll into balls and freeze. Before serving, place still frozen on cookie sheet and bake 10 minutes at 350°. Makes 60-70 balls.

PAT'S BLUEBERRY-APPLE RELISH

8 cups blueberries
8 cups apples, pared, cored, sliced
8 cups sugar
1 teaspoon powdered allspice
1 teaspoon mace
1 teaspoon nutmeg

Combine all of the ingredients in a large kettle. Mix well. Cook slowly over low heat, stirring frequently. Test some of the mixture on a plate to note if it has thickened. Pour into sterilized jars; seal and process in a boiling water bath for 10 minutes.

DILL PICKLES

When cucumbers in the garden are ready, we cover the whole patch each time, picking all cucumbers of eating and pickling size and larger. They are then sorted into gherkin, dill chunk, relish and, if some get by and become yellow, into ripe cucumber pickle sizes. We leave about a ¼-inch stem on each cucumber, cutting them from the vine with a knife.

20 to 25 dill-size cucumbers
 1 quart cider vinegar
 1 cup pickling salt
 3 quarts cold water
   Tiny red peppers
   Powdered alum
   Garlic
   Onion slices
   Horseradish root
   Dill

Wash the cucumbers with a brush to remove dirt. Put the cucumbers in a pail or bucket and cover with cold water; leave overnight. Wash and scald the jars and sterilize in boiling water. To each quart jar, add ⅛ teaspoon powdered alum, 1 slice onion, a 1-inch piece of horseradish root, 1 tiny red pepper, 1 clove garlic and 2 heads of fresh dill. (Dill heads have extra flavor when the seeds are fat and green.) Pack the pickles into each jar and top with 2 more heads of dill and a horseradish leaf or a couple of grape leaves, washed. In a kettle, bring to boiling salt, vinegar and water and pour, boiling hot, over contents of each jar. Run a knife down the sides of each jar to release any air bubbles. Liquid should cover the contents of each jar, leaving a ⅛-inch space at the top of the jar. Seal jars immediately. Store in cool dry place after marking date of canning.

CRANBERRY AND APPLE RELISH

This fresh mixture may be made a few days ahead of time and kept in a covered container in the refrigerator. It's a nice change from plain cranberry sauce.

    4 cups fresh cranberries (1 pound)
    2 apples, cored, with skins on
    2 oranges, seeded
 2½ cups sugar
    1 lemon, seeded

Wash and dry the fruit. Put the cranberries through the medium blade of the food grinder. Core, quarter and chop the apples. (Cortland apples are suggested as they do not darken as quickly as other apples when cut.) Quarter the oranges and the lemon, remove seeds and put the fruit through the food chopper. Mix all thoroughly, then add the sugar and stir to completely blend the mixture.

BREAD AND BUTTER PICKLES

Bread and butter pickles are always popular and are a good way to use those bushels of cucumbers that all seem to come at once from the garden. Zucchini pickles can be made from this same recipe.

    4 quarts thinly sliced cucumbers
    8 thinly sliced onions
    2 green peppers, seeded and sliced
  ½ cup canning or pickling salt
    4 cups sugar
 1½ teaspoons turmeric powder
  ½ teaspoon clove
 3½ teaspoons mustard seeds
 4½ cups vinegar

Wash cucumbers. Slice into ⅛-inch thickness. Mix with onions and green peppers; sprinkle salt over the prepared vegetables; toss to mix. Empty two or three trays of ice cubes over the mixture; let stand for 3 to 4 hours. In a large kettle, combine sugar, spices and vinegar; heat to boiling. Drain vegetables thoroughly. Add to the hot vinegar mixture. Heat over low heat to scalding. Stir frequently, carefully lifting the vegetables and turning them. Do not allow the mixture to boil. Ladle into hot sterilized jars; seal at once. Process in a boiling water bath for 10 minutes. Makes about 5 pints of pickles, depending on how they are packed. Leftover pickling syrup, if any, may be added to salad dressing, used as part of the liquid for barbecuing pork ribs or for another batch of pickles.

CAROLYN'S KANSAS RELISH

This is a bit different from the usual bean relish. This recipe comes from Kansas City and may be used as a relish or a salad.

1 8-ounce can French-style green beans, drained
1 8-ounce can tiny green peas, drained
1 8-ounce can whole-kernel corn, drained
1 sweet onion, sliced or chopped
½ cup salad oil
½ cup sugar
½ cup vinegar
    Crushed garlic

Put vegetables and onions in a bowl. In a saucepan, combine oil, vinegar and sugar. Season with salt, pepper and crushed garlic as desired. Bring to boiling and pour, while hot, over vegetables. Cool. Refrigerate.

COLD VINEGAR PICKLES

One of the pickles that Mother made on the farm was the cold vinegar (so-called) pickle. Every homemaker had a different name for it. When dinner pails were being packed with sandwiches, cookies, fruit and frequently a piece of pie, the children would run down to the cellar and, reaching down in the cold pickling liquid, find a pickle to put into the dinner pail. At the present time, with cellars heated by the furnace, crocks of pickles no longer fill the cellar. It took several crocks of pickles to give a family of eight the variety needed for winter menus—cold vinegar, sliced green tomatoes, chop (piccalilli), and generally a new recipe for a pickle. We now can in quart and 2-quart glass jars with tight seals.

1 gallon apple cider vinegar
1 cup canning or pickling salt
1 cup dry mustard
1 cup sugar
¼ cup pickling spice
    Horseradish leaves or grape leaves (optional)
    Cucumbers

In container mix vinegar with salt, sugar, mustard and pickling spices. Mix well. Pack fresh, crisp cucumbers in sterilized jars. Add a piece of horseradish leaf or a grape leaf (both have astringent properties, keeping pickles crisp). This pickling mixture may be kept in a glass container in the refrigerator for a few days to use as the cucumbers grow to the desired size.

IZETTA'S POTTSFIELD PICKLES

6 cups peeled ripe tomatoes, chopped
6 cups unpeeled green tomatoes, chopped
4 large onions, chopped
2 green peppers, chopped
1 sweet red pepper, chopped
2 to 2½ cups sugar
2 cups vinegar
1 teaspoon powdered cloves
1 teaspoon powdered cinnamon
¼ cup salt

Chop ripe and green tomatoes; measure into large glass or stainless steel bowl. Mix with chopped onions and peppers. Sprinkle with salt. Allow to set overnight. In morning, drain for 1 hour. In a kettle, combine drained vegetables, sugar, vinegar, clove and cinnamon. Cook until soft and thickened. Taste for sweetness as you may like a sweeter relish. Ladle into hot sterilized jars; seal. Process in boiling water bath for 5 minutes. We use the bottom of a large roaster and cook this relish in a slow oven, 225°, stirring occasionally, until liquid has simmered down and relish has thickened. A taste-test is best for determining how you like this relish!

OPAL'S SWEET GARLIC DILL PICKLES

Now you can add these pickles from "the County" to the pickle shelves in the cellar.

5 cups granulated sugar
½ cup canning salt
4 cups vinegar
2 cups water
¼ teaspoon powdered alum
Cucumbers, cut in chunks
Sliced onion
Garlic cloves
Dill heads

Wash and cut cucumbers (slicing size or larger — not ripe) into chunks. Place in sterilized glass jars after putting a ¼-inch-thick slice of onion in the bottom of each. If chunks are seedy, remove seeds. Add 2 or 3 cloves of garlic to each jar and 2 or 3 heads of dill, depending on size of jar. Put another slice of onion on top of the pickle chunks. In kettle combine sugar, salt, vinegar, water and alum. Bring to boiling and pour over the packed cucumbers. Wipe tops of jars and seal according to manufacturer's directions.

MARGE'S ADIRONDACK PICKLES

5 pounds small (3- or 4-inch) cucumbers
4 large onions
1 bunch celery
2 hot peppers
2 sweet green peppers
½ cup salt
Water to cover vegetables
1 quart vinegar
3 cups sugar
½ cup all-purpose flour
1 teaspoon dry mustard
2 teaspoons turmeric

Wash vegetables and cut into small pieces. Soak overnight in brine made with ½ cup pickling salt and water to cover. In the morning, drain well. Make a paste with vinegar, sugar, flour, dry mustard and turmeric. Mix well and cook until slightly thickened. Add drained and cut-up vegetables. Let come to a boil and cook until all ingredients are hot, 10 to 15 minutes. The vegetables must remain crisp; do not boil. Seal in jars and process in boiling water bath for 20 minutes.

PICKLED EGGS

1½ tablespoon dry mustard
2 cups distilled white vinegar or cider vinegar
¼ cup water
1 cup sugar
3 teaspoons salt
1 tablespoon celery seed
1 tablespoon mustard seed
6 whole cloves
2 medium onions, sliced
12 to 14 hard-cooked eggs, peeled

If desired, 3 or 4 peppercorns or ¼ teaspoon pepper may be added and two cloves of garlic are suggested. In a saucepan, blend mustard with a little vinegar; add remaining vinegar, water, sugar, salt, celery seed, mustard seed and cloves. (If pepper is used, add at this time.) Cover; heat to boiling; simmer 10 minutes; cool. While mixture is cooling, put hard-cooked eggs and sliced onions in a glass jar (add garlic cloves at this time, if used.) Pour cooled mixture over eggs. Cover; refrigerate overnight. These eggs will keep for several days in the refrigerator.

DOT'S DUTCH SALAD (PICKLES)

This Dutch salad is a sweet mustard pickle that is a real treat with baked beans, or any meat or fish menu. It is a good item for food sales. Nearly all gardens will yield the ingredients for the pickle.

1 quart onions
2 quarts green tomatoes
1 small cabbage
1 medium cauliflower
1 quart small cucumbers
2 sweet green peppers

Chop all vegetables into pieces about ¾ inches square; measure into kettle and cook in one cup of pickling salt (so-called bag salt) with water to cover the vegetables, until vegetables are done. Drain the vegetables, and while they are draining prepare the following:

5 cups sugar
1 cup flour
8 teaspoons dry mustard
1 quart cider vinegar
1 quart water
1 teaspoon turmeric

Using the same large kettle in which the vegetables were cooked, cook this mixture, stirring constantly until thickened. Add drained vegetables and bring the mixture back to boiling. Immediately put into hot sterilized jars and seal jars immediately according to manufacturer's directions. Makes 5 quarts or a little more of pickles.

PARTY PUNCH

1 cup orange juice
¼ cup fresh lemon juice
2 cups cranberry juice cocktail
1 cup pineapple juice
2 cups apple cider or apple juice
2 quarts chilled ginger ale

In large bowl, combine all juices; mix well. Just before serving, pour over ice (or a mold of frozen juice) in the punch bowl. Add ginger ale. Makes about 30 punch-cup servings. SUGGESTION: All fruit juices may be combined in a gallon container and refrigerated overnight to be ice cold when added with the chilled ginger ale. A mold of any frozen fruit juice is better than plain ice because as it melts, the juices add to the punch rather than dilute the flavor. The addition of ¼ cup lime juice adds a refreshing flavor and a "zip" to the punch.

RUSSIAN TEA

In 1960 we made our first so-called Russian tea, a mixture of instant iced tea, with lemon and sugar added, and Tang orange crystal. This was served iced. In addition to using the tea for iced tea, a recipe came for making hot Russian tea. This was served as a spiced, hot beverage at many occasions. There are many recipes for the same drink. This is the original recipe according to the makers of the first combination.

1 cup iced tea mix
1 (17.3 oz.) jar of Tang
1½ cups sugar
2 teaspoons cinnamon
1 teaspoon allspice
1 teaspoon ground cloves

Mix all ingredients together. When a cup of hot beverage is desired, use a heaping tablespoon of the mixture to one cup of boiling water. The amount of sugar may be reduced by ½ cup to make a less sweet drink. Keep in a tightly sealed jar.

PUNCH FOR ONE-HUNDRED

For a special occasion try this fruit punch. Freeze an extra 16-ounce can of pineapple juice mixed with a 6-ounce can of orange juice in a ring mold or bowl to use as ice for the punch. As the juice melts it adds flavor instead of diluting the punch.

1 can (16 oz.) frozen orange juice concentrate
1 can (6 oz.) frozen limeade concentrate
1 can (12 oz.) frozen lemonade concentrate
2 cans (46 oz. each) unsweetened pineapple juice
2½ quarts water
2 quarts ginger ale

Chill pineapple juice, water and ginger ale. Combine all juices in a large 16-quart kettle. Chill ginger ale until ready to mix punch for serving. Ice ring may be made a few days ahead.

EASY BOUILLABAISSE

This recipe is called easy bouillabaisse. It differs much from the real dish but will be an interesting mixture. In the recipe, 1 (8 oz.) can of tuna and 1 (6 oz.) can of tiny shrimp may replace the salmon or 1 (6 oz.) can of crabmeat may be used. This is a good winter dish.

1 medium onion, chopped
1 16-oz. can salmon, flaked
2 tablespoons olive oil
1 16-oz. can whole tomatoes
1 teaspoon dry basil
  Pinch of saffron, optional
1 14½-oz. can spaghetti in tomato sauce
1 14-oz. can chicken broth
1 cup shredded Gruyere or Swiss cheese

Flake, bone and remove skin of salmon. If crabmeat is used instead of salmon, remove cartilage. One tablespoon chopped, fresh basil may be used in place of 1 teaspoon of dry basil.
Saute onion in olive oil until tender but not brown; add tomatoes, basil and saffron. Bring to a boil and simmer 5 minutes. Add spaghetti, chicken broth, salmon or tuna, shrimp or crabmeat; heat to boiling, stirring gently to mix. Serve topped with shredded cheese. Makes 4 to 6 servings.

CHICKEN ASPARAGUS SOUP

Serve soup and sandwiches for a meal when calorie counting is needed. Just because it is only soup and a sandwich doesn't mean it has to be plain, everyday food; a touch of seasoning will make this soup special. A cabbage or fruit salad may be served to add texture to the meal.

1 can (15 oz.) all green asparagus cut spears
1 can (10¾ oz.) cream of chicken soup
½ teaspoon curry powder
  Dash of pepper
¾ cup milk
  Chopped parsley
  Toasted coconut
  Toasted slivered almonds

Drain asparagus, reserving liquid. In saucepan, combine reserved liquid, soup, curry and pepper. Bring to boil, stirring constantly. Slowly add milk and asparagus, including the tips. Reduce heat and simmer 5 minutes. Serve topped with parsley, coconut and nuts. Six servings (approximately ⅔ cup each)

SOUPS AND CHOWDERS

CLAM CHOWDER

3 cups shucked clams
4 cups diced potatoes
¼ pound salt pork
3 medium onions
4 cups milk
2 tablespoons butter
Salt and pepper

Chop the hard part of the clams and cook with potatoes in a small amount of water until potatoes are tender. While potatoes cook, "try out" salt pork in a frying pan; cut onions in thin wedges and cook in pork fat until golden. Add onions, salt pork fat and pork scraps to the potatoes. Add soft part of clams and milk. Cook slowly for 15 to 20 minutes until milk is hot and flavors have blended. Add butter; salt and pepper to season.

AUDREY'S BEAN SOUP

A different treat for the cold-weather menu is a bean soup made from a combination of a variety of beans. In this pound of dry beans, we noted yellow eye, black, soldier, Jacob's cattle, pea, pinto, and a few other varieties of beans. This hardy soup is a delicious combination of flavors. Serve it with crisp crackers, bran muffins or johnnycake plus a green salad. It reheats and freezes well.

1 pound mixed dried Maine beans
2 tablespoons salt
4 cups water
2 quarts water
1 ham hock or pieces of ham
1 large onion, chopped
1 large can of tomatoes
1 pod of red pepper or 1 teaspoon chili powder
Juice of 1 lemon
Salt and pepper to taste

Pick over beans. Wash and soak overnight in 4 cups of water to which 2 tablespoons of salt have been added. In the morning, drain beans and put into a kettle with the ham hock or pieces of ham. Beef or lamb may be used in place of the ham. (We used a small slice of smoked ham shoulder, removing the fat from the meat.) Add 2 quarts of water; cover and simmer for 2½ to 3 hours or until beans are tender. Then add tomatoes, chopped onion, lemon juice, and red pepper or chili powder with salt and pepper to season. Simmer 45 minutes to an hour to blend flavors.

LOBSTER STEW

The lobster feed is enjoyed by inlanders as well as those on the coast. One of the delicious aftermaths of a lobster feed is a lobster stew. The coral (eggs in some lobsters) and tomalley (lobster liver) add good flavor, plus the meat from claws and body of the crustacean, picked by patient lobster "pickers." We find that it takes about five 1¼-pound lobsters to make 1 pound or 3 cups of clear meat.

2 quarts milk
¼ to ½ cup butter or margarine
2 to 3 cups lobster meat
    Salt and pepper to season
    Coral and tomalley

In a kettle, melt butter over low heat and saute the lobster meat, stirring until meat is pink in color. Add milk and continue cooking, stirring frequently. Reduce heat; do not boil. A double boiler at this stage is recommended. The stew will have blossomed to a rosy color. Add tomalley and coral. Heat to serve hot. Many cooks prepare the stew early in the day, refrigerate and reheat when needed.

TOMATO BISQUE

A Sunday-night dish on the farm was tomato bisque as a means of using the supply of ripe tomatoes not used in canning. It also was made in the winter from canned tomatoes and from some frozen tomatoes we were experimenting with. Don't wait for a Sunday night; use this for any meal!

¼ cup butter or margarine
½ cup flour
½ teaspoon salt
    Few grains pepper
    Few grains Cayenne pepper
4 cups milk
2 or 3 cups tomatoes, fresh, cooked or frozen

Melt butter and add flour, salt, pepper and Cayenne pepper. When mixed, add milk slowly, stirring all the while until a thickened mixture evolves. When smooth, add tomatoes, cut if fresh or broken apart if canned or frozen. We generally heat the tomatoes and blend a small amount of the mixture with them before adding to the cooking pot. Taste for more seasoning.

MEXICAN FRANKFURTER SOUP

This Mexican frankfurter soup is a change from fish chowder or chicken soup.

1 can (16 oz.) baked beans
1 cup water
1 tablespoon chili powder
6 frankfurters
   Shredded Cheddar cheese
   Crushed taco chips

Combine beans and water in a saucepan. Add chili powder and frankfurters and bring to a boil. Reduce heat and simmer for 5 minutes. Serve topped with cheese and crushed taco chips. Makes 4 servings.

CORN AND CHICKEN CHOWDER

1 broiler-fryer chicken (2½ to 3 pounds)
2 cups water
2 large onions, quartered, divided
1 large carrot, cut in chunks
2 stalks celery, cut in chunks
¼ teaspoon salt
¼ pound bacon, diced
1 medium green pepper, diced
2 tablespoons flour
¼ teaspoon Tabasco pepper sauce
4 medium potatoes, cubed
2 12-ounce cans whole-kernel corn
1½ cups milk
½ cup cream

In large saucepot, combine chicken, which has been cut in quarters, water, 1 onion, carrot, celery and salt. Bring to boil. Cover and simmer 30 minutes, or until tender. Remove chicken and vegetables. Reduce broth by boiling rapidly until you have 2 cups. Remove chicken from bones and cut in small pieces; measure 2 cups; reserve. In large saucepot, fry bacon until lightly browned. With slotted spoon, remove bacon bits; set aside. Dice remaining onion; saute onion and green pepper in bacon fat until soft. Blend in flour; gradually stir in broth. Add Tabasco sauce and potatoes. Bring to boil. Cover and simmer 10 to 15 minutes until potatoes are tender. Add corn and reserved chicken. Heat 5 minutes. Scald milk and cream; add to chowder. Heat to simmer. Sprinkle with bacon bits to serve. Makes 8 servings.

GRAND CENTRAL OYSTER BAR STEW

1 pint medium oysters
1 cup oyster liquid
6 tablespoons butter
2 teaspoons Worcestershire sauce
½ teaspoon celery salt
1 teaspoon paprika
1 cup light cream
   Salt to season
2 cups milk

Pick over oysters to remove any bits of shell; reserve oyster liquid. Put 4 tablespoons butter in a saucepan; add Worcestershire sauce, celery salt and paprika. Add oysters and bring to simmer; add oyster liquor and bring to boiling. Add milk and cream. Bring to simmer. Add salt to taste. Dip stew into four bowls for serving; add ½ tablespoon butter to each serving.

COLLECTOR'S SOUP

It is easy and convenient to open a can of soup to heat. There is no need for any additions. But, when there are leftovers, a very tasty soup may evolve, with the addition of herbs, maybe a boullion cube or other favorite soup additions. Put a name to it, and it will taste great with crisp crackers or dry toasted bread, spread with garlic butter. Of course, not all homemakers will have the same leftovers, but this soup could be a pattern for others.

1 small piece cooked London broil
3 small slices cold roast lamb
1 onion, uncooked
   Pepper
   Thyme, to season
   Basil, to season
1 cup red cabbage, raw
1 large carrot, sliced
2 raw potatoes, pared, cubed
   Salt
   Garlic salt, to season
   Chicken or beef bouillon cube

This soup really started with the leftover red cabbage, meats and raw onion, plus water to simmer the soup slowly and more water as the liquid boiled down. Then the herbs were added. Simmer until vegetables are tender.

SALMON BISQUE

Salmon bisque and crisp crackers with fruit for dessert can make a meal.

¼ cup (½ stick) butter or margarine
1 medium onion, finely chopped
1 cup finely chopped celery
3 tablespoons all-purpose flour
½ medium green pepper finely chopped
1 teaspoon salt
⅛ teaspoon pepper
4 cups skim milk
1 can (15 oz.) salmon
2 tablespoons chopped pimiento

In saucepan, melt margarine; saute onion, green pepper and celery until tender. Stir in flour, salt and pepper. Remove from the heat and gradually add milk. Return to heat and cook, stirring constantly, until thickened. Add salmon which has been flaked and the soft bones crushed. Stir in pimiento at this time. Simmer until serving temperature. Makes six 8-ounce servings. Pimiento may be omitted, if desired.

SPLIT PEA SOUP

A hot soup on a cold day is one of the most comforting of all cold-weather foods. Any soup will do, but a pea soup is especially good. There are many recipes for the soup; this recipe has a fine flavor. Add to or subtract from the recipe to suit your taste. We like to add sliced carrots to this soup.

1 pound split peas
8 cups water
1 onion, chopped
1 cup chopped ham pieces or ham bone
1 tablespoon salt
¼ teaspoon pepper
    Roux, if desired for thickening

Pick over and wash split peas. In a large soup kettle, combine peas, water, onion, salt, pepper and ham pieces, ham bone or ham hock. Cover and simmer until desired thickness. If desired, a roux may be made for thickening. For the roux, combine 2 tablespoons butter or margarine with 2 tablespoons flour; add to simmering soup and stir until soup is slightly thickened. Years ago, a piece of salt pork was put into the simmering soup when ham was not available.

CORN CHOWDER

3 slices salt pork or 3 tablespoons butter
4 large potatoes
2 large onions
1 can cream-style corn
1½ cups milk
    Salt and pepper to season
6 common crackers or saltines

Cut salt pork in small cubes and try out (fry) in kettle. Pare and cube potatoes. Slice onions; add to salt pork fat and cook until golden. Remove pork "scraps" and save to garnish chowder. Add potatoes to onions and water to cook vegetables. When vegetables are tender, add canned corn, milk, and salt and pepper. Cook chowder slowly after adding milk. If common crackers are available, soak them, after splitting, in cold milk for 10 minutes; add to top of each bowl of chowder, with salt pork scraps. If butter is used, saute onions in it and proceed as above. Saltines will not need soaking in milk before being added to each serving. Serves 4.

FISH AND LOBSTER CHOWDER

To stretch the meat from a lobster, try this stew which includes halibut.

1½ pounds halibut
1½ pound lobster
 4 tablespoons butter
 4 cups cubed raw potatoes
 1 large onion, sliced
 2 slices salt pork or 4 tablespoons butter
 2 teaspoons salt
⅛ teaspoon pepper
 1 quart milk

Simmer the halibut in 1½ cups water for about 15 minutes, or until it flakes easily when tested with a fork. Reserve cooking liquid. Cook lobster; cool and remove meat. Cut in generous pieces. Saute lobster meat slowly in butter to bring out the rosy color. Try out the salt pork; add onion and cook until golden. In a stew kettle, combine salt pork fat and pork scraps, if used, with onion and potatoes; add water to barely cover. Cook until potatoes are tender. Add cooking liquid from fish. Remove skin and bones from fish and break fish into bite-size pieces. Add fish and lobster, milk and seasonings. Taste for further seasonings. For a richer stew, add half and half or cream to the stew as part of the milk. Makes 6 servings.

PARSNIP STEW

3 thin slices salt pork
3 medium-sized potatoes
  Salt and pepper
2 or 3 large parsnips
2 cups milk

"Try out" salt pork; leave crispy brown pieces of pork with fat. Add potatoes, pared and cut in ⅛-inch slices. Pare and slice parsnips in same thickness. Add to potatoes. Add water to cover vegetables and cook until tender. Add milk and season with salt and pepper. If you prefer to omit the salt pork, use ¼ cup butter or margarine. This stew rewarms. If desired, more milk may be added.

SEAFOOD CHOWDER

2 tablespoons butter or margarine
2 onions, sliced
4 medium potatoes, pared, diced
½ pound fish (hake or other fish)
1 can minced clams
¾ cup frozen shrimp or 1 can
1 teaspoon salt
⅛ teaspoon pepper
3 cups milk
½ cup evaporated milk

Cook onions in butter until golden. Add liquid from canned clams, potatoes and a small amount of water for cooking potatoes. When potatoes are nearly tender, add clams. Lay the piece of fish on top of vegetables; cover and simmer until fish flakes. Add shrimp and cook for 5 minutes. Then, add milk and evaporated milk (or an equal amount of cream). Taste for further seasoning. You may wish to add more milk to the chowder. Crabmeat or scallops may be substituted for the shrimp.

SOUTHWESTERN PORK SALAD

2 cups cut up lean cooked pork
1 (16 oz.) can kidney beans, drained, rinsed
1 small can pitted black olives
½ cup chopped onion
½ cup chopped green pepper
1 large tomato, peeled, seeded, chopped (1 cup)
2 tablespoons sugar
¼ cup cider vinegar
¼ cup cooking oil
½ teaspoon dry mustard
½ teaspoon cumin
½ teaspoon oregano
¼ to ½ teaspoon salt
2 tablespoons chopped parsley

Mix cooked pork, kidney beans, olives, onion, green pepper and tomatoes in a large bowl. Combine the remaining ingredients in a jar; shake to mix. Pour over pork mixture, toss and refrigerate several hours, stirring occasionally. Serves 6.

FIESTA BEAN SALAD

For barbecues, picnics and patio suppers, fiesta bean salad is summer-perfect. The colorful combination of kidney beans, corn, red pepper, rice and scallions takes on a Southwestern flair with a spicy cumin-accented dressing. Prepare this salad up to a day in advance of serving to allow flavors to mix and mingle.

2 cups cold cooked rice
1 can (16 oz.) kidney beans, rinsed
1 cup fresh cooked or frozen kernel corn
1 medium red (or green) pepper
½ cup sliced green onions with tops
½ to ⅔ cup PACE piquante sauce, as desired
¼ cup Italian dressing
1 teaspoon ground cumin
½ teaspoon salt

Rinse and drain the beans. Thaw corn kernels or use 1 can (8 oz.) drained, canned corn. Cut red pepper into 1"x ¼" strips. Combine rice, beans, corn, red pepper and green onions in medium bowl. Combine piquante sauce, Italian dressing, cumin and salt. Pour over rice mixture; toss. Cover and chill. Makes 6 to 8 servings, about 5½ cups salad.

SALADS

BLUE CHEESE POTATO SALAD

4 cups diced potato
1 cup diced celery
3 tablespoons minced onion
½ cup mayonnaise
½ cup blue cheese salad dressing
2 hard-cooked eggs, cut in wedges
   Salt and pepper
   Parsley for garnish

Cook potatoes in salted, boiling water until tender. Chill. To the diced potatoes add celery and onion. Combine mayonnaise and blue cheese dressing and mix into the potatoes. Garnish with egg wedges and parsley.

CHICKEN SALAD

1 5 to 6-pound roasting chicken
1 stalk celery
1 small carrot, cut
1 small onion, sliced
1 teaspoon seasoned salt
½ teaspoon pepper
   Mayonnaise or salad dressing
4 cups water
   Juice of one lemon
   Salt and pepper
   Grated onion
½ cup chopped, toasted pecan meats
   Lettuce

Wash chicken after removing the small package of giblets. To the cooking water add chicken, celery, carrot, sliced onion and seasoned salt and pepper. Bring water to boiling, then lower temperature to simmering for about 1½ hours, until chicken is tender. It is not necessary to cut up the chicken before cooking. Remove cooked chicken and allow to cool until it can easily be handled. Reserve cooking liquid to use as broth or for soup. Remove the meat from the bones, leaving it in large pieces. Cover and refrigerate until needed. For salad cut the meat in desired size pieces. Add the juice of 1 lemon, salt, pepper and grated onion, if desired. Saute the chopped pecans in butter and add to the salad mixture, larger pieces for salad, small for sandwiches. Add mayonnaise to mix and serve on lettuce as a salad, or use as filling for sandwiches. Always keep the cooked meat under refrigeration until used. As a rule, 1 pound of whole chicken yields 1 cup of meat.

ORIENTAL CARROT SLAW

⅓ cup peanut oil
3 tablespoons orange juice concentrate
2 tablespoons vinegar
2 tablespoons soy sauce
½ teaspoon ground ginger
3 cups finely shredded cabbage
3 cups shredded carrots
¼ cup thinly sliced scallions (green onions)

In a large bowl combine oil, orange juice concentrate, vinegar, soy sauce and ginger. Beat with fork or wire whip until smooth. Add cabbage, carrots and scallions; toss well to coat evenly. Cover and refrigerate until ready to serve. Yields about 5 cups.

LEONE'S PINEAPPLE-CABBAGE-CARROT SALAD

4 packages (3 oz. each) lemon flavored-gelatin
2 cans (1 lb., 4 oz. each) crushed pineapple
2 envelopes plain gelatin
1 cup cold water
6 tablespoons lemon juice
4 teaspoons vinegar
2 teaspoons salt
3 cups finely shredded cabbage
3 cups finely shredded carrot
1 medium green pepper, shredded

Drain crushed pineapple. To pineapple juice, add enough water to make a total of 2 quarts of liquid. Bring to boiling and pour over lemon flavored gelatin. Soak plain gelatin in cold water for 10 minutes; add to pineapple mixture; mix. Add lemon juice, vinegar and salt. Chill until slightly thickened, then fold in prepared vegetables and pineapple. Pour into water-rinsed molds or pans; chill to set. Makes 25 servings. Serve with mayonnaise or Leone's ginger dressing.

LEONE'S GINGER DRESSING

¼ pound cream cheese
½ pound cottage cheese
¼ cup pineapple juice
½ cup sour cream
¼ cup ginger marmalade or ginger topping
¼ teaspoon salt

Mix and beat well cream cheese, cottage cheese, pineapple juice and sour cream, until smooth. Add ginger marmalade and salt.

SPINACH SALAD

1½ pounds fresh spinach
8 ounces fresh bean sprouts
1 (8½ oz.) can water chestnuts
5 slices bacon, cooked and crumbled
Salt and pepper to taste
2 hard-cooked eggs, sliced
⅔ cup salad oil
⅓ cup sugar
⅓ cup catsup
⅓ cup vinegar
⅓ cup finely chopped green onion or scallions
2 teaspoons Worcestershire sauce

Trim the spinach leaves, discarding coarse stems. Wash thoroughly in several waters; pat dry. Tear leaves into bite-size pieces and place in salad bowl. Drain and slice water chestnuts and add to spinach along with sprouts. Crumble the drained bacon into the vegetables. Cover and refrigerate. In a jar or bowl, combine oil, sugar, catsup, vinegar, green onions and Worcestershire sauce. Stir and chill. Just before serving, shake dressing well and pour over the greens. Toss to mix. Sprinkle the salad with salt and pepper and garnish with slices of the hard-cooked eggs.

SPINACH SALAD II

When lettuce prices go up, try this spinach salad with bacon.

1 cup slice green onions
¾ pound bacon, cooked crisp and crumbled
1 package (10 ounces) frozen peas, uncooked
2 cups cherry tomatoes
2½ cups fresh spinach leaves
½ cup sour cream
½ cup mayonnaise (not salad dressing)
½ teaspoon oregano
¼ teaspoon cumin
1 teaspoon salt

Place frozen peas on a towel and allow to thaw and dry. Combine all vegetables in a large bowl. In another bowl, combine sour cream, mayonnaise, oregano, cumin and salt; mix and spread over the contents of the first bowl. Do not mix. Cover the bowl with a damp cloth and refrigerate overnight. Toss just before serving.

MARILYN'S MASHED POTATO SALAD

Try a mashed potato salad. It is a cold salad with lots of flavor. Serve with slices of baked ham, with toasted frankfurters or with barbecued pork ribs. This recipe came from The County—Aroostook—and is a long-time favorite.

8 large potatoes
6 eggs, hard cooked
1 large onion, grated
  Pepper to season
  Salt to season
  Vinegar
  Mayonnaise

Pare and boil potatoes; mash with potato ricer or masher. Mash eggs with a fork after reserving one yolk to use as a garnish. Combine potato, onion, salt and pepper in a large bowl with mashed eggs, with mayonnaise to make a creamy mixture. Add 2 or 3 tablespoons vinegar for flavor. (Try tarragon vinegar.) Mix all well, smooth top and sprinkle with the reserved egg yolk, mashed. Cover and chill.

WINTER SALAD

This winter salad uses a mixture of red and green cabbage for color and flavor. Make it fresh, adding the oil and vinegar when ready to serve.

½ head small green cabbage, shredded
½ head small red cabbage, shredded
1 medium onion, chopped
3 carrots, shredded
1 clove garlic, mashed
2 apples chopped, not too fine
1 cup dill beans or pickles, cut in small pieces
½ teaspoon basil
¼ teaspoon oregano
1 teaspoon celery seed
¼ teaspoon marjoram
1 cup olive oil
¼ cup vinegar
  Salt and pepper to taste

If not all vegetables are available, use what are on hand. Combine prepared vegetables. Mix olive oil with vinegar, crushed garlic, basil, oregano, marjoram and celery seed with salt and pepper to season. Add to salad and toss. (You may not need all the dressing on one salad.) Add chopped apples last.

COMMON SENSE COLE SLAW

½ cup mayonnaise
2 tablespoons honey
½ teaspoon grated lemon peel
2 tablespoons lemon juice
½ teaspoon salt
¼ teaspoon ground ginger
2 cups shredded red cabbage
2 cups shredded green cabbage

In a medium bowl, stir together mayonnaise, honey, lemon peel and juice, salt and ginger. Add cabbage; toss to coat well. Cover; chill at least 2 hours. Makes 8 servings.

COBB SALAD—SURIMI SEAFOOD STYLE

Surimi seafood is a restructured fish product that has been flavored, textured and shaped to resemble shellfish. Although surimi seafood looks and tastes like crab, shrimps, scallops or lobster, it is made from abundant and economical whitefish. It is convenient, nutritious and relatively inexpensive. In some markets it is labeled as surimi seafood, crab legs or seafood royale. Use in salads, casseroles, sandwiches and other dishes.

12 ounces surimi blended seafood, crab flavored
1 avocado, diced
4 teaspoons lemon juice
  Chopped salad greens
2 tomatoes, diced
2 hard-cooked eggs, chopped
1 small cucumber, peeled, diced
4 tablespoons crumbled blue cheese
  Creamy dressing

Toss surimi seafood with 2 teaspoons lemon juice. Arrange chopped salad greens in large shallow bowl or on individual serving plates. Arrange rows of tomato, egg, avocado, surimi seafood, cucumber and blue cheese over salad greens. Pass creamy dressing. Yield: 4 main dish servings.

CREAMY DRESSING

Combine ¾ cup dairy sour cream, 1 tablespoon vinegar, 1 teaspoon Dijon-style mustard, ¼ teaspoon sugar and a dash of bottled hot pepper sauce. (Lacking hot pepper sauce, use a dash of Cayenne pepper.) Mix well. Chill until served. Yield: about ¾ cup.

TRIPLE FRUIT SALAD

2 (3 oz. each) packages strawberry or lemon gelatin
2 cups boiling water
2 (10 oz. each) frozen, sliced strawberries
1 (13½ oz.) can crushed pineapple
2 large bananas, diced
2 tablespoons lemon juice

Drain pineapple well, reserving juice. Dissolve gelatin in boiling water, or use part of juice of pineapple mixed with the boiling water to make the 2-cup measure of liquid. Add frozen, sliced strawberries and stir until they thaw. Stir in pineapple, bananas and lemon juice. Pour into a 6½-cup mold which has been rinsed with cold water. Allow salad to set for several hours or overnight. Unmold and serve with a choice of salad dressings or make one of sour cream with ginger marmalade or ground ginger for flavor. Mix 1 cup sour cream with 1 teaspoon sugar and ¼ teaspoon ground ginger or 1 tablespoon ginger marmalade.

CURRIED CASHEW CHICKEN SALAD

Chicken salad with cashews and curry powder added as seasoning is worth a try as a summer salad. This salad also has seedless green grapes, which are just bursting with juice, and a sour cream-mayonnaise dressing.

  2 cups seedless grapes, halved
  2 cups chicken, cooked, diced, and chilled
  ½ cup sour cream
  ½ cup mayonnaise
  2 tablespoons minced onion
  1 tablespoon fresh lemon juice
  1 teaspoon curry powder
  ¼ teaspoon salt
1½ cups cashews, divided
    Salad greens
    Grape clusters

In a mixing bowl, combine chicken and grapes. In a small bowl, combine sour cream, mayonnaise, onion, lemon juice, curry and salt; blend well. Pour over chicken and grapes and mix well. Chill several hours. At serving time, stir in ¾ cup cashews. Serve on individual plates lined with lettuce or salad green. Chop remaining ¾ cup nuts and sprinkle over salad. Garnish with grape clusters. Makes 4 servings.

HOT AND SPICY WILTED HAM SALAD

A hot and spicy wilted ham salad is a change from the usual wilted lettuce salad. This will be a suggestion to go with chicken salad sandwiches for lunch.

    1 pound extra lean ham, thin sliced
    1 (16 oz.) package frozen mixed vegetables
    5 cups torn red leaf or iceberg lettuce
    3 cups torn fresh spinach (about ¼ pound)
 1½ cups cherry tomatoes, halved
    1 cup orange juice
    1 teaspoon chili powder
    1 small dried red chili pepper
    2 tablespoons vinegar
    2 tablespoons vegetable oil

Thaw mixed vegetables in cool running water; drain well. In large bowl combine lettuce, spinach, mixed vegetables and tomatoes. Toss lightly to mix; add ham and set aside. In skillet combine orange juice, chili powder and small dried chili pepper broken into small pieces; heat just to boiling. Add vinegar and oil and heat thorugh. Pour mixture over salad; toss to mix. Serve immediately. Hot rolls will be a nice addition to the menu.

LOBSTER SALAD OR FILLING FOR LOBSTER ROLL

If a trip to the coast of Maine means boiled lobster one day, followed by lobster stew another day and a lobster salad the following day—you must really enjoy lobster! Enough lobster is cooked the first day to have meat left over, plus the coral and tomale to use in the stew. The rest of the meat is set aside to make a lobster salad or lobster roll.

    2 cups lobster meat, cut in pieces
      Juice of ½ lemon
      Salt
      Pepper
    ½ cup celery
      Mayonnaise to mix

Cut lobster meat into medium pieces; add lemon juice and set aside in refrigerator. When ready to prepare salad, add the celery and salt and pepper to taste. Mix with desired amount of mayonnaise or salad dressing for a salad or a lobster roll filling. A few drops of onion juice add interest to either use of the mixture. Serve salad on lettuce. Butter the roll before adding the filling.

COOL CARROT RING

¾ cup water
1 envelope unflavored gelatin
½ cup low-fat cottage cheese
½ cup mayonnaise
1 tablespoon minced green onions
2 teaspoons lemon juice
1 teaspoon dill weed
1½ cups shredded carrots
4 hard-cooked eggs, chopped
  Fresh dill sprigs (optional)
  Carrot curls (optional)
  Hard-cooked egg wedges (optional)

In medium saucepan, sprinkle gelatin over water. Let stand 1 minute. Cook and stir over medium heat until gelatin is dissolved, about 1 minute. Remove from heat and blend in cottage cheese, mayonnaise, onions (minced with tops), lemon juice and dill weed. Stir in carrots and chopped eggs. Pour mixture into 3-cup mold and chill until set, several hours or overnight. Unmold onto platter and garnish with dill sprigs, carrot curls and egg wedges if desired.

SUSAN'S TANGY TOMATO SALAD

6 firm, ripe tomatoes
1 large green pepper, sliced
1 red onion, sliced, separated into rings
1 cucumber, pared
¾ cup vinegar
1½ teaspoons celery salt
1½ teaspoons mustard seed
⅛ teaspoon pepper
½ teaspooon salt
4½ teaspoons sugar
  Few grains Cayenne pepper
¼ cup cold water

Remove skin from tomatoes and cut each into 4 to 8 parts. Place in bowl with green pepper and red onion. Heat vinegar with seasonings and water to boil. Boil hard for 1 minute, and pour boiling hot over tomato mixture. Chill, stirring occasionally. When ready to serve, add the sliced cucumber. The tomatoes will keep, refrigerated, for several days. The cucumber will need to be replaced, as it becomes soft in the mixture.

COLESLAW DELUXE

This coleslaw recipe is quite different from our usual coleslaws, and it comes from San Francisco. It's a good recipe to use some of your cabbage and apples.

    1 cup cored and diced tart apples
    2 teaspoons lemon juice
    3 cups finely shredded red and green cabbage
    ¾ cup raisins
    ½ cup thinly sliced celery
    ⅓ cup sliced red onion
    1 medium carrot, pared, shredded
    2 green onions, with tops, sliced
    ¼ cup coarsely chopped walnuts

In large bowl, toss apples with lemon juice. Add remaining ingredients. Toss to blend thoroughly; chill. Makes 6 servings.

DILL DRESSING

In a small bowl, whisk together ½ cup sour cream, ½ cup mayonnaise, 2½ tablespoons vinegar, 1½ tablespoons sugar, 2 teaspoons dill weed, ½ teaspoon salt and ¼ teaspoon pepper. Mix into prepared salad ingredients and chill.

PINEAPPLE AND HAM PASTA SALAD

This salad is best if chilled at least 3 hours or overnight to allow flavors to blend. This is an easy-to-make recipe for parties, picnics or brown bag lunches. Macaroni, spiral or small shell pasta may be used.

    1 can (20 oz.) pineapple tidbits
    1 pound cooked ham, diced
    1 red or green pepper, seeded and diced
    2 cups frozen peas, thawed
    2 cups diced celery
    8 ounces elbow macaroni or other small pasta, cooked
    1¼ cups mayonnaise
    1 tablespoon vinegar
    1 teaspoon onion powder
    ¼ teaspoon pepper
    ¼ teaspoon dill weed

Drain pineapple. Combine pineapple, ham, green pepper, peas, celery and pasta in a large bowl. Combine mayonnaise, vinegar, onion powder, ¼ teaspoon pepper and dill weed; mix well and stir into pineapple mixture. Refrigerate 3 to 4 hours before serving. Serves 8.

RAW CRANBERRY SALAD MOLD

A raw cranberry mold makes a good salad for Thanksgiving or Christmas. It goes well with turkey and vegetables.

2 cups raw cranberries
1 whole orange, juice and rind
2 medium apples, pared
1 cup chopped celery
½ cup chopped nuts (optional)
1 (3 oz.) package lemon gelatin
½ cup sugar
1 cup hot water

Remove seeds from orange and grind with the cranberries through medium blade of food chopper (be sure to catch all juice). Chop apples, nuts and celery. Dissolve gelatin and sugar in 1 cup hot water. Add 1 cup of juice from grinding the cranberries and orange. Chill until partially set. Add cranberries-orange mixture, apple, celery and nut meats. Chill in a water-rinsed mold or in 9 individual salad molds.

HOT GERMAN POTATO SALAD

Use leftover boiled potato for hot German potato salad.

4 slices bacon, cut into 1-inch pieces
⅓ cup cider vinegar
1½ teaspoons sugar
¼ teaspoon pepper
¼ teaspoon salt
¼ cup water
2 teaspoons cornstarch
3 cups sliced, cooked potatoes
⅓ cup sliced green onions
3 tablespoons chopped parsley

NOTE: A 12-ounce package frozen cottage fries may be used in place of the sliced cooked potatoes.

In large skillet, cook bacon over medium-high heat until crisp. Remove from heat. Remove bacon with slotted spoon; set aside. Drain all but 3 tablespoons of the fat. To fat in skillet add vinegar, sugar, salt and pepper. Mix water with cornstarch; stir into skillet. Cook and stir over medium heat until slightly thickened. Add potatoes; toss. Cover and cook over medium heat about 8 minutes until potatoes are tender, stirring once or twice. Add bacon, onions and parsley. Mix gently to heat through. Serve hot.

JELLIED CIDER SALAD

Sweet cider makes a good jellied salad to go with any menu. This recipe makes a large salad, but you will not mind because, kept in the refrigerator, it will go for more than one meal. Other fruit may be added, except fresh pineapple.

3 packages (3 oz. each) orange gelatin
4½ cups apple cider, divided
½ cup seedless raisins
2 large apples, cored, chopped
½ cup chopped walnut or pecan meats

Dissolve gelatin in 2 cups boiling cider; add 2¼ cups cold cider, mixing well. Chill until gelatin mixture is slightly congealed. Soak raisins in ¼ cup of cider for 30 minutes. Add raisins, apples and nut meats to gelatin mixture, stirring carefully. Pour into a water-rinsed 2½-quart mold and chill until firm. Serves 10 to 12.

FRUIT SALAD

There is so much good fruit in the markets that you can design your own fruit salad using your family's favorites.

2 oranges, peeled, sectioned, cut
1 banana, sliced
2 kiwi fruit, pared, sliced
½ cup grapes
1 cup fresh pineapple chunks
2 pears, washed, sliced

Prepare the fruit, dipping pears and banana slices into lemon juice or lightly salted water. If you do need a dressing, you may like this "old faithful" that is added just before serving the salad.

FRUIT SALAD DRESSING

2 egg yolks, beaten
¼ cup sugar
¼ cup pineapple juice
¼ cup lemon juice
¼ teaspoon salt
½ cup cream, whipped

In top of double boiler, mix egg yolks, sugar, lemon juice, pineapple juice and salt. Cook over hot water, stirring constantly, until thickened. Set aside to cool. Just before serving, fold in whipped cream.

CUCUMBER SALAD

1 pint carton of cottage cheese
1 medium onion, grated
1 medium cucumber, shredded or grated
¾ cup mayonnaise
1 (3 oz.) package lime gelatin
1 cup boiling water

Dissolve gelatin in 1 cup boiling water; set aside until partially congealed. Mix together cottage cheese, onion, cucumber and mayonnaise. Fold mixture into partially congealed gelatin; refrigerate until firm.

A GREAT SALAD

Lemon juice, freshly squeezed, adds zest to this salad. This may be made on individual plates to serve 6. The dressing is delicious, too.

2 avocados, peeled, sliced lengthwise
2 small heads romaine lettuce torn in bite-size pieces
1 cup sliced mushrooms
1 cup sliced (unpared) cucumbers
1 cup cherry tomatoes, halved
6 ounces cooked chicken or turkey, sliced
1 small red or green pepper
1 or 2 green onions, sliced
  Sunkist dressing

Cut chicken or turkey in julienne strips or leave plain sliced. Cut pepper in rings. Arrange the meat and vegetables on the romaine on individual plates. Serve dressing on the side.

SUNKIST DRESSING

⅓ cup salad oil
  Juice of 1 lemon
1 clove garlic, minced
½ teaspoon dried oregano
  Grated peel of ½ lemon
1½ tablespoons brown sugar
½ teaspoon ground cumin
¼ teaspoon pepper

In jar with lid, combine all dressing ingredients. Shake well. Makes ⅔ cup of dressing.

CHICKEN-VEGETABLE SALAD PIQUANT

Hold the pickle juice when you are about to empty a bottle of sweet mixed pickles. The juice goes well in salads mixed with French dressing or mayonnaise. It adds a tart, not too sweet, tang to the salad.

  2 cups cubed cooked chicken
1½ cups shredded cabbage
 ½ cup cubed avocado
 ½ cup shredded carrot
  2 tablespoons raisins
  3 tablespoons French dressing
  1 tablespoon sweet mixed pickle liquid
  1 tablespoon lemon juice
 ½ cup sweet mixed pickle

In large bowl, combine chicken, carrot, cabbage, avocado and raisins. In small bowl, combine French dressing, pickle liquid and lemon juice; blend. Pour over chicken and toss well. Stir in pickles. Cover and chill. Makes 6 servings.

GOLDEN APPLE LAYERED SALAD

This is one of the make-ahead salads that is an assist to the hostess who may like to spend extra time on other dishes in the meal.

2 (about ¾ pound) Golden Delicious apples, cored
1 can (1 lb. 4 oz.) pineapple chunks
1 large banana, peeled and sliced
1 cup red grapes, halved
1 large orange, peeled
  Creamy dressing

Seed grapes if necessary; slice and quarter orange. Cut 1½ apples into chunks; thinly slice remaining apple for garnish. Drain pineapple; reserve syrup. Pour syrup over bananas; let stand 5 minutes. Drain banana; reserve 3 tablespoons syrup for dressing. In a 2½-quart glass bowl, layer pineapple, grapes, banana, apple chunks and orange. Garnish top with apple slices. Refrigerate, covered, 1 hour. Serve with creamy dressing.

CREAMY DRESSING

Blend ½ cup dairy sour cream, 3 tablespoons reserved pineapple syrup, 2 tablespoons mayonnaise and ⅛ teaspoon salt. Makes about ¾ cup.

NEW ENGLAND CRABMEAT AND ZITI SALAD

A shopping trip to the supermarket is always an adventure. We note the advent of new products and the loss of old ones. We have noticed the numbers of different forms of pastas in many shapes and sizes. Ziti is a favorite for pasta salads.

8 ounces uncooked ziti pasta
½ pound cooked or canned crabmeat
½ cup plain lowfat yogurt
¼ teaspoon dried tarragon
1 tablespoon chopped fresh chives
2 lettuce cups
1 tablespoon chopped pimientos (optional)

Cook ziti according to package directions; drain. Cut crabmeat into chunks, discarding any cartilage. Add to pasta. Combine the yogurt, tarragon and chives and mix with the crabmeat and ziti. Spoon into lettuce cups and top each serving with chopped pimientos. Makes 4 servings.

MUSTARDY COLE SLAW

This mustardy cole slaw may be made ahead to go with any meat cooked in the kitchen or over the barbecue coals. Made a day ahead, this cole slaw gets even more flavorful with time. Try it with baked beans on a Saturday night or your special time for baking beans.

1 medium head green cabbage, finely shredded (about 8 cups)
1 medium green pepper, cut into thin strips
⅔ cup sliced celery
⅔ cup grated or shredded carrot
½ cup mayonnaise
⅓ cup Dijon-style mustard
1 tablespoon milk
1 teaspoon sugar
  Green pepper rings for garnish

In large bowl, combine cabbage, green pepper strips, celery and carrot. In small bowl, mix mayonnaise, mustard, milk and sugar until well-blended and smooth. Toss cabbage mixture with mustard mixture until well-blended. Cover and refrigerate 2 hours or overnight to blend flavors, stirring occasionally. Garnish with green pepper rings.

AMY'S CREAMY CUCUMBER MOLD

This salad is an easy one and is a light green with bits of pimiento. A bit of fresh parsley or lettuce makes it even more tempting.

1 (3 oz.) package lime flavor gelatin
1 cup boiling water
½ teaspoon salt
1 cup sour cream
1 cup chopped cucumber
1 cup mayonnaise
3 tablespoons chopped pimiento
1 tablespoon finely minced onion

Dissolve gelatin in boiling water; stir in salt. Combine mayonnaise and sour cream, mixing well, and stir into the gelatin mixture. Chill until consistency of unbeaten egg white. Fold in cucumber, pimiento and onion. Pour into oiled or water-rinsed mold. Chill.

PENNY ANTE SALAD

Carrot slices, like copper pennies, form the base of this salad.

2 cans (4 cups) sliced carrots, drained
1 large sweet onion, thinly sliced
1 large green pepper, sliced
  Salt and pepper to season
½ cup vinegar
1 can condensed tomato soup
¾ cup sugar
1 teaspoon prepared mustard
1 teaspoon Worcestershire sauce
½ cup salad oil

Drain carrots. (Two cans of tiny carrots may be used in place of sliced carrots, or cooked and drained raw carrots to measure 4 cups may be used.) Place in bowl with green pepper and onion slices. Sprinkle with salt and pepper. In saucepan, mix vinegar, tomato soup, sugar, mustard, Worcestershire sauce and salad oil; bring to boiling to dissolve sugar, and pour boiling hot over vegetables. Allow to set overnight to blend flavors. Keeps up to 2 weeks in refrigerator.

JUDY'S BROCCOLI SALAD

From friends in Oregon, we have this salad.

1 bunch (4 cups chopped) broccoli
½ pound bacon, cooked crisp and crumbled
½ cup sunflower seeds
½ cup raisins or currants
1 small red onion, sliced and separated into rings

Combine all ingredients and mix with a dressing of 1 cup mayonnaise, 2 tablespoons vinegar and 2 tablespoons sugar.

ALLURA'S POTATO SALAD

This is really an overnight or all-day salad. It is made to fit the number to be served. Extra dressing may be refrigerated to use for other salads.

Use only boiled potatoes, hard-cooked eggs and thinly sliced white, red or sweet Spanish onions. For each serving, allow one large potato, one hard-cooked egg and onion to suit taste. Slice or dice potatoes, eggs and onions. Mix in dressing and refrigerate at least 6 hours (overnight would be best). Use plenty of dressing to make vegetables very moist. The dressing soaks into the vegetables and blends flavors.

SALAD DRESSING

½ cup sugar
½ teaspoon salt
1½ tablespoons flour
1 teaspoon dry mustard
2 eggs, beaten
2 tablespoons butter or margarine
Few grains Cayenne pepper
½ cup vinegar
2 cups cream
1 cup mayonnaise

In saucepan, combine sugar, salt, flour, pepper, and mustard. Stir in eggs; mix well and cook, stirring constantly, until thickened and creamy. Add butter and cream, unwhipped. Stir in mayonnaise. Add to potato mixture and mix well. Stir in sliced eggs. Refrigerate overnight or 6 to 8 hours for flavors to blend. Use plenty of dressing as the dressing soaks into the potatoes. This is a salad that is best made in the morning for supper or for a meal the next day.

MORSE'S SAUERKRAUT SALAD

Many salads come to potluck suppers. This sauerkraut salad can be made the day before and refrigerated, ready to tote for others to sample. No cooking here.

    2 cups sauerkraut, rinsed and well-drained
    ½ cup grated or shredded carrots
    1½ cups minced celery
    1½ cups chopped green pepper
    ½ cup finely chopped onion
    ½ chopped red bell pepper
    ⅓ cup white vinegar
    ⅓ cup sugar
      Dash of black pepper

In a bowl, combine all ingredients. Refrigerate all day or preferably overnight before serving. Makes 12 (½-cup) servings.

CHEF'S SALAD BOWL AND DRESSING

    2 quarts lettuce, cut in 1-inch pieces
    ¾ cup julienne-cut cooked chicken
    ¾ cup julienne-cut cooked ham
    1 large tomato, cut in thin wedges
    4 tablespoons sweet pickle relish

Mix all ingredients in a salad bowl. Add salad dressing and toss to mix.

SALAD DRESSING

    1 tablespoon chopped chives
    3 hard-cooked eggs, finely chopped
    ½ cup mayonnaise
    ¼ cup tarragon vinegar
    ¼ cup salad oil
    1 tablespoon Worcestershire sauce

Combine ingredients in a bowl. Mix well together. Pour over salad mixture; toss.

FAMOUS FRENCH DRESSING

This recipe makes about 3 cups of dressing.

```
 1 cup sugar
 1 cup vinegar
 4 teaspoons salt
 1 teaspoon pepper
 1 teaspoon paprika
 1 garlic bud, crushed
1⅔ cup salad oil
```

Dissolve sugar in vinegar. Add salt, seasonings and garlic. Add oil and shake well before using. Prevent garlic bud from dropping into salad, or remove from dressing.

CELERY SEED DRESSING

Take advantage of the variety of fruits and vegetables available at your local supermarket. A varied selection of lettuce can make the tossed salad a different one each time. A large choice of fruits will make a fine salad or a dessert of cut fruit. If it is fruit, try a celery seed dressing as a change from the ready made mixtures. This dressing keeps well in the refrigerator. We have also made the dressing with poppy seed with good flavor resulting.

```
¼ cup vinegar
 1 teaspoon celery seed
½ cup sugar
¾ teaspoon salt
¾ teaspoon dry mustard
 1 teaspoon onion juice
 1 cup salad oil
```

(NOTE: a quick way to get onion juice is to cut an onion crossways, and with a knife, scrape across the grain to direct the juice into the salad dressing mixture. Cut another slice and again scrape the juice into the dressing. Reserve the onion slices to add to a chowder for another meal.)

In a saucepan, combine celery seed and 2 tablespoons of the vinegar; heat just to boiling; remove and cool. In beater bowl, combine remaining 2 tablespoons vinegar, sugar, salt, mustard and onion juice. Beat together well. Then, add the oil, a tablespoon at a time, beating all the time. Beat until a thick, transluscent mixture results. Slowly add the vinegar and celery seed mixture. We suggest that the dressing is served in a bowl separate from the salad. Store dressing in the refrigerator.

COOKED FRUIT SALAD DRESSING

This dressing is as good on a mixture of canned fruits as it is on fresh fruits. This is an "oldie but goodie."

2 eggs
3 tablespoons melted butter
3 tablespoons lemon juice
1 cup cream, beaten
¼ teaspoon salt
¼ cup confectioners' sugar
½ teaspoon celery salt
½ teaspoon vanilla
3 drops onion juice

Beat eggs lightly in top of a double boiler. Gradually beat in melted butter, lemon juice and ¼ teaspoon salt. Cook over hot water until mixture thickens. (Do not overcook). Cool. Fold in the whipped cream, confectioners' sugar, celery salt, vanilla and the onion juice. Chill. NOTE: For onion juice, cut an onion in half and scrape the juice with a few passes of the knife blade. This method is also used when preparing chicken, fish or seafood salad in which you don't want chopped onion but want the onion flavor.

SALAD DRESSING

What a treat! The first ripe tomato from the garden! It joins lettuce, radishes and sliced cucumber, also garden-fresh, for a salad. We could have added fresh zucchini slices, also garden-fresh, if the bowl had not already been full with the other vegetables. Make your own favorite salad dressing as a change from the large and varied prepared dressings on the market.

¼ cup olive oil
¼ cup vegetable oil
1 teaspoon salt
1½ teaspoons sugar
⅛ teaspoon pepper
⅓ cup apple cider vinegar or more
1 large clove garlic, sliced

If desired, all vegetable or all olive oil may be used. Mix all together in a jar. This is even better if mixed several hours ahead of use, to give the garlic a chance to blend with other ingredients. Try different vinegars in the market for a change.

BLUE CHEESE DRESSING

With a choice of several kinds of dressing at a salad bar, do you choose blue cheese? You can make your own blue cheese dressing at home and keep it in the refrigerator in small jars to use as needed.

¼ pound blue cheese
3 tablespoons lemon juice
1 teaspoon celery salt
1 clove garlic, minced
1 teaspoon grated onion
1 pint (2 cups) sour cream
1 pint (2 cups) mayonnaise

Cut or crumble blue cheese into large pieces (not fine) and set aside. In a bowl combine lemon juice, salt, minced garlic, grated onion and sour cream and mayonnaise; mix well. Fold in blue cheese. Refrigerate.

FRESH TOMATO DRESSING

Try a fresh tomato dressing for tomatoes, salad greens, sliced avocado, or any combination of chilled cooked vegetables left from a meal.

1 cup diced, ripe tomatoes
¼ cup vegetable oil
1½ tablespoons vinegar
2 tablespoons sliced scallions
1 teaspoon thyme leaves, crushed
¼ teaspoon salt
¼ teaspoon paprika
⅛ teaspoon sugar (optional)
  Dash ground black pepper

Use fully ripe tomatoes. In container of electric blender place tomatoes, oil, vinegar, scallions, thyme, salt, paprika, sugar and pepper. Blend at high speed until smooth, stopping blender and scraping down sides of container if needed. Cover and refrigerate until ready to serve.

COOKED SALAD DRESSING

½ cup vinegar
2 tablespoons dry mustard
1½ teaspoons salt
2 cups milk
3 tablespoons flour
¼ cup sugar
  Yolk of 3 eggs
  Whipping cream

In top of double boiler, combine vinegar, mustard, salt, milk, flour, sugar and egg yolks; mix well. Cook over boiling water stirring frequently, until mixture thickens. Cool. Keep refrigerated. Thin with whipping cream.

SHERRY'S FRENCH DRESSING

½ cup salad oil, part or all olive oil
5 tablespoons vinegar
1 teaspoon water
1 teaspoon salt
1 teaspoon sugar
  Few grains pepper

Combine all ingredients in a jar; shake well.

VARIATIONS:
Add 1 clove garlic or ½ teaspoon instant minced garlic to French dressing.
Add 1 teaspoon chopped green pepper and 1 teaspoon chopped sweet red pepper to French dressing.
Add 1½ tablespoons crumbled blue cheese to French dressing.

ZIPPY LEMON CHILI DIP FOR FISH

Baked or broiled fish may be enhanced by the addition of a white sauce, lemon juice or a lemon chili dip or sauce. This dip or sauce is best served hot over the fish.

½ cup chili sauce
½ cup ketchup
  Grated peel of 1 lemon
  Juice of ½ lemon

In small bowl, combine all ingredients; chill. Serve as a dip for crispy fish sticks or as a sauce over any cooked fish fillets. Makes about 1 cup of sauce. Try this sauce on broiled haddock, or serve it on the side.

HONEY LIME BARBECUE SAUCE

For brushing over chicken or pork on the grill, try a sauce of lime juice and honey, instant minced onion and garlic, and a zip of crushed red pepper. Any leftover sauce may be used for dipping the chicken or toasty chunks of bread at the table.

⅔ cup water
1 tablespoon cornstarch
⅓ cup lime juice
⅓ cup honey
¼ cup vegetable oil
3 tablespoons instant minced onion
2 teaspoons instant minced garlic
¼ teaspoon salt
¼ to ½ teaspoon crushed red pepper

In a small saucepan combine water and cornstarch until smooth; stir in lime juice, honey, oil, onion, garlic, salt and red pepper. Bring to a boil; reduce heat and stir until sauce is slightly thickened and flavors are blended, about 5 minutes, stirring often. Brush over grilled chicken or pork during last 5 minutes of cooking. Serve remaining sauce with chicken as a dipping sauce.

LEMON-HONEY MUSTARD SAUCE

If plain baked or broiled fish has the family at the ho-hum stage, wake up the appetites with a sauce over the fish.

1½ pounds fish fillets
2 tablespoons butter or margarine
2 tablespoons flour
½ teaspoon salt
⅛ teaspoon pepper
1 cup hot water
2 teaspoons Dijon-style mustard
1 tablespoon honey
   Grated peel of ½ lemon
   Juice of ½ lemon
½ cup mayonnaise or salad dressing

Wipe fish with a damp towel. Broil or bake fish and keep warm while sauce is being prepared, or prepare sauce first so that fish will not have to wait. In saucepan, melt butter. Remove from heat; stir in flour, salt and pepper. Gradually blend in water, honey and mustard. Cook over medium heat, stirring until thickened. Add lemon peel and juice. Remove from heat; blend in mayonnaise.

MAINE SARDINE SPREAD

Use this sardine spread for a sandwich filling or on bread, toast or crackers as an appetizer.

2 cans Maine sardines, drained
¼ cup fresh lemon juice
½ teaspoon hot pepper sauce
½ cup chili sauce
   Bread, toast or crackers

Drain sardines and mash; season with lemon juice, hot pepper sauce and chili sauce. Serve on rounds of bread, toast or crackers.

OWL 'WICHES

Have fun and make owl 'wiches for refreshments for a party or for supper.

Slaw (yield: approximately 4 cups)

4 cups finely shredded cabbage
1 cup (4 oz.) shredded Provolone cheese
¼ cup sliced green onion
¼ cup chopped pimento, drained
½ cup dairy sour cream
1 teaspoon prepared mustard
¼ teaspoon salt

Sandwiches

6 Kaiser rolls, split
½ cup butter, softened
6 ounces thinly sliced hard salami
36 thin round slices Colby cheese
   Pimiento-stuffed green olives
   Ripe olives
   Green pepper strips

For slaw, combine cabbage, cheese, onion and pimento. Fold in sour cream, mustard and salt. Chill, covered, 2 hours. For sandwiches, hollow out rolls, leaving ½-inch thick. Spread butter on cut surfaces. Use salami to line shells. Arrange 3 cheese slices on each; top with ⅓ cup slaw. Decorate with owl faces, using green olives for eyes, a sliver of ripe olive for beak and 2 green pepper strips between the eyes. Makes 12 servings.

GIANT DELI SANDWICH

This is a giant no-fuss picnic sandwich which may be made and served at once or packed in plastic or foil to go on a picnic. Keep all picnic foods in a refrigerated carrying case.

1 loaf (1 pound) unsliced round bread or French bread
2 tablespoons butter, softened
½ pound Muenster cheese, sliced
½ pound sliced deli meats (ham, salami, liver sausage)
1 large tomato, sliced
1 large dill pickle
Lettuce leaves
German dressing

Slice dill pickle lengthwise. Cut bread into halves, horizontally. Hollow out halves, leaving shells about ¾-inch thick. (Reserve crumbs for another use.) Butter cut sides of bread. Layer remaining ingredients, starting and ending with cheese, and spreading German dressing between layers. Cut into 6 wedges or slices and serve immediately, or wrap loaf securely in plastic wrap or foil and pack for a picnic.

GERMAN DRESSING

In small bowl whisk ¼ cup mayonnaise, 1 tablespoon coarse grained mustard and 2 teaspoons prepared horseradish. Mix in 1½ tablespoons drained capers. Makes about ⅓ cup.

DELI-GARDEN SANDWICH ROUND

½ cup salad dressing
¼ cup finely chopped, seeded cucumber
¼ cup finely chopped, seeded tomato
½ teaspoon dried basil leaves, crushed
1½ pound round sourdough bread loaf (or rye or pumpernickel)
6 salami slices
6 green pepper rings
6 slices pasteurized process American cheese
6 red onion rings
6 cooked turkey slices

Combine salad dressing, cucumber, tomatoes and basil; mix lightly. Chill. Cut slice from top of bread loaf; remove center leaving ½-inch shell, saving crumbs for other uses. Layer salami, peppers and half of salad dressing mixture in shell. Cover with cheese, onions and remaining salad dressing mixture, top with turkey. Replace top of bread loaf. Wrap and chill. Cut into 6 wedges to serve.

RUTH'S OLIVE BUTTER FILLING

Years ago olive butter was on the grocer's shelf and was a favorite spread for sandwiches right from the jar or mixed with cream cheese. These sandwiches went to many parties and in dinner pails for school. Try this version of olive butter.

¼ cup butter
2 tablespoons finely chopped olives
¼ teaspoon lemon juice
    Cream cheese for mixing, if desired

Put stuffed olives through the fine blade of the food chopper; mix with butter and lemon juice. Use as is, or mix with cream cheese as a filling.

CRABMEAT FILLING

1 can (5 oz.) crabmeat, or fresh crabmeat
½ cup finely chopped celery
2 tablespoons lemon juice
    Salt and pepper
    Mayonnaise to mix

Add celery and lemon juice to crabmeat. Refrigerate; when ready to use, add mayonnaise, salt and pepper.

CHICKEN SALAD SANDWICHES

5 cups cooked diced chicken
¼ cup lemon juice
2½ cups chopped celery (optional)
⅛ teaspoon pepper
½ cup chopped toasted pecan meats
2 cups mayonnaise, or more
    Salt and onion juice to season
2 long loaves sandwich bread

Cook chicken in boiling water to which 1 small onion, 1 carrot, 1 tablespoon chopped parsley and a small piece of celery have been added. (A 5½-pound chicken usually yields 5 cups cubed meat.) Cool in the cooking liquid; remove meat from bones and dice. Add lemon juice and refrigerate overnight. When ready to make sandwiches, add celery, nut meats and mayonnaise to make a filling of good spreading consistency. Season to taste with salt and pepper. Spread a thin coating of butter on each slice of bread; spread filling on one slice and top with second buttered slice. Trim edges and cut each sandwich in four parts. Makes 128 tea sandwiches.

SANDWICH FILLING

When it's bridge club night, try this sandwich filling to go with hot coffee. Your guests will enjoy it, and leftovers could fill the brown bag the next day.

    1 12-ounce can corned beef
    6 ounces Swiss cheese, grated
    ⅓ cup mayonnaise
    1 teaspoon prepared mustard
    ½ teaspoon grated horseradish
    2 sweet gherkins or other sweet pickles
    Rye or whole-wheat bread
    Lettuce
    Thinly sliced tomato

Cut the corned beef in cubes and combine it with the cheese, mayonnaise, mustard, horseradish and pickles (sweet pickle relish is also good in this) in a blender, or put through the coarse blade of the food chopper to spreading consistency. Use as a spread for rye, whole wheat or pumpernickel bread. Add sliced tomato and lettuce to the sandwich or serve it on the side, if desired.

VEGETABLE SANDWICHES

This filling for sandwiches also may be used as a salad if desired. It uses varied amounts; if you do not have enough of one vegetable, another may be substituted.

    2 large carrots, shredded
    3 cups cabbage, shredded
    ½ cup chopped celery
    1 green pepper, chopped
    1 small onion, grated
    1 small cucumber, grated
    2 tablespoons chopped chives, if available
    Salt and pepper to taste
    1 package (3 ounces) cream cheese and chives, beaten
    2 or 3 tablespoons mayonnaise

Prepare vegetables. In beater bowl, beat the cream cheese until fluffy. Stir in mayonnaise. Place in salad bowl. Add prepared vegetables. When ready to serve, toss all together. You may like more salt and pepper or mayonnaise. Butter bread slices and spread filling. Cut in desired shapes.

TUNA BUNS

When the fish don't bite but you've planned fish for lunch, open a can of dependable tuna and prepare some tuna buns.

1 can tuna (6½ oz.)
⅓ cup mayonnaise (about)
⅓ cup diced celery
2 tablespoons diced onion
1 small can peas (1 cup) or freshly cooked peas
3 hamburger buns
  Cheese slices
2 tablespoons butter or oil

Melt butter in a saucepan; add onions and celery and cook until tender. Combine the tuna, celery and onions with mayonnaise in a medium bowl. Drain peas, if canned, and add to tuna mixture. Mix well. Spread mixture generously on bun halves and top with cheese slices. Bake at 350° until cheese is bubbly.

PICKLE PACKED TUNA PITA POCKETS

Prepare the filling for these pita pockets and chill until lunch or supper time.

1 can (6½ oz.) tuna packed in water
1½ tablespoons mayonnaise
1 tablespoon dill pickle liquid
1 tablespoon grated onion
½ cup red or green pepper pieces
4 small romaine leaves
¾ cup alfalfa sprouts
⅓ cup diagonally sliced dill pickles
4 whole wheat pita bread pockets (1-oz.size)

In small bowl, combine tuna, mayonnaise, dill pickle liquid and onion. Stir until well-blended. Stir in red pepper pieces. Cut a 1-inch strip from one side of each pita bread pocket. Place a romaine leaf in each. Fill with alfalfa sprouts. Spoon tuna mixture into center and insert pickle slices. Makes 4 servings.

SOUR DOUGH STARTER

Our colonial homemakers made potato yeast and kept a "seed" going in a yeast pot for another day. Others called the yeast pot "emptins" and added to it by scraping bits of dough and flour left on the bread board or pastry cloth into the yeast pot. Kept warm, this "lifeblood of the Western pioneers" can be kept for years if starter is replenished each time it is used.

3½ cups unsifted bread-type flour
  1 tablespoon sugar
  1 package dry yeast or 1 cake compressed yeast
  2 cups warm water

Combine flour, sugar and dry yeast in a large bowl. Gradually add warm water to dry ingredients and beat until smooth. Cover with transparent wrap; let stand in warm place for 48 hours. To use, measure amount called for in recipe and use as directed. To replenish starter: Add to remaining starter 1½ cups bread-type flour and 1 cup warm water. Beat until smooth. Store covered in warm place. Stir before using. If not used within 1 week, remove 1½ cups starter and follow directions for replenishing.

SOUR DOUGH BREAD

1½ cups sour dough starter
  ¾ cup milk
  3 tablespoons sugar
  1 teaspoon salt
  ¼ cup warm water
  1 package active dry yeast
  5 to 6 cups unsifted flour
  2 tablespoons margarine

Have sour dough starter ready. Scald milk; stir in sugar, salt and margarine; cool to lukewarm. Measure water into large warm bowl. Sprinkle in yeast; stir to dissolve. Add lukewarm milk mixture, starter and 2½ cups flour; beat until smooth. Stir in enough additional flour to make a stiff dough. Turn onto lightly floured board; knead until smooth and elastic, 8 to 10 minutes. Place in greased bowl, turning to grease top. Cover; let rise in warm place until double in bulk, about 1 hour. Punch dough down; divide into 3 equal parts. Form each piece into a smooth round ball or a 14-inch tapered roll or loaf. Place on greased baking sheet. With a sharp knife, make several cuts in criss-cross fashion on tops of round loaves or make several diagonal cuts on top of long loaves. Cover; let rise in warm place until double in bulk, about 1 hour. Bake at 400° for about 25 minutes, or until done. Remove from baking sheets and cool on wire rack.

YEAST BREADS

DANISH PASTRY

This is one of the most rewarding of yeast dough products. This recipe makes over 5 dozen Danish pastries. The pastries freeze well.

1 pound margarine
1 cup milk
2 packages yeast, compressed or dry
½ cup warm water
1 teaspoon salt
2 eggs
6 cups sifted all-purpose flour
⅓ cup sugar

Heat milk to scalding; chill. Dissolve yeast in warm water; chill. Cream 1 stick margarine with sugar and salt. Add eggs; beat well. Stir in chilled milk and chilled yeast. Add 3 cups flour; mix well. Add remaining 3 cups flour. Mix just enough to moisten and form a soft dough. Turn onto a floured pastry cloth. Do not knead. Pat down to 10-inch square. Fold all four sides to center; turn dough over and pat down to about an 8-inch square. Wrap square loosely in wax paper and refrigerate 10 to 15 minutes. This relaxes the dough and chills it slightly. While the dough chills, cut 3 sticks (¾ pound) margarine into 18 to 20 thin pats each. Spread on wax paper and let stand 10 to 15 minutes. Margarine slices best when taken directly from refrigerator. Now you are ready to roll and fold the dough. Roll dough to 10x15-inch rectangle. Place half of the margarine pats in center third of dough (a 5x10-inch section). Fold one side of dough over margarine. Press edges together. Place remaining squares of margarine over folded portion of dough. Fold other third of dough over top. Press edges together to seal margarine. Turn dough ¼ turn. Roll to a rectangle about 12x20 inches. Fold again into thirds and press edges together. Let stand 5 minutes. The rolling should be smooth and even in order to form unbroken alternate layers of margarine and dough. Repeat this step twice. Then roll dough into rectangle 10x15 inches. Cut into three sections 5x10 inches each. Wrap each section in wax paper. Refrigerate for at least 1 hour, or overnight.

FILLINGS AND TOPPINGS FOR DANISH PASTRY

PECAN CREAM FILLING: Cream together ½ stick margarine (¼ cup), 1¼ cups sifted confectioners' sugar and 1 tablespoon flour. Beat in 1 egg yolk. Add ¼ cup finely chopped pecan meats.

CREAM CHEESE FILLING: Combine and beat well 1 8-ounce package cream cheese, ⅓ cup sugar, 1 egg and 1 teaspoon vanilla.

JAMS, JELLIES, PRESERVES: These make easy fillings and toppings. Black raspberry, raspberry, strawberry, apricot and pineapple preserves or jams are delicious.

EGG WHITE GLAZE: Mix 1 egg white and 2 tablespoons water. Stir with fork. Brush over top of all rolls just after shaping.

FROSTING: Beat until smooth 4 cups sifted confectioners' sugar, 1 teaspoon vanilla and ⅓ cup water. Brush over surface of baked rolls.

BAKING TIPS: Danish pastry will be flakier if not permitted to rise until doubled in bulk. Let stand 1 hour in warm room, free from drafts. Overbaking dries out Danish pastry. Sugar content is low so rolls will be lightly browned when done.

STORAGE: Keep in covered container or plastic bag. Use within one to two days. To freshen and warm rolls, place on a baking sheet in a 350⁰ oven for 5 minutes. To freeze; wrap in foil or put in tightly covered box; overwrap to seal out air. These freeze very well.

HORSESHOE ROLLS

⅓ recipe Danish pastry dough
⅓ pecan cream filling (about ⅓ cup)
    Egg white glaze
    Frosting

Roll chilled dough into rectangle about 12x20 inches. Spread filling on dough in two long strips, about 2½x20 inches, leaving equal strips free along both edges and center. Fold each wide edge over nearer strip of filling, then fold again so that folds meet in the center. Moisten surface with water; fold again and press down firmly. This forms a 20-inch strip with six layers of dough. Cut into 1-inch slices. Place cut side up on baking sheet about 2 inches apart. Brush surfaces with egg white glaze. Cover with wax paper; let rise 1 hour. Bake at 375⁰ for 15 minutes, or until lightly browned. Brush with frosting. Cool on rack.

FRUIT-FILLED TWISTS

⅓ recipe Danish pastry
    Jams or preserves or cream cheese filling
    Egg white glaze
    Frosting

Roll chilled dough into rectangle 12x7 inches. Cut 18 to 20 strips, 7 inches long. Twist ends of each strip in opposite directions. Form on greased baking sheets into snails, rosettes, horseshoes or pretzels. Tuck loose end under roll. Place 2 inches apart on cookie sheets. Brush surfaces with egg white glaze. Let rise 1 hour. With a teaspoon make depression in center of each roll. Add ½ teaspoon of jam or other filling. Bake at 375⁰ for 15 minutes, or until lightly browned. Brush with frosting. Cool on rack.

SWEET ROLLS

This recipe has been used for dinner rolls, coffee cake, pecan rolls and hot cross buns.

2 packages active dry yeast or 2 cakes compressed yeast
½ cup warm water
2 tablespoons sugar
2 cups milk, scalded and cooled
4 cups sifted all-purpose flour
2 eggs, well beaten
½ cup sugar
½ cup shortening, melted and cooled
3 cups sifted all-purpose flour
2 teaspoons salt

In mixing bowl, dissolve yeast in water (warm for active dry, lukewarm for compressed yeast), to which 2 tablespoons sugar have been added. Add cooled milk. Mix in 4 cups flour; beat well. Cover with towel and let this sponge rise for 45 minutes, or until light. Add eggs, shortening, ½ cup sugar and remaining flour sifted with salt. Put ½ cup flour on pastry board; turn out dough. Knead well. Put in lightly greased bowl; let rise to double in bulk. Shape in desired forms. Place in greased pans. Let rise to double in bulk. Bake at 375° for 15 to 30 minutes, depending on shape and size of rolls. This recipe makes five dozen small Parker House rolls, four dozen large pan rolls or three dozen large muffin-size pecan rolls.

PECAN NUT ROLLS

1 recipe sweet roll dough
   Melted butter or margarine
   Sugar
   Cinnamon
   Brown sugar
   Pecan halves

Grease muffin pans. Put 1 tablespoon melted butter and 1 dessert spoon brown sugar in each muffin cup. Place 3 pecan halves, rounding side down, in each cup. Roll sweet dough into a rectangle about ½ inch thick. Spread with melted butter and sprinkle with sugar and cinnamon. Beginning on long side, roll as for jelly roll. Cut into 1-inch slices; place each slice, cut side down, in muffin cup. Let rise to double in bulk. Bake at 375° for about 25 minutes. Turn from pan at once onto cookie sheet, allowing caramel-like mixture from pan to fall on top of each roll. Makes 3 dozen large rolls.

CINNAMON ROLLS

1 recipe sweet roll dough
Melted butter or margarine
Sugar or brown sugar
Cinnamon

Roll portions of dough to rectangle, ¼ to ½ inch in thickness. Spread with melted butter. Sprinkle with sugar or brown sugar. Sprinkle with cinnamon. Roll, beginning from long side, as for jelly roll. Cut in 1-inch slices. Let rise to double in bulk. Bake in greased cake pan or muffin cups at 375° for about 25 minutes, depending on size of roll. Raisins or nut meats may be sprinkled on dough before rolling and cutting.

BASIC WHITE BREAD

¼ cup warm water
1 package yeast, active dry or compressed
2 cups milk, scalded, cooled
2 tablespoons melted butter or margarine
2 tablespoons sugar
2 teaspoons salt
6 to 6½ cups sifted all-purpose flour

Sift flour before measuring. Measure water into a large bowl—warm for active dry yeast, lukewarm for compressed. (If bowl is rinsed with warm water before mixing, the yeast will act faster.) Stir in scalded and cooled milk. Add butter, sugar and salt. Stir in 3 cups flour, 1 cup at a time; beat well after each addition. Stir in remaining 3 cups flour. Turn dough onto floured board or pastry cloth; knead until smooth and not sticky. Lightly grease bowl; turn dough around in bowl to grease top of dough. Cover bowl with towel. Let rise until double in bulk. Test by inserting two fingers about ½ inch into risen dough. If indentations remain, dough is ready to shape. Punch down dough; knead, squeezing out air bubbles. Divide dough into two even pieces. Pat each piece into a rectangle. Fold dough over and fold in ends. Place in greased bread tins with seam side down. Cover and let rise until double in bulk. Bake at 375° for about 45 minutes, or until brown. To test for doneness, tap loaf smartly with fingers—a hollow sound indicates the loaf is baked. Rub loaf with a bit of butter after taken from oven.

For dark bread, use 3 cups white flour and 3 cups of whole wheat or graham flour. Alternate the flour, starting with 1 cup of white flour. The more dark flour used, the longer the rising time and the smaller the loaf.

ALL-BRAN REFRIGERATOR ROLLS

½ cup boiling water
½ cup shortening
1 teaspoon salt
½ cup All-Bran cereal
1 egg, beaten
1 cake compressed yeast
½ cup lukewarm water
3½ cups sifted all-purpose flour
⅓ cup sugar

Pour boiling water over shortening; stir until shortening has melted. Stir in sugar, salt and All-Bran. Let stand until lukewarm. Add egg and yeast which has been dissolved in lukewarm water. Mix in flour. Cover and refrigerate overnight or until ready to use. Shape. Put in greased pan. Let rise until double in bulk. Bake at 400° for 15 to 20 minutes.

BURLAP BREAD

This is the name that came with the bread recipe. What's in a name? In this case, it's good eating and good nutrition.

5 to 5½ cups all-purpose flour
2 packages quick-rise type yeast
1 cup rolled oats
⅓ cup wheat germ
½ cup bran flakes cereal
1 tablespoon salt
2 cups water
½ cup molasses
2 tablespoons butter or margarine

In large mixer bowl, combine 2 cups flour, yeast, oats, wheat germ, cereal and salt; mix well. In saucepan, heat water, molasses and butter until very warm (120°-130°); butter does not need to melt. Add to flour mixture. Blend at low speed until moistened; beat 3 minutes at medium speed. By hand, gradually stir in enough remaining flour to make a firm dough. Knead on floured surface, 5 to 8 minutes. Place in greased bowl, turning to grease top. Cover; let rise in warm place until double, about 30 minutes.

Punch dough down. Divide into 2 parts. On lightly floured surface, roll or pat each half to a 14x7-inch rectangle. Starting with shorter side, roll up tightly, pressing dough into roll with each turn. Press edges and ends to seal. Place in greased 9x5-inch bread pans. Cover; let rise in warm place until doubled, about 30 minutes. Bake at 375° for 35 to 40 minutes. Remove from pans; cool. Makes 2 loaves.

GARLIC-BUTTERED FRENCH BREAD

This is a great accompaniment to pork chops, barbecued ribs or steak. It may be prepared the day before, wrapped in foil, refrigerated and be ready to go when the time comes.

French bread, homemade or from the bakery
Cloves of garlic
Butter or margarine

You will need about one stick of butter for a long loaf of bread. The butter will spread easily if beaten in the mixer before adding the garlic. Mash or crush the peeled garlic bud or clove and mix well with the butter. Cut the bread in 1-inch slices in a slanting motion but only to, not through, the bottom crust. Spread the garlic butter liberally on each slice. Wrap the buttered bread in foil for heating when ready to use. If garlic is not everyone's choice, bake one loaf with garlic and the other spread with butter and finely minced sweet Spanish onions and grated Parmesan cheese—the amounts are your choice. Heat thoroughly.

SQUASH YEAST BREAD

This bread is a delicious loaf made in the shape of a French bread. It also may be made with mashed potatoes in place of the squash. If potatoes are used, substitute ½ cup minced chives for the cinnamon and cloves in the squash bread.

2½ cups mashed squash
2 tablespoons dry yeast
1½ cups warm water
2 cups flour, half white, half whole wheat
2 tablespoons honey
3 tablespoons maple syrup
¼ cup oil
2 teaspoons salt
1 teaspoon cinnamon
½ teaspoon cloves
6 to 8 cups flour

Dissolve yeast and honey in water. Add mashed squash, oil, maple syrup, salt and spices. Stir in flour. (Add last of flour slowly so as not to get too much.) Knead for 10 minutes. Let rise for 1 hour, punch down and shape into 2 large loaves or into French-bread-shaped loaves. Place in 2 greased loaf pans or in 2 long loaves on a cookie sheet. Let rise until double in size. Bake at 375° for 45 to 50 minutes. Cool on wire rack.

ANADAMA BREAD

½ cup yellow corn meal
2 cups boiling water
2 tablespoons shortening
½ cup molasses
1 teaspoon salt
1 cake yeast or 1 package active dry yeast
1 cup lukewarm or warm water
5 to 5½ cups sifted all-purpose flour

Stir cornmeal slowly into water just before it boils. Boil 5 minutes. Add shortening, molasses and salt. Cool. When lukewarm, add yeast softened in lukewarm water (warm water for active dry yeast). Add flour to make a stiff dough. Knead well; let rise until slightly more than double in bulk. Shape into loaves. Place in greased loaf pans; let rise until double. Bake at 400° for 15 minutes. Reduce heat to 350° and bake for 30 minutes longer, or until done. Makes 2 loaves.

OAT BRAN LOAF

There are a few hints to making oat breads a success. Because of its very nature as a soluble fiber, oat bran absorbs water like a sponge. It needs to be first softened in boiling hot water before combining with the remaining bread ingredients.

2 cups water, divided
1 cup plus 2 tablespoons oat bran
2 packages active dry yeast
¼ cup honey
¼ cup vegetable oil, at room temperature
1½ teaspoons salt
4½ to 5 cups all-purpose flour
1 egg white

Bring 1½ cups water to boil; remove from heat and stir in 1 cup oat bran; blend well. Set aside to cool. Place ½ cup warm water in large bowl. Sprinkle in yeast; stir until dissolved. Stir in oat bran mixture, honey, vegetable oil, salt and 2 cups flour; beat until smooth. Stir in enough additional flour to make a soft dough. Knead on lightly floured surface until smooth and elastic, about 8 to 10 minutes. Place in greased bowl, turning to grease top. Let rise in warm, draft-free place until doubled in size, about 35 minutes.

Punch dough down. Divide dough into two equal pieces. Roll each piece to 8x12 inches; roll up from short ends to make loaves. Place seam side down in 2 greased loaf pans. Cover, let rise in warm, draft-free place until doubled in size, about 35 minutes. Brush with egg white; sprinkle with remaining oat bran. Bake at 375° for 35 minutes or until done. Remove from pans; cool on a wire rack.

SHREDDED WHEAT BREAD

2 shredded wheat biscuits, crumbled
2 cups milk, scalded
2 teaspoons salt
2 tablespoons shortening
¼ cup molasses
1 yeast cake or 1 package active dry yeast
½ cup lukewarm water; warm for dry yeast
5 to 6 cups sifted all-purpose flour

Crumble shredded wheat into mixing bowl. Scald milk; add salt and shortening. Stir until shortening has melted; pour over shredded wheat. Stir to mix. Add molasses. Cool to lukewarm. Add yeast which has been dissolved in water. Add flour to make a stiff dough. Let rise until double in bulk. Knead and shape into loaves and place in two greased bread pans. Let rise until double. Bake bread for 40 to 50 minutes, starting at 400° for the first 15 minutes, then reduce heat to 350° for remaining time. Bread will sound hollow when done if rapped sharply with fingers. Remove from tins and cool on a rack.

PINEAPPLE UPSIDE-DOWN ROLLS

1 package yeast
¼ cup warm water
1 cup scalded milk
½ cup shortening or margarine
½ cup sugar
1½ teaspoons salt
  Crushed pineapple
3 beaten eggs
4¾ cups flour
½ cup shortening or margarine
1½ cups brown sugar
  Maraschino cherries

Dissolve the yeast in warm water. In a large mixing bowl, combine scalded milk, ½ cup shortening, ½ cup sugar and the salt. Stir in yeast mixture, beaten eggs and flour. Cover and let rise until doubled. Stir down. Cream together ½ cup shortening and brown sugar. Place a teaspoon of creamed mixture in each greased muffin cup, place ¼ of a Maraschino cherry in the center and add 1 teaspoon crushed pineapple. Spoon roll dough onto pineapple mixture until each cup is ¾ full. Cover and let rise. Bake at 375° for 12 to 15 minutes. Invert muffin pans onto cookie sheets immediately after taking them from the oven. Allow a few minutes for topping to run onto the rolls and then remove the muffin pan. Makes 3 dozen rolls. If there are leftover rolls, tuck them into the freezer for another day.

DORIS'S YEAST ROLLS

¼ cup milk, scalded
¼ cup water
1 egg, beaten
1 teaspoon salt
¼ cup sugar
1 cake compressed yeast or 1 pkg. active dry yeast
¼ cup warm water or lukewarm water
2 cups sifted all-purpose flour
¼ cup melted shortening
1 or more cups additional flour

Dissolve yeast in warm or lukewarm water. Scald milk; add water. When lukewarm, beat in egg, salt and sugar. Stir in dissolved yeast. Add 2 cups flour; beat well. Add melted shortening; again beat and add flour to make a soft dough—1 cup or more. Knead on lightly floured board; place in greased bowl and allow to rise to double in bulk. Shape into any variety of rolls. Pan rolls, Parker House or cloverleaf rolls are suggestions. When doubled in bulk, bake at 375° for 15 to 20 minutes, depending on size and kind. For whole wheat rolls, add whole wheat flour for last flour addition to rolls.

FIFTY-FIVE-MINUTE ROLLS

This recipe is for the homemaker on the run who needs rolls in a hurry or plans ahead to bake the rolls after the roast has been removed from the oven to cool or "rest" before serving. Or, make ahead and freeze. These are shaped like the old Parker House rolls so often served at a bridge luncheon.

2 cups milk
¼ cup sugar
2 teaspoons salt
¼ cup melted shortening
2 packages active dry yeast
½ cup warm water
6 cups sifted flour
   Melted butter for dipping

Heat milk until warm. Add sugar, salt and melted shortening (¼ cup). Have yeast dissolving in the warm water. Add yeast and mix all well. Add flour and mix well. Cover bowl and allow to rise for 15 minutes, in a warm place. Remove from bowl, knead and roll to 1-inch thickness. Cut with a 2¾-inch cutter. Fold in half after dipping in melted butter. Pinch edges together. Place in baking pan and bake at 450° for about 10 minutes. Makes about 25 large rolls.

CHERRY CINNAMON SWIRL BREAD

Homemade cherry bread may be your choice for a special treat. With the new rapid-rising yeasts, the time needed to "proof" the dough is almost cut in half. Mashed potatoes add lightness to the loaf. This bread is excellent for French toast and try it for a sandwich with cream cheese filling.

7½ cups unsifted flour
  1 cup unseasoned mashed potatoes
  2 tablespoons sugar
  2 teaspoons salt
  2 packages (¼ oz. each) rapid rising yeast
  1 cup milk
  1 cup water
 ½ cup butter
  1 jar (10 oz.) maraschino cherries, chopped
 ½ cup sugar
  2 teaspoons cinnamon
  2 tablespoons butter, melted
  1 egg, beaten

Reconstituted instant mashed potatoes may be used. Maraschino cherries must be well-drained. Set aside 1 cup of flour. In large bowl, mix remaining flour, potatoes, 2 tablespoons sugar, salt and yeast. Heat milk, water and ½ cup butter until hot to touch (125° to 130°); stir into dry mixture. Dry cherries on paper towel; toss with a little flour and add to batter. Mix in enough reserved flour to make a soft dough. On floured board, knead 10 minutes, until dough is no longer sticky. Set in greased bowl; grease top. Cover, let rise in warm, draft-free place until doubled in bulk, about 30 to 40 minutes. Punch dough down; divide in half. On floured board, roll each half into a 16" x 8" rectangle. Combine remaining sugar (½ cup) and cinnamon. Sprinkle over rectangles. Roll up from narrow sides, jelly roll fashion. Pinch edges and ends together. Tuck ends under. Place, seam-side-down, in greased bread tins. Brush with melted butter. Cover; let rise in warm, draft-free place until doubled, about 30 to 40 minutes. Brush each loaf with beaten egg. Bake at 375° for 25 to 30 minutes, until golden brown. Remove from pans; cool on wire rack. Makes 2 loaves.

BRIOCHES

These rolls may be made a day ahead and reheated in the oven after your roast has been removed to rest for easy carving. These small French rolls will add much to the menu. You really do not need to butter them—they are that good!

　1 package active dry yeast
　¼ cup warm water
　2 tablespoons sugar
　1 teaspoon salt
　4 eggs
　1 egg white
　¾ teaspoon lemon extract
　1 cup butter at room temperature
3½ cups all-purpose flour
　1 egg yolk
　1 tablespoon water

Dissolve yeast in warm water in large mixer bowl. Add sugar, salt, 4 eggs, egg white, lemon extract, butter and 2 cups of the flour. Beat on low speed 30 seconds, scraping bowl constantly. Beat on medium speed 10 minutes. Stir in remaining flour until smooth; scrape sides of bowl. Cover with plastic wrap and let rise in warm place until double, about 1 hour. Stir batter down by beating 25 strokes. Cover bowl tightly with plastic wrap and refrigerate overnight or at least 8 hours. About one hour before serving turn batter onto pastry cloth. It will be soft and slightly sticky. Work quickly with floured hands to divide dough into halves. Shape each into a roll about 8 inches long. Divide each roll into 4 pieces. Place one piece from each roll back into the refrigerator while shaping the rest.

Divide each of the remaining pieces into 3 equal parts and form into a total of 18 balls. Place in greased 2½-inch muffin cups. Make a deep indentation in the center of each ball with thumb. Take remaining 2 pieces from refrigerator and divide each into 3 parts. Divide each of these into 3 equal parts and form 18 small balls. Place a ball in each indentation. Let rise until double, about 40 minutes.

Heat oven to 375°. Beat egg yolk and 1 tablespoon water slightly; brush over top of rolls. Bake until golden brown, 15 to 20 minutes. Immediately remove from pans. Yield: 18 rolls.

BUTTERHORN ROLLS

2 yeast cakes or 2 packages dry yeast
2 tablespoons lukewarm or warm water
2 tablespoons sugar
1 cup milk, scalded
½ cup butter
½ cup sugar
1 teaspoon salt
3 eggs, beaten
5 cups sifted all-purpose flour
    Butter, melted
    Celery, poppy or sesame seed, optional

Dissolve yeast in 2 tablespoons water (lukewarm for compressed, warm for dry) to which the 2 tablespoons sugar have been added. Add scalded milk to ½ cup butter, ½ cup sugar and salt. Stir until butter melts and mixture becomes lukewarm. Add beaten eggs and yeast mixture. Add flour, mixing well. Cover bowl with wax paper; refrigerate overnight. About two hours before you wish to bake the rolls, remove dough to floured board and knead. Divide dough into four parts and roll each portion into a circle. Spread each circle with melted butter. If seeds are to be used, sprinkle each circle with ½ teaspoon salt and 1 teaspoon of any one seed. Cut circles into 8 or 10 pie-shaped pieces. Start at widest part of each piece and roll to pointed end. Place on greased sheets with points on underside of rolls; leave three inches between each roll to allow for rising. Cover with towel and allow to rise to double. Bake in a 375° oven for 15 minutes, or until golden brown.

MILDRED'S OATMEAL BREAD

2 packages dry yeast or 2 cakes yeast
½ cup warm water
2 tablespoons sugar
1½ cups boiling water
1 cup quick cooking rolled oats
½ cup molasses
2 eggs, beaten
5½ cups sifted all-purpose flour
⅓ cup shortening or oil
2 teaspoons salt

Dissolve yeast in warm water (lukewarm for yeast cakes) to which 2 tablespoons sugar have been added. In a large bowl, combine rolled oats, salt, shortening and molasses; pour boiling water over this

Continued on next page

mixture. Stir to melt shortening. When mixture is lukewarm, add beaten eggs and dissolved yeast. Stir in flour. You may need another ½ cup flour, depending on brand used. This is a soft dough. Knead the dough on floured board or pastry cloth for 5 minutes. Place dough in greased bowl and turn dough in bowl to grease top. Cover with towel and refrigerate for 2 hours. Remove dough from refrigerator; knead for 2 minutes. Cut into equal quarters and shape into loaves, making a long roll of each quarter, and put two into each greased bread tin, or make two round-shaped loaves for each tin. Butter the rolls or rounds between each section as they are put into tins. Cover; let rise until double in bulk. Bake at 350° for 40 to 45 minutes. Remove baked bread from oven and butter crusts. This recipe makes two loaves of bread.

HOLIDAY FRUIT BREAD

For gifts for the Christmas holidays and for morning coffees.

½ cup sugar
5 tablespoons butter
5 tablespoons shortening
2 teaspoons salt
2 cups milk, scalded
2 packages dry yeast
½ cup warm water
2 eggs, beaten
6½ cups sifted all-purpose flour
    Grated rind of 1 lemon
1 cup seedless raisins
1 cup mixed candied fruit
½ cup nut meats, chopped

In a mixing bowl, combine sugar, butter, shortening and salt. Add scalded milk; stir until butter and shortening are melted. Cool to lukewarm. Soften yeast in warm water; add to cooled mixture. Stir in beaten eggs. Add 3 cups flour; beat until smooth. Stir in lemon rind. Add remaining flour to make a soft dough. Mix thoroughly. Cover; let rise until double in bulk. Punch down dough; add fruit and nut meats. Knead dough; divide into four portions; shape into small loaves. Place in small greased bread tins. Let rise to double. Bake at 375° for 10 minutes; lower heat to 325° and bake for 30 minutes. Small aluminum foil pans make good containers for baking this bread as well as giving the bread as gifts.

BANANA THREE-WAY BATTER

A coffeecake for morning coffee, a batch of muffins to take to a neighbor or a loaf of banana bread for a tea all can be made from this banana batter.

½ cup soft butter or margarine
1 cup sugar
2 eggs
1½ cups mashed ripe banana (4 medium)
1 tablespoon lemon or lime juice
2 cups unsifted all-purpose flour
1 teaspoon soda
½ teaspoon salt
½ teaspoon cinnamon
½ teaspoon grated lemon rind
½ cup chopped nuts

In a large mixing bowl, cream together butter and sugar until light and fluffy. Beat in eggs, one at a time, beating well after each addition. Stir in mashed bananas and lemon juice. Mix together flour, soda, salt, cinnamon and lemon rind; blend into creamed mixture. Stir in chopped nuts. Make one of the following variations:

LOAF: Turn batter into greased 9-inch loaf pan. Bake in 350° oven for 55 minutes. Cool before slicing.

COFFEE CAKE: Turn batter into a 9-inch square baking pan. Bake in a 350° oven for 40 minutes, until cake tester inserted in middle comes out clean. Slice 2 bananas and arrange on top of cake. Sprinkle with a topping of ½ cup brown sugar mixed with 2 tablespoons of butter, melted, and ¼ cup flaked coconut. Broil 2 minutes or until topping is bubbly or lightly browned.

MUFFINS: Spoon batter into 24 greased 2½-inch muffin cups. Bake in 350° oven for 15 to 20 minutes.

VARIATIONS: Substitute any of the following for chopped nuts: raisins, snipped dates, chopped dried apricots, coconut, chopped prunes, chocolate pieces or cranberries.

QUICK BREADS

STRAWBERRY BREAD

3 cups flour
¾ teaspoon salt
1½ cups sugar
1¼ cups salad oil
2 cups (1 quart frozen) thawed, drained strawberries
1 teaspoon soda
3 teaspoons cinnamon
4 eggs, beaten
1½ cups chopped nut meats

Preheat oven to 350°. In mixing bowl, combine dry ingredients. Combine salad oil and well-beaten eggs. Add to dry ingredients and mix until just moistened. Fold in strawberries and nut meats. Bake in two greased loaf pans for about 1 hour, or until loaves test done. Cool in pans for 10 minutes; remove to a rack to finish cooling.

LEMON-GLAZED PINEAPPLE BREAD

2½ cups all-purpose flour
3½ teaspoons baking powder
1 teaspoon salt
⅓ cup butter or margarine
½ cup sugar
1 large egg
1 (8¼ ounces) can crushed pineapple, undrained
⅓ cup milk
1 teaspoon grated lemon peel
½ cup chopped walnuts
Lemon glaze

Mix and sift flour with baking powder and salt. Cream shortening (butter or margarine) with sugar. Beat in egg; beat well. Add sifted dry ingredients alternately with undrained pineapple and milk, beginning and ending with dry ingredients. Stir in lemon peel and walnuts. Turn into a greased loaf pan. Let stand 10 minutes. Bake in a moderate oven, 350° for 55 to 60 minutes, just until loaf tests done. Let stand in pan 10 minutes, then turn onto a rack to cool. When cold, brush top of loaf with lemon glaze.

LEMON GLAZE

Stir ½ cup sifted powdered sugar, 2 teaspoons milk and ½ teaspoon coarsely grated lemon peel together until smooth.
NOTE: After the lemon peel has been grated, squeeze and freeze the juice for later use, as a lemon, removed of peel, dries up quickly.

BLUEBERRY NUT BREAD

2 eggs, beaten
1 cup sugar
1 cup milk
3 tablespoons margarine or oil
3 cups sifted all-purpose flour
¾ teaspoon salt
4 teaspoons baking powder
1 cup blueberries
¾ cup broken nut meats
1 teaspoon vanilla

Beat eggs; add sugar and beat until fluffy. Stir in milk and oil or margarine which has been melted. Mix and sift flour, baking powder and salt and add to egg mixture with vanilla. Fold in blueberries and nut meats. Bake in greased bread pan at 350° for 1 hour or until bread tests done. Remove to rack to cool for 20 minutes; remove from pan to finish cooling. Quick breads generally slice better if set for overnight.

CALIFORNIA DATE NUT BREAD

1½ cups pitted California dates
½ cup hot milk
3 cups flour
1 teaspoon baking powder
1 teaspoon soda
1 teaspoon salt
  Spice of your choice: 1½ teaspoons nutmeg with banana; 1½ teaspoons cinnamon with applesauce; 1½ teaspoons pumpkin pie spice with pumpkin
1 cup packed brown sugar or granulated sugar
2 eggs, beaten
½ cup melted butter or margarine
1 cup mashed ripe bananas or canned pumpkin or applesauce
1 cup chopped walnuts

In container of electric blender, combine ½ cup of the dates with the milk. Blend to chop dates; set aside. Sift together flour, baking powder, salt and soda with spice of your choice. In mixing bowl, combine sugar, eggs, butter, banana and date-milk mixture. Add in dry ingredients, mixing just to blend. Stir in remaining 1 cup of dates and the nuts. Spoon batter into a greased 5x9-inch loaf pan. Bake at 350°, 55 to 60 minutes, until wooden pick inserted in center comes out clean. Cool in pan 5 minutes; turn out onto rack to cool completely. Makes 1 loaf.

DATE AND NUT BREAD

1 pound pitted dates, chopped
1 teaspoon soda
½ cup sugar
1 cup boiling water
1 egg, beaten
2 cups sifted all-purpose flour
½ teaspoon salt
2 teaspoons baking powder
1 teaspoon vanilla
1 cup nut meats, coarsely broken
2 tablespoons butter or salad oil

Cut dates into a bowl. Add soda, sugar, butter and boiling water. Cool to lukewarm. Beat in egg. Mix and sift together flour, salt and baking powder and stir into date mixture. Add vanilla and nut meats. Bake in greased bread pan. Wax paper lining in bottom of greased pan is recommended, as dates often become overcooked.

WALNUT CRUNCH BREAD

What to do with the eggnog remaining from the New Year's Eve party? Bread, ice cream, custards, pie, salad or souffle to list a few uses. Or, make a loaf of quick bread to use when the holiday festivities have become dim.

2 cups all-purpose flour
¾ cup firmly packed brown sugar
2 teaspoons baking powder
¼ teaspoon salt
⅔ cup butter
⅔ cup chopped walnuts
¾ teaspoon cinnamon
¼ teaspoon nutmeg
2 eggs
¾ cup dairy eggnog
1 teaspoon vanilla

Preheat oven to 350°. Combine flour, sugar, baking powder and salt in a large mixing bowl. Cut in butter until mixture resembles coarse crumbs. Place ½ cup of the mixture in a small bowl. Stir in nuts and spices and set aside. To remainder of dry mixture, add eggs, eggnog and vanilla. Stir until well-blended. Pour a third of the batter in well-buttered and floured 9-inch loaf pan. Sprinkle with a third of crumb mixture. Repeat twice. Bake 60 to 65 minutes, or until wooden pick inserted in center comes out clean. Let cool in pan 15 minutes. Remove from pan and cool completely on wire rack. Wrap tightly in plastic wrap and store 24 hours before slicing.

ZUCCHINI BREAD

3 eggs, beaten
1 cup oil (not olive)
2 cups sugar
3 cups sifted all-purpose flour
1 teaspoon salt
2 teaspoons baking powder
1 teaspoon soda
1 teaspoon cinnamon
2 cups fresh zucchini squash (unpared)
1 cup chopped walnuts

Wash vegetable; remove blossom end and grate unpared zucchini to make 2 cups. (This is about 1 pound of zucchini.) In a bowl, beat eggs until light. Mix in oil and sugar. Mix and sift together flour, salt, baking powder, soda and cinnamon and add to beaten eggs. Stir in grated zucchini and nut meats. Bake in two greased and floured bread pans in a 350° oven for about 1 hour or until bread tests done. Cool on a rack. To freeze, wrap in plastic and then foil. Label.

CAROL'S BLUEBERRY-APPLESAUCE BREAD

Carol Louise Zimmerman, a 4th grade teacher from McMurray, Pennsylvania and a summer resident of Masons Bay, Jonesport, entered this overall prize-winning blueberry-applesauce bread at the Machias Blueberry Festival. She told us that her 4th graders have a cooking class each week and that the boys in the class are as enthusiastic as the girls, as well as very good cooks. This recipe makes a large loaf of bread.

1 cup sugar
2 eggs, well-beaten
1 cup applesauce
¼ cup melted butter or margarine
3 cups sifted all-purpose flour
3 teaspoons baking powder
1 teaspoon salt
½ teaspoon soda
½ teaspoon mace
2 cups blueberries
½ cup dried apricots, chopped

Mix and sift together flour, baking powder, salt, soda and mace. In a mixing bowl, mix sugar and beaten eggs. Stir in applesauce and melted butter. Add sifted dry ingredients. Mix well. Fold in blueberries and apricots. Spoon batter into a greased large bread pan or two smaller ones. Bake at 350° for about 50 minutes or until the bread tests done.

PINEAPPLE CARROT BREAD

3 cups sifted all-purpose flour
1 teaspoon soda
1 teaspoon salt
1½ teaspoons cinnamon
3 eggs, beaten
2 cups sugar
1 cup cooking oil (not olive)
1 cup grated raw carrots (about 2 large carrots)
1 cup crushed pineapple (undrained)
2 teaspoons vanilla

Mix and sift together flour, soda, salt and cinnamon. In a mixing bowl, beat eggs and sugar together; stir in oil, grated carrots and crushed pineapple. (An 8½-ounce can of crushed pineapple measures 1 cup.) Stir in sifted dry ingredients and vanilla. Grease two bread tins and line bottom of each with greased wax paper. Spoon batter into pans. Bake at 325° for 1 hour, or until bread tests done. Cool in pans for 15 minutes; remove from pans and cool on rack.

SPICED PRUNE AND WALNUT LOAVES

These loaves of spiced prune and walnut bread are baked in the small bread tins. That allows the homemaker to use some, freeze some and take one to a shut-in.

3 cups unsifted all-purpose flour
4 teaspoons baking powder
¾ teaspoon cinnamon
½ teaspoon salt
½ teaspoon ground allspice
¼ cup butter or margarine, softened
1 cup sugar
1 egg, beaten
1½ cups milk
2 cups diced pitted prunes
¾ cup chopped walnuts

Preheat oven to 350°. Grease four (small) 5¾x3x2-inch loaf pans; set aside. On a square of wax paper combine flour, baking powder, cinnamon, salt and allspice; set aside. In a large bowl cream butter. Add sugar; beat until light and fluffy . Beat in egg. Alternately stir in ⅓ of the flour mixture with ½ of the milk. Repeat, ending with flour. Stir in prunes and walnuts. Bake until a cake tester inserted in the center comes out clean, about 30 minutes. Let stand in pan 10 minutes. Loosen edges with a metal spatula. Turn out onto a wire rack to cool. YIELD: 4 loaves.

CINNAMON BREAD

½ cup margarine
1 cup sugar
2 eggs
1 teaspoon vanilla
2 cups flour
1 teaspoon salt
1 teaspoon soda
1 teaspoon baking powder
1 cup sour cream

Mix as for a cake. Put half of batter in greased bread pan. Sprinkle with half of filling. Add rest of batter and then rest of filling. Bake at 350⁰ for 1 hour, or until done.

FILLING

¼ cup sugar
¼ cup chopped nuts (optional)
1 teaspoon cinnamon

ORANGE-DATE-NUT BREAD

A loaf of quick bread is always welcomed for gifts, parties and family meals. This date bread has the extra surprise of orange juice and peel.

2 cups sifted all-purpose flour
2 teaspoons baking powder
½ teaspoon soda
½ cup chopped nut meats
2 tablespoons grated orange rind
2 tablespoons butter, melted
½ teaspoon salt
⅔ cup sliced, pitted dates
⅓ cup orange juice
⅔ cup water
1 teaspoon vanilla
1 egg beaten
½ cup sugar

Mix flour, baking powder, soda and salt; sift together 3 times. Add nut meats, orange rind and dates; mix all together. Beat egg well; add sugar, orange juice, water, vanilla and melted butter. Mix well. Add all at once to flour mixture and blend together. Spoon batter into a greased bread pan and allow the batter to stand for 15 minutes. Bake at 325⁰ for about 1 hour or until the bread tests done. Makes 1 large loaf.

BLUEBERRY-BANANA OATMEAL BREAD

½ cup blueberries
1½ cups flour
⅔ cup sugar
2¼ teaspoons baking powder
½ teaspoon salt
½ cup rolled oats, uncooked
2 eggs, beaten
½ cup melted butter or margarine
1 cup mashed bananas (2 or 3)
⅓ cup chopped walnuts

Wash and dry blueberries. Sprinkle with 2 tablespoons of the flour; set aside. Into a mixing bowl, sift remaining flour with sugar, baking powder and salt. (A sprinkle of nutmeg into this recipe adds an interesting flavor.) Stir in rolled oats. To beaten eggs add melted shortening and mashed bananas. Stir egg mixture into dry ingredients, only until moistened. Fold in prepared blueberries and nut meats. Spoon into greased and floured pan. Bake at 350° for about 50 minutes, or until bread tests done. Cool bread in pan for 10 to 12 minutes before removing from pan to finish cooling on a rack.

ORANGE APRICOT NUT BREAD

1 cup reconstituted frozen concentrated orange juice
1 cup chopped dried apricots
1 cup sugar
1 tablespoon butter or margarine, melted
1 egg, slightly beaten
2 cups all-purpose flour
1 teaspoon baking powder
1 teaspoon soda
½ teaspoon salt

In small saucepan, heat orange juice to boiling. Remove juice from heat and stir in apricots. Let stand 15 minutes. In mixing bowl, cream together sugar and butter; beat in egg. Add cooled orange juice and apricots. Mix and sift flour, baking powder, soda and salt and add to apricot mixture; mix well. Fold in chopped nut meats. Spoon into greased 9x5x3-inch pan. Bake for 1 hour in 350° oven, or until bread tests done. Best for slicing after 24 hours. To freeze, wrap in plastic wrap and then in foil. Label. Tests have shown that breads should be fully thawed before unwrapping, as they tend to lose their moisture if thawed after they are unwrapped.

BLUEBERRY ORANGE BREAD

3 medium oranges
1 beaten egg
2 tablespoons cooking oil
2 cups sifted all-purpose flour
1½ teaspoons baking powder
¾ cup granulated sugar
1 teaspoon salt
½ teaspoon soda
1 cup blueberries
½ cup chopped walnuts

Grate the peel of 1 orange and squeeze the juice of all 3 to make ¾ cup. (Extra juice may be used to make a glaze on the baked bread.) In a mixing bowl, combine grated peel, orange juice, egg and oil. Sift together flour, baking powder, soda, sugar and salt and add to egg mixture. Stir until just moist. Fold in blueberries and nuts. Spoon into a lightly greased 8-inch loaf pan. Bake 50 to 60 minutes at 350°. Cool. Combine 1 cup confectioners' sugar with orange juice and drizzle over the bread.

MILDRED'S CARROT AND ZUCCHINI BREAD

The person who gave me this recipe says that the bread freezes well and makes excellent toast. She uses a dark brown sugar in the recipe and all-purpose flour in place of the whole wheat flour. Is that not the way many homemakers tailor a recipe to their own needs?

3 eggs
1 cup vegetable oil
1½ cups brown sugar, packed
1 cup grated zucchini
1 cup grated carrots
2 teaspoons vanilla
2½ cups whole-wheat or all-purpose flour
½ cup bran cereal
1 teaspoon salt
1 teaspoon soda
1 teaspoon cinnamon
1 cup chopped walnuts

Preheat oven to 350°. Grease a 9-inch loaf pan or two small pans. In large bowl, beat eggs with oil. Stir in brown sugar, zucchini, carrots and vanilla. Mix flour, bran cereal, salt, soda and cinnamon and stir into egg mixture. Stir in nuts. Bake for 1 hour or longer until the bread tests done. The original recipe calls for 1½ hours, but as ovens differ, check after 1 hour of baking. This is a moist bread.

APRICOT AND NUT BREAD

An all-time favorite quick bread. This recipe makes a large loaf of bread.

    2 cups chopped dried apricots
    1 cup boiling water
    ¼ cup shortening or margarine
    1½ cups sugar
    2 eggs
    3 cups sifted all-purpose flour
    2 teaspoons soda
    ½ teaspoon salt
    1 cup walnut meats, coarsely broken

Pour boiling water over the chopped apricots; allow to stand for 15 minutes. Cream the shortening and sugar; beat in the eggs. Mix and sift together the flour, soda and salt and add to the creamed mixture alternately with the apricots, starting and ending with the dry ingredients. Stir in the nut meats. Spoon the batter into a greased and wax paper-lined bread pan. Bake at 325° for 50 minutes to 1 hour. Cool and wrap in foil.

DANISH ORANGE BREAD

    1 cup cooking oil (not olive)
    2 cups sugar
    4 eggs
    2 teaspoons soda
    1⅓ cups buttermilk
    4 cups sifted all-purpose flour
    1 teaspoon salt
      Grated peel of 1 large orange
    1 cup nut meats, chopped
      Juice of 2 oranges
    ⅔ cup granulated sugar

Mix oil and 2 cups sugar. Beat in eggs, one at a time. Dissolve soda in buttermilk and stir into oil mixture. Stir in the flour, salt and orange peel with nut meats. Pour batter into 2 greased bread pans. Bake in a moderate oven, 350°, for about an hour or until bread tests done. A few minutes before the bread comes from the oven, combine orange juice and granulated sugar. Boil for 1 minutes. When bread is done, cool for 10 minutes in pans; remove from pans to a rack and brush with the hot glaze.

LEMON BREAD

1 cup sugar
⅓ cup butter or margarine
2 eggs
1½ cups sifted all-purpose flour
1 teaspoon baking powder
½ teaspoon salt
½ cup milk
    Grated rind of 1 lemon
½ cup nut meats, chopped
⅓ cup sugar

Cream butter and 1 cup sugar; beat in eggs. Mix and sift together flour, baking powder and salt; add to creamed mixture alternately with milk and grated lemon rind. Stir in nut meats. Bake in a greased bread tin at 350° for about 50 minutes. Cool in pan for 5 minutes, then combine one-third cup sugar with lemon juice and spoon mixture over bread. Allow bread to cool in pan for 10 more minutes, then remove to cool on a rack.

HERB BREAD

This herb bread will go with any menu, especially with chicken. Serve the bread with no advance publicity to the family and note the results. Too much advance notice may elicit the "I know I'll not like it" response.

3 cups unsifted flour
3 tablespoons sugar
3 teaspoons baking powder
2 teaspoons caraway seeds
½ teaspoon salt
½ teaspoon nutmeg
½ teaspoon dried thyme leaves
1 cup skim milk
⅓ cup corn oil
1 egg, lightly beaten

In large bowl, stir together flour, sugar, baking powder, caraway seeds, salt, nutmeg and thyme. In small bowl, stir together milk, corn oil and egg. Add to flour mixture, stirring just until moistened. Turn into greased, 9-inch loaf pan. Bake in moderate oven, 350°, for 55 minutes or until cake tester inserted in center comes out clean. Remove from pan and cool on wire rack for at least 30 minutes before slicing.

TANGY APRICOT BREAD

1 (8 oz.) package dried apricots
½ cup chopped pecans
¼ cup all-purpose flour
1 cup sugar
2 tablespoons butter or margarine, softened
1 egg, beaten
1¾ cups all-purpose flour
2 teaspoons baking powder
¼ teaspoon soda
¼ teaspoon salt
½ cup orange juice
¼ cup water

Soak apricots in warm water for 30 minutes; drain and cut into small pieces. Combine with pecans; dredge with ¼ cup flour and set aside. Cream butter and sugar together; beat in egg; mix well. Combine 1¾ cups flour, baking powder, soda and salt. Add dry mixture to creamed mixture, beginning and ending with dry mixture, alternately with orange juice and water combined. Stir in apricots and pecans. Pour batter into greased loaf pan. Allow to stand for 15 minutes, then bake in moderate oven, 350° for one hour or until bread tests done.

WALNUT-RHUBARB BREAD

1½ cups packed light brown sugar
⅔ cup oil, not olive
1 egg, beaten
1 cup buttermilk or sour milk
1 teaspoon soda
1 teaspoon salt
2 teaspoons vanilla
2½ cups sifted all-purpose flour
1½ cups thinly sliced rhubarb
½ cup chopped walnut meats
1 tablespoon melted butter or margarine
⅓ cup granulated sugar

In mixing bowl, combine brown sugar, oil and egg. In another bowl, combine buttermilk, soda, salt and vanilla; add to oil mixture alternately with flour, mixing well after each addition. Fold in sliced rhubarb and nut meats. Spoon into two greased and floured bread pans. Combine granulated sugar and melted butter; mix thoroughly and scatter evenly over top of dough in pans. Bake at 325° for 45 to 50 minutes, or until bread tests done. Turn onto a rack to cool. Makes 2 loaves.

SOUR CREAM BANANA BREAD

1 stick (½ cup) butter or margarine
2 cups sugar
2 eggs
4 ripe bananas
3 cups sifted all-purpose flour
2 teaspoons soda
2 teaspoons baking powder
1 teaspoon salt
1 teaspoon vanilla
1½ cups chopped nut meats
¾ cup dairy soured cream
3 tablespoons chopped nut meats

Cream butter and sugar; add slightly beaten eggs. Thoroughly mash bananas and add to butter-sugar mixture. Stir in vanilla. Mix and sift together flour, soda, baking powder and salt and stir into banana mixture. Fold in sour cream and 1½ cups nut meats. Spoon into two greased and lightly floured bread pans. (We lined bottom of greased tin with waxed paper and greased the paper.) Srinkle 1½ tablespoons chopped nut meats over dough in each pan. Bake at 325° for about 1¼ hours. Do not open oven door until time is up. Cool for 10 minutes. Remove from pan to finish cooling on a wire rack.

CRANBERRY ORANGE NUT BREAD

2 cups sifted all-purpose flour
1 cup sugar
1½ teaspoons baking powder
½ teaspoon soda
¼ cup shortening or margarine
1 teaspoon salt
¾ cup orange juice
1 tablespoon grated orange peel
1 egg, well-beaten
¾ cup chopped nut meats
1½ to 2 cups fresh cranberries, chopped

In a mixing bowl, sift together flour, sugar, baking powder, soda and salt. Cut in shortening until mixture resembles coarse meal. Combine orange juice and grated peel with beaten egg and pour into flour mixture. Mix just enough to dampen. Carefully fold in nuts and chopped cranberries. Bake in greased loaf pan, 9 x 5 x 3 inches. Spread batter to corners of pan so that sides are slightly higher than center. Bake at 350° for about 1 hour. Test with a cake tester. Cool in pan for 10 minutes before turning onto a wire rack to completely cool.

HONEY APRICOT BREAD

For the home table, food sales and parties add this bread to your group of recipes. This is a contrast to the usual banana and date breads and goes well with the other breads on the sandwich tray.

1 cup milk, scalded
⅔ cup grape-nuts cereal
1 egg well-beaten
3 tablespoons butter or margarine, melted
¼ cup honey
1¾ cups all-purpose flour
2½ teaspoons baking powder
½ teaspoon salt
¾ cup firmly packed brown sugar
⅔ cup dried apricots, finely chopped

Pour scalded milk over cereal and cool. Add egg, butter and honey; mix well. Mix flour, baking powder, salt and sugar; stir in apricots. Add milk mixture and stir just to moisten the flour. Fill greased 8x4-inch loaf pan. Bake at 350° for 50 minutes or until bread tests done. Cool in pan for 10 minutes before removing to cool on a rack. Wrap in foil to store. Quick breads slice best when stored overnight.

BANANA BERRY BREAD

⅓ cup shortening or margarine
⅔ cup sugar
2 eggs, slightly beaten
½ cup chopped walnuts
1¾ cups sifted all-purpose flour
½ teaspoon salt
1 cup mashed, ripe bananas
½ cup chopped, fresh cranberries
2¼ teaspoons baking powder

Beat shortening until creamy; gradually add sugar, beating until light and fluffy. Add eggs and beat until thick and a light lemon in color. Mix and sift flour, salt and baking powder and add to creamed mixture alternately with the mashed bananas. Stir in nuts and cranberries. (Lacking cranberries, you might try blueberries.) Grease the bottom of a bread pan, cover bottom only with wax paper and grease the wax paper. Spoon batter into pan, making it even with some of the batter coming up a bit more at sides of the pan. Bake at 350° for about 1 hour to 1 hour, 10 minutes, or until bread tests done with a wooden pick. Cool in pan on rack for 20 minutes, then turn out onto rack to finish cooling.

GRAPENUTS-ORANGE MUFFINS

2 cups sifted all-purpose flour
6 teaspoons baking powder
½ teaspoon salt
2 tablespoons butter or margarine
⅔ cup sugar
2 eggs
¾ cup orange juice
   Grated rind of 1 orange
1 cup grapenuts

Mix and sift together flour, baking powder and salt. Cream butter; add sugar gradually. Beat in eggs. Add sifted dry ingredients alternately with orange juice and grated rind. Fold in grapenuts. Fill hot, greased muffin tins two-thirds full. Bake at 425° for 20 to 25 minutes. Makes 12 muffins.

AARON'S BUNDLES

A request for this recipe for Aaron's bundles sent us on a long hunt! Because a friend said the recipe was baked in an iron gem pan, usually used for baking gems or muffins, our search centered on muffin recipes. This is a cake batter but the shape is the pillow shape

½ cup granulated sugar
½ cup brown sugar
¾ cup shortening or margarine
1 egg, beaten
3 tablespoons molasses
2¼ cups all-purpose flour
1 teaspoon soda
1 teaspoon salt
1 teaspoon cinnamon
½ teaspoon nutmeg
¼ teaspoon cloves
1 cup buttermilk
1 cup seedless raisins
½ cup chopped nut meats

In mixing bowl cream shortening and sugars. Beat in egg. Mix and sift together flour, salt, soda and spices; add to creamed mixture alternately with buttermilk. Stir in raisins. Fill greased muffin tins or iron gem pans; sprinkle top of each with nut meats. Bake for 20 to 25 minutes at 350°. If raisins are dry, soften in boiling water for 5 minutes, drain well and add to batter.

MUFFINS

GRAHAM MUFFINS

Please don't leave out the vanilla. It's supposed to be in this recipe for graham muffins.

¼ cup butter or shortening
½ cup sugar
1 egg, beaten
1 teaspoon vanilla
½ teaspoon salt
1 cup sour milk or buttermilk
1 teaspoon soda
2 cups graham flour, unsifted

Cream butter and sugar; beat in egg. Stir in vanilla and salt. Dissolve soda in sour milk and blend with creamed mixture. Add graham flour. Fill greased muffin or gem pans two-thirds full of batter. Bake at 400° for 20 to 25 minutes, or until done.

DOUGHNUT MUFFINS

My mother, when I told her of a new recipe I had tried, would say, "It's just like mine, except - I don't use as much of this and less of that, but it's just like mine." This recipe for doughnut muffins came to me in that way, with additions and subtractions from the original, pub-

1 egg, slightly beaten
⅓ cup oil
½ cup milk
1 teaspoon vanilla
1 teaspoon lemon extract
1½ cups sifted all-purpose flour
½ cup sugar
2 teaspoons baking powder
½ teaspoon salt
1 teaspoon nutmeg
3 tablespoons sugar for topping
¼ teaspoon cinnamon

In a mixing bowl, beat egg slightly with a fork; with the fork mix in the oil, milk, vanilla and lemon. Mix and sift together flour, sugar, baking powder, salt and nutmeg. Add these dry ingredients to egg mixture, again using the fork for mixing. Spoon mixture into greased cupcake pans. Mix 3 tablespoons of sugar with cinnamon and sprinkle lightly over muffin batter. Top each muffin with a tiny piece of butter. Bake in a hot oven, 400° for about 15 minutes. Muffins in regular muffin pans will probably need 20 minutes.

BLUEBERRY MUFFINS

This recipe is only one of the many recipes for blueberry muffins; you may have a favorite.

1¾ cups sifted all-purpose flour
3 teaspoons baking powder
2 tablespoons sugar
1 teaspoon salt
1 egg, well beaten
1 cup milk
¼ cup melted shortening or margarine
1¼ cup fresh blueberries

Wash, drain and pat dry the blueberries. Sift together into a bowl the flour, sugar, baking powder and salt. Mix together egg, milk and melted shortening and add all at once to the dry ingredients; mix thoroughly. Fold in the blueberries. Drop dough into each of 12 muffin cups, filling each about two-thirds full. Bake at 425° until muffins are done, about 25 minutes. Serve warm.

APPLESAUCE MUFFINS

Are you looking at what is in the freezer to be used before the new crop is harvested, or what is in jars or cans on the shelf? If it is applesauce, you may like to make some applesauce muffins.

1 cup cornmeal
¾ cup sifted all-purpose flour
2 teaspoons baking powder
½ teaspoon salt
⅔ cup canned, sweetened applesauce
½ cup milk
1 egg, beaten
¼ cup vegetable oil
2 tablespoons sugar
½ teaspoon cinnamon

Sift together into a bowl cornmeal, flour, baking powder and salt. Add applesauce, milk, egg and vegetable oil; stir only until dry ingredients are moistened. Fill greased muffin cups ⅔ full. Combine sugar and cinnamon and sprinkle top of each muffin batter. Bake in preheated oven, 425°, for about 15 minutes. The only sweetening in the muffins is from the sweetened applesauce. Because ovens vary, it may take a longer baking time.

TWIN MOUNTAIN MUFFINS

One of the first foods we learned to make in Home Economics was Twin Mountain muffins. Was the recipe from a famous eating place? Was it named for Twin Mountains in New Hampshire? We never knew, but we did know that the muffins were delicious with any meal.

2 cups sifted all-purpose flour
½ teaspoon salt
5 teaspoons baking powder
¼ cup (½ stick) butter or margarine, melted
1 cup milk
1 beaten egg
¼ cup sugar

In a mixing bowl, sift flour, salt, sugar and baking powder. In another bowl combine beaten egg and milk. Add the melted and cooled butter. Stir into dry mixture. Mix, but do not overmix. Spoon into greased muffin pans. Bake for about 25 minutes at 400°. These muffins freeze well.

PEANUT BUTTER BRAN MUFFINS

Can't you just taste these muffins as you read the list of ingredients —bran, raisins and wheat germ blended with buttermilk, honey, peanut butter and other goodies.

1½ cups bran cereal
1 cup golden raisins
1 cup boiling water
½ cup honey wheat germ
2¼ cups buttermilk
1 cup honey
2 eggs
½ cup chunky peanut butter
⅓ cup butter, melted
1¾ cups all-purpose flour
¾ cup whole wheat flour
2½ teaspoons soda
½ teaspoon salt

Preheat oven to 375°. Combine bran, raisins, boiling water and wheat germ in medium-sized bowl. Let stand 10 minutes. Meanwhile, combine buttermilk, honey, eggs, peanut butter and butter in large bowl. Stir in bran mixture. Mix in dry ingredients. Fill paper-lined 2¾-inch muffin cups three-fourths full. Bake 20 to 25 minutes, or until golden. Cool in pan 10 minutes. Remove from pan and cool completely on wire rack. If desired, freeze in meal-size packages.

SOUR CREAM CORN MUFFINS

1 cup yellow cornmeal
1 cup flour
¼ cup sugar
2 teaspoons baking powder
1 teaspoon salt
½ teaspoon soda
1 cup sour cream
2 eggs, slightly beaten
¼ cup butter, melted

Butter 12 muffin tins. In a medium bowl, combine cornmeal, flour, sugar, baking powder, salt and soda. In a small bowl, combine sour cream, beaten eggs and melted butter; blend well. Add to dry ingredients and stir until evenly blended; do not overmix. Drop batter into prepared muffin tins and bake at 425°, 25 to 30 minutes. Cool in pans for 5 minutes before removing. Serve hot.

BLUEBERRY STREUSEL MUFFINS

⅓ cup sugar
¼ cup butter or margarine, softened
1 egg
2⅓ cups all-purpose flour
1 tablespoon plus 1 teaspoon baking powder
1 cup milk
1 teaspoon vanilla extract
1½ cups fresh blueberries

Preheat oven to 375°. In a large bowl, combine the sugar and butter, creaming until light. Add the egg, mixing well. In a separate bowl, combine the flour and baking powder. Add the dry ingredients to the creamed mixture alternately with the milk, stirring well after each addition. Stir in vanilla and blueberries. Spoon into lined muffin pans, filling each ⅔ full. Sprinkle streusel topping over muffin batter. Bake for 25 to 30 minutes or until done. Makes 16 to 18 muffins.

STREUSEL TOPPING

½ cup sugar
⅓ cup all-purpose flour
½ teaspoon ground cinnamon
¼ cup butter or margarine

Combine sugar, flour and cinnamon in a small bowl. Cut in butter until mixture resembles crumbs. Sprinkle over batter in muffin pans.

PLUM OATMEAL MUFFINS

5 medium fresh California plums
1¾ cups rolled oats
2 cups flour
¾ cup brown sugar, packed
3 teaspoons baking powder
1 teaspoon salt
1 teaspoon vanilla
1 teaspoon grated orange rind
1 egg
⅓ cup vegetable oil
Granulated sugar

Cut up 2 or 3 plums to measure 1 cup; whirl in blender until smooth. Coarsely chop remaining plums; set aside. Combine pureed plums with remaining ingredients except granulated sugar; stir just until blended. Stir in chopped plums. Spoon batter into 18 greased 2½-inch muffin cups or 7 greased 6-ounce custard cups. Sprinkle tops with granulated sugar. Bake at 350° for 35 minutes or until pick inserted in center comes out dry. Makes 1½ dozen small or 7 large muffins.

DATE-ALL BRAN MUFFINS

2 cups All-Bran cereal
2 cups crushed shredded wheat
½ cup boiling water
1 cup shortening
3 cups sugar
4 eggs, slightly beaten
5 cups sifted all-purpose flour
4½ teaspoons soda
½ teaspoon baking powder
2 teaspoons salt
1 quart buttermilk
1 cup chopped dates or raisins

In a bowl, combine All-Bran and crushed shredded wheat; pour boiling water over cereal. In another bowl, cream shortening and sugar; stir in eggs. Add cereals. Mix and sift together flour, soda, baking powder and salt into a large bowl. To this add creamed mixture alternately with buttermilk. Mix well. Stir in dates or raisins. Store in airtight container in refrigerator, and bake as many as you need at one time. When ready to use, fill greased muffin tins two-thirds full. Bake at 400° for 20 to 25 minutes. Recipe makes 4 dozen muffins.

FIT 'N FIBER MUFFIN

Are you ready for a muffin with onion as an ingredient; one that goes well with chili or a pot roast? It's different and an interesting change.

2 eggs, beaten
1⅓ cup milk
¼ cup honey
¼ cup oil
¼ cup onion, finely chopped
1 cup whole wheat flour
1 cup cornmeal
4 teaspoons baking powder
½ teaspoon salt
¼ cup sunflower seeds, shelled

In a medium mixer bowl, combine eggs, milk, honey, oil and onion. Add flour, cornmeal, baking powder and salt. Stir until moistened. Batter will be very thin. Spoon into well-greased or paper-lined muffin cups until ⅔ full. Sprinkle with sunflower seeds. Bake at 400°, 18 to 20 minutes. YIELD: 12-18 muffins.

CARROT MUFFINS

1½ cups sifted all-purpose flour
½ cup whole wheat flour
¼ cup packed brown sugar
1 teaspoon baking powder
½ teaspoon soda
¾ teaspoon cinnamon
¾ teaspoon nutmeg
½ teaspoon salt
¾ cup shredded carrots
½ cup walnuts, chopped
1 cup buttermilk or sour milk
1 egg, beaten
2 tablespoons melted butter or margarine

In a mixing bowl combine all-purpose flour, whole wheat flour, brown sugar, baking powder, salt, soda, cinnamon and nutmeg. Stir together, mixing well. Stir in walnuts and shredded carrots. Stir buttermilk into beaten egg; add melted butter; mix and add to dry mixture. Stir to mix; do not overmix. Spoon into paper-lined muffin pans, filling each cup two-thirds full. Bake at 350° for 30 minutes or until done. Makes 12 muffins.

SQUASH MUFFINS

This recipe for squash muffins was used at the Old Gardner House at East Machias in the early 1800's. This inn was the stop for the stagecoach, for the steamer that came up the river to Machiasport, and for transients. This is a soft, sweet muffin, almost appearing as if it were not completely cooked, it is that tender.

½ cup shortening
½ cup sugar
 1 egg
 1 cup milk
 1 cup mashed squash
 2 cups sifted all-purpose flour
 1 teaspoon salt
 1 teaspoon soda
 2 teaspoons cream of tartar

Cream shortening and sugar; add egg and mix well. Add milk and squash. Mix and sift together flour, salt, soda and cream of tartar; add to creamed mixture. Stir only enough to mix. Bake in greased muffin tins or iron gem pans at 425° for 20 to 25 minutes. This recipe makes about 16 muffins.

LARGE CEREAL MUFFINS

 1 cup sifted all-purpose flour
½ cup whole wheat flour
 3 teaspoons baking powder
½ teaspoon salt
⅔ cup firmly packed brown sugar
½ teaspoon cinnamon
¼ teaspoon nutmeg
 1 cup milk
 1 egg, slightly beaten
⅓ cup cooking oil
 2 cups corn flakes
⅓ cup chopped nut meats

Mix all-purpose and whole wheat flours with baking powder and salt. In another bowl combine brown sugar, cinnamon, nutmeg, oil, milk and egg; mix well and add to flour mixture. Stir until just moistened. Stir in corn flakes and nut meats. Spoon into six paper baking cups or twelve greased muffin cups. Bake at 400° for 30 to 35 minutes or until muffins test done.

SPICED ORANGE MUFFINS

Treat your friends with coffee and spiced orange muffins, served at the next meeting you attend. Other committee members will enjoy the coffee and muffins to make it a fun meeting.

1 cup all-purpose flour
1 cup whole wheat flour
1½ teaspoons baking powder
¾ teaspoon soda
1¼ teaspoon ground mace or nutmeg
1 teaspoon ground cinnamon
½ teaspoon ground ginger
¼ teaspoon salt
⅓ cup cold butter or margarine, cut in pieces
½ thin-skin juice orange, seeded, coarsely chopped
Scant ¼-cup milk
⅔ cup sugar
2 teaspoons vanilla extract
2 eggs
⅔ cup raisins
¼ cup finely chopped walnuts

Preheat oven to 375°. Lightly grease 15 standard-sized muffin-tin cups or fit with paper liners. Stir together white flour, whole wheat flour, baking powder, soda, spices and salt in a medium bowl. Cut in butter with pastry blender or forks until mixture resembles coarse meal. Place all remaining ingredients, except walnuts and raisins, in blender container or food processor bowl and blend or process. Blend on medium speed or process 30 seconds. Scrape down container sides of bowl and blend or process one minute longer or until mixture is completely smooth. Pour pureed mixture, then raisins and walnuts into dry ingredients. Gently stir until thoroughly blended, but not overmixed. Divide mixture evenly among prepared cups. Bake for 22 to 25 minutes until muffins are golden brown and tops are springy to the touch. Serve warm. Muffins may be frozen and reheated for later use. Makes 15 muffins.

PLUM-GOOD COFFEE CAKE

½ cup butter, softened
⅔ cup sugar
4 eggs
1 teaspoon vanilla
1 cup all-purpose flour
1 teaspoon baking powder
½ teaspoon pumpkin pie spice
1½ cups diced plums (about 8 oz.)
    Confectioners' sugar (optional)

Grease a 9-inch cake pan. In small mixing bowl, beat together butter and sugar at medium speed until light and fluffy. Beat in eggs and vanilla until thoroughly blended. Stir together dry ingredients. Add flour mixture to egg mixture and beat until smooth. Fold in ¾ cup of the plums. Pour into prepared pan. Top with remaining plums. Bake at 375º until lightly browned and top springs back when lightly touched with finger, about 30 to 35 minutes. Cool on wire rack. Dust with confectioners' sugar if desired.

MARIE'S COFFEE CAKE

FILLING:

¾ cup graham cracker crumbs
½ cup flour
½ cup margarine
⅓ cup sugar
1½ teaspoons cinnamon
½ teaspoon nutmeg

Combine ingredients in a small bowl and mix on low speed until crumbs form.

CAKE PART:

¾ cup margarine
1½ cups sugar
3 cups sifted all-purpose flour
1½ cups sour cream
3 eggs
1½ teaspoons baking powder
1½ teaspoons soda
1½ teaspoons vanilla

Cream margarine and sugar until fluffy. Add eggs, flour, sour cream, baking powder, soda and vanilla. Beat at low speed until blended. Increase speed to medium and beat for 3 minutes. Spread a third of the batter in an ungreased tube pan; scatter on a third of the filling. Repeat two more times. Bake in a moderate oven, 350º, for 50 to 60 minutes.

SOUR CREAM COFFEE CAKE

½ cup butter or margarine
½ cup shortening
1¼ cups sugar
2 eggs, beaten
1 cup sour cream
1 teaspoon vanilla
2 cups sifted cake flour (or 1¾ cup sifted all-purpose flour)
1 teaspoon baking powder
½ teaspoon soda
½ cup chopped pecan meats
2 tablespoons sugar
1 teaspoon cinnamon

Grease a 9-inch tube or spring-form pan. Preheat oven to 350°. Cream together butter, shortening and sugar; add eggs, sour cream and vanilla. Beat well. Sift together flour, baking powder and soda and add to creamed mixture. Place half of mixture in greased pan. Combine chopped nut meats, 2 tablespoons sugar and cinnamon; mix and sprinkle half over the dough. Place rest of dough on top and sprinkle with remaining topping. Bake for 1 hour or until cake tests done. Sprinkle confectioners' sugar on top of the hot cake. Let cool before cutting.

"EMMIE'S" BLUEBERRY COFFEE CAKE

2 cups sifted all-purpose flour
1½ cups sugar
½ cup (1 stick) butter
1 teaspoon salt
2 teaspoons baking powder
2 eggs, separated
1 cup milk
1 cup blueberries, fresh or frozen

Mix and sift the flour and sugar together into a mixing bowl. Cut in butter until mixture is like a biscuit mixture, the size of small peas. Remove ½ cup of the mixture and set aside. To the remaining flour mixture add baking powder, salt, egg yolks and milk. Beat on low speed for 3 minutes. Beat egg whites stiff; fold into the batter. Spread into a well-greased and lightly floured 9-by-13-inch baking pan. Spread blueberries (thawed, if frozen) evenly over top of batter; sprinkle reserved flour mixture over blueberries and bake in a moderate oven, 350°, for 45 minutes. Good hot or cold.

CHOCOLATE CHIP COFFEE CAKE

In addition to the familiar ones, it's nice to have a new recipe for coffee cake to share with friends or new folks in the neighborhood. This cake may be made in the food processor or the electric mixer.

½ cup milk
½ cup (1 stick) butter or margarine
⅓ cup sugar
1 teaspoon salt
2 packages active dry yeast
½ cup warm water
2 eggs, beaten, at room temperature
3 cups all-purpose flour
¾ cup semi-sweet chocolate morsels
Coffee-cake topping

Scald milk; stir in butter, sugar and salt. Cool to lukewarm. Sprinkle yeast into warm water in large, warm bowl. Stir until dissolved. Add lukewarm milk mixture, eggs and 2 cups flour. Beat at medium speed of electric mixer until smooth, about 15 to 20 seconds. Stir in remaining 1 cup flour and chocolate morsels until well blended, about 1 minute. Turn into well-greased tube pan with removable bottom or 9-inch springform pan. Cover; let rise in warm, draft-free place until doubled in size, about 45 to 60 minutes. Bake at 400° for 15 minutes; remove from oven and sprinkle with coffee-cake topping. Return to oven and bake additional 15 minutes or until done. Cool in pan 10 minutes, then remove and cool upright on wire rack.

COFFEE-CAKE TOPPING

¼ cup (½ stick) butter or margarine
⅓ cup all-purpose flour
⅓ cup sugar
1½ teaspoons cinnamon
½ cup semi-sweet chocolate morsels
½ cup pecans, chopped

Cut butter into flour; stir in sugar, cinnamon, chocolate morsels and nuts.

RAISIN COFFEE CAKE

Make a raisin coffee cake for breakfast, for a midnight snack or toasted with a mid-morning cup of coffee. Use it warm from the oven for the committee meeting. Good for snacking for returning school children.

    2 cups sifted all-purpose flour
2½ teaspoons baking powder
    1 teaspoon salt
⅓ cup shortening
⅓ cup sugar
    1 egg
¾ cup milk
½ to ¾ cup raisins
½ teaspoon grated orange rind
    3 tablespoons brown sugar
½ teaspoon cinnamon
¼ teaspoon nutmeg

Mix and sift flour, baking powder and salt. Cream shortening and ⅓ cup sugar; beat in egg. Add sifted dry ingredients alternately with milk, beating well. Fold in raisins and orange rind. Spoon into greased 9x9x2-inch baking pan. Mix brown sugar, cinnamon and nutmeg and sprinkle over mixture in pan. Bake at 425° for 20 minutes or until done.

HARRINGTON STEAMED BROWN BREAD

1 cup graham flour
1 cup rolled oats, uncooked
1 cup sifted all-purpose flour
2½ teaspoons soda
1 teaspoon salt
2 cups cold water
⅔ cup molasses

Mix together and sift the flour, soda and salt. Add the graham flour and rolled oats. Add molasses and water; mix well. Fill well-greased pound-size shortening cans or molds two-thirds full, or spoon batter into one 3-pound shortening can. Cover tightly; steam 3 to 3½ hours. To steam, put can or mold on trivet in kettle containing boiling water that comes half way up on mold. Keep water boiling; add more as needed. Keep kettle covered.

FRANNIE'S PANCAKES

A Candlemas Day custom in many places, expecially in England, is to run while flipping pancakes up in the air from the frying pan. You may have to run from the stove to the table to keep the plates filled with these hot pancakes. Maine maple syrup goes well with these but molasses was used years ago when the syrup, made from the spring run of sap, had been used up.

2½ cups sour milk or buttermilk
½ cup sour cream
3 eggs, well beaten
¼ cup sugar
1 teaspoon salt
1 teaspoon baking powder
1½ teaspoons soda
3 cups, more or less, sifted all-purpose flour

Add well-beaten eggs to the buttermilk and sour cream mixture. Stir in the sugar. Mix and sift the flour, salt, baking powder and soda and add to the buttermilk mixture. "More or less" flour depends on how thick you will like your batter. Try 2½ cups of sifted flour with the salt, baking powder and soda first, then add other half cup of flour if needed. Drop batter by spoonsfull onto a hot greased griddle; when bubbles appear, flip the cake over. Whatever pancake recipe you use on Candlemas Day, think of the young ladies in England flipping their pancakes as they run!

MA'S JOHNNY CAKE

Every morning there was a Johnny cake for breakfast to go with fried 'taters, bacon, make-me-grow (cooked rolled oats) and apple or wild strawberry sauce.

½ cup sifted all-purpose flour
½ teaspoon soda
2 teaspoons baking powder
1½ cups cornmeal
1 egg, slightly beaten
1 cup buttermilk or sour milk
3 tablespoons melted shortening
1 teaspoon salt

Mix and sift together the dry ingredients. Add buttermilk to egg. Combine liquid with cornmeal mixture; add fat and stir until mixture is moistened. Pour into greased 8- or 9-inch square pan. Bake at 425° until top is brown, about 30 minutes.

TIM'S CINNAMON APPLE SCONES

2 cups sifted all-purpose flour
2 tablespoons sugar
2 teaspoons baking powder
½ teaspoon cinnamon
⅛ teaspoon nutmeg
⅛ teaspoon ginger
⅛ teaspoon allspice
⅓ cup butter or margarine
1 egg
½ cup milk
⅔ cup diced McIntosh apples
1 tablespoon heavy cream
¼ teaspoon cinnamon
2 tablespoons sugar

Mix and sift together flour, 2 tablespoons sugar, baking powder, ½ teaspoon cinnamon, and the nutmeg, ginger and allspice. (We added ½ teaspoon salt.) Cut in the butter until mixture resembles coarse crumbs—not unlike a biscuit mixture. Stir in egg and milk. Fold in diced apples. Turn dough onto lightly floured surface. Divide in half, and pat each half into two 6-inch circles. Cut each into 6 wedges; placed on ungreased baking sheet. Combine cream, ¼ teaspoon cinnamon and 2 tablespoons sugar and brush over scones. Bake in a hot oven, 425°, for 10 to 12 minutes. Cool before serving.

CORN BREAD

1½ cups corn meal
½ cup all-purpose flour
2 tablespoons sugar
2 teaspoons baking powder
½ teaspoon salt
1 cup milk
1 egg, beaten
¼ cup vegetable oil

Heat oven to 425°. Grease 9-inch square pan. Combine corn meal, flour, sugar, baking powder and salt. Add milk, egg and oil; mix just until dry ingredients are moistened. Pour into prepared pan. Bake about 20 minutes or until golden brown. Cool. This is good toasted for breakfast with honey or jam on it.

HARLAND'S CREAM OF TARTAR BISCUITS

3 cups sifted all-purpose flour
5 teaspoons cream of tartar
2 teaspoons soda
1 teaspoon salt
5 tablespoons lard
1 cup plus 2 tablespoons milk

Mix and sift dry ingredients into a mixing bowl. Cut the lard in with a blender or tips of the fingers. Add milk. More milk may be needed depending on flour used. Knead on lightly floured board, quickly and lightly. Roll to ½-inch thickness. Cut with 2½-inch biscuit cutter. Place in baking pan, close together for little crust, farther apart for crusty biscuits, and bake at 500° until golden brown.

BUTTERMILK JOHNNY CAKE

½ cup molasses
1 egg
1 cup corn meal
½ teaspoon salt
1 cup buttermilk
1 cup flour
1 teaspoon soda

Beat egg and molasses. Add corn meal, buttermilk in which soda has been mixed, and flour to which ½ teaspoon of salt has been added. Stir to mix but do not overmix. Bake in greased 8- or 9-inch square pan at 400° for about 30 minutes, or until done.

SPOON BREAD OR SPIDER CORN BREAD

In the past we used this recipe in home economics demonstrations. This is a soft bread, cooked in an iron frying pan ("spider") and sometimes eaten with a spoon.

1½ cups corn meal
1 cup flour
1 cup sour milk or buttermilk
1 scant teaspoon soda
2 eggs
2 cups sweet milk
¼ cup sugar
½ teaspoon salt
1½ tablespoons butter

Mix and sift corn meal with flour; add sour milk mixed with soda, well-beaten eggs, and half of the sweet milk, sugar and salt. Heat an iron frying pan. Add butter, and when it melts turn in the corn meal mixture. Pour the remaining milk over all, but do not stir. Cook in a 350° oven for about 50 minutes. Cut in wedges to serve, and top with butter or a bit of maple syrup.

HELENE'S DOUGHNUTS

1 cup sugar
2 eggs
⅔ cup sour milk or buttermilk
2 tablespoons melted butter
1 teaspoon lemon extract
3 cups sifted all-purpose flour
1 teaspoon soda
1 teaspoon salt
1 teaspoon baking powder
½ teaspoon nutmeg
¾ teasapoon ginger

Beat sugar, eggs and buttermilk together; add melted butter and lemon extract; beat well. Mix and sift together flour, soda, salt, baking powder, nutmeg and ginger and add to buttermilk mixture. This is a soft dough. Chill thoroughly in refrigerator before rolling on a floured board. Roll to ¼-inch thickness. For doughnut holes, use a 1¼-inch cutter; for regular doughnuts use doughnut cutter. Fry in hot (365° on thermometer) fat. Turn doughnuts to cook both sides. Doughnut holes do not need turning.

DELLA'S SCOTCH SCONES

This scone is good served hot as well as split and toasted.

1 cup sour milk or buttermilk
⅔ cup sour cream
2 teaspoons soda
1 teaspoon salt
2 tablespoons sugar
1½ cups sifted all-purpose flour
1½ cups graham flour

In mixing bowl, combine sour milk and sour cream. Mix and sift together flour, graham flour, soda, salt and sugar; add coarse siftings from graham flour; add to sour milk and cream. This is a soft dough. Knead dough on pastry cloth; roll to ½-inch thickness in shape of circle. Cut in 2-inch wedges. Bake on greased cookie sheet at 450° for about 15 minutes, or until done.

BLUEBERRY SCONE

2 cups sifted all-purpose flour
½ cup sugar
2 teaspoons baking powder
½ teaspoon soda
½ teaspoon salt
½ cup margarine or butter (1 stick)
2 eggs, beaten
½ cup sour milk or buttermilk
1½ cups fresh blueberries
    Topping (optional)

Mix and sift flour, sugar, baking powder, soda and salt into a mixing bowl. Cut in margarine as for making biscuits, until well distributed. Beat eggs; add buttermilk, mix and add to dry ingredients. Mix to form a soft dough. Stir in blueberries which have been rinsed in water, drained and dried. (If frozen berries are used they do not need to be defrosted.) Spoon batter into a greased 7x11-inch pan. Add the topping, if used, and bake in a moderately hot oven, 375°, for 35 to 40 minutes. Serve hot or cold, or sliced and toasted.

IRISH SODA BREAD

　3 cups all-purpose flour
1½ teaspoons baking powder
　1 teaspoon soda
　1 teaspoon salt
　4 tablespoons caraway seeds (optional)
　1 cup raisins or currants
　1 egg
　1 tablespoon shortening or softened margarine
　1 cup buttermilk

Preheat oven to 350°. Lightly grease baking pan and set aside. Mix dry ingredients, raisins and caraway seeds in a large mixing bowl. Add egg, margarine, softened (not melted) butter and mix well. Place dough on a floured board and mold into a round loaf. Place loaf in the greased pan and bake 1 hour. Serve at once, or cool and serve toasted.

BUTTERMILK BISCUITS

Cut the rolled dough in squares or cut with a regular round biscuit cutter in this buttermilk biscuit recipe.

　2 cups all-purpose flour
　3 teaspoons baking powder
　¼ teaspoon soda
　½ teaspoon salt
　⅓ cup butter, margarine or shortening
　¾ to 1 cup buttermilk

Mix flour, baking powder, soda and salt in a bowl. Cut in butter with a pastry fork or two knives until mixture is crumbly. Stir in, all at once, ¾ cup buttermilk. Because every brand of flour is different, you may need more buttermilk to make a soft dough. Knead dough gently about 10 times on lightly floured surface. Pat or roll to ½-inch thickness. Cut into squares or cut with a floured 2-inch biscuit cutter. Place biscuits on baking sheet; brush tops with a little buttermilk. Bake in a very hot oven, 450°, 12 to 15 minutes until lightly browned. Makes 12 biscuits.

CORN PUDDING

1 package frozen corn, or 1½ to 2 cups canned
3 eggs
1 cup light cream or milk
¼ cup sugar
½ teaspoon salt
2 tablespoons margarine
¼ cup grated cheese

Blend corn, eggs, milk, sugar, salt and margarine in blender. Pour into buttered 1-quart casserole. Sprinkle grated cheese on top and let it sink in. Bake at 350° for 1 hour. Makes 4-5 servings.

COLEEN BEAN'S ZUCCHINI CASSEROLE

If you are taking a casserole to a potluck supper you might like to try this recipe, or you may like to make it for supper at home. It's nearly all vegetable, only two hot sausages are used. Put a loaf of French bread in the oven to heat to go with the casserole. Both microwave and regular baking directions are given.

1 tablespoon water
4 onions (2½ to 3-inch size), sliced thick
2 cups chopped zucchini
½ green pepper, cut in 1-inch strips
6 oz. super sharp cheese (cut in ½-inch cubes)
¼ teaspoon salt
Parsley flakes
6 ozs. tomato paste
2 hot sausages, sliced thin
Sprinkle of oregano
Sprinkle of garlic powder
1 scant tablespoon sugar
Grated Parmesan cheese

In a 2-quart casserole put water, zucchini and onion separated into rings. Cover with plastic wrap or glass lid. Microwave on high until done. (See below for regular oven instructions.) Do not drain. Add green pepper, sharp cheese, tomato paste and sliced hot sausages and mix; sprinkle with oregano, garlic powder, sugar and salt. Microwave on high until green peppers are tender and casserole is hot. Remove from oven. Sprinkle top with grated Parmesan cheese and parsley flakes. Let stand covered 5 minutes before serving. Makes 4 to 6 servings. (FOR REGULAR OVEN: Onions and zucchini can be cooked together with a small amount of water until done. Leave about 6 ounces of liquid and add rest of ingredients except Parmesan and parsley. Bake at 350° until hot and peppers are tender. Add Parmesan cheese and parsley flakes.)

PINEAPPLE-CHEESE CASSEROLE

1 20-oz. can crushed pineapple
1 20-oz. can chunk pineapple
8 slices American cheese, cut small
1 cup sugar
½ cup flour
⅓ stick butter or margarine
¼ teaspoon salt

Do not drain pineapple. Mix all ingredients together and pour into a greased casserole. Bake at 350° for 30 minutes, or until it bubbles and is slightly brown on top.

FRESH MUSHROOM SCALLOP

Casseroles traditionally take very little preparation time and few ingredients, but long, slow simmering molds the flavors together to make an extraordinary dish that is greater than the sum of its parts. This casserole is made simply by layering sliced potatoes, flour and seasonings, sauteed mushrooms, Parmesan cheese and milk. As the casserole bakes, the mushroom flavor intensifies and transforms the ingredients into a delicious part of the menu. Serve as a main dish or add sliced meat, whole-wheat bread and a tossed salad.

2 teaspoons vegetable oil
1 pound fresh mushrooms, sliced
1 tablespoon flour
¼ teaspoon salt
¼ teaspoon pepper
1½ pounds potatoes (4 to 5 medium), thinly sliced
½ cup grated Parmesan cheese
3 tablespoons butter or margarine
1 cup milk
1 tablespoon chopped parsley

Heat oil in a large skillet; add mushrooms and saute over high heat until tender and liquid has evaporated; set aside. In small bowl, combine flour, salt and pepper. Cover bottom of greased, shallow 1½-quart baking dish with a layer of potatoes; sprinkle with some of the flour mixture. Add a layer of mushrooms; sprinkle with some of the Parmesan cheese and dot with butter. Repeat layers until all of the ingredients are used. Pour milk over all. Cover and bake in 375° oven about 45 minutes. Remove cover and continue baking until potatoes are tender and top is browned, about 30 minutes. Sprinkle with chopped parsley.

CLAM SCALLOP

When the clam flats or the fish market have no clams, use canned minced clams for a clam scallop. Cans of minced clams are good insurance on the shelf for such an emergency.

2 cans minced clams
6 saltines, rolled fine
1½ cups milk
⅛ teaspoon pepper
2 tablespoons minced onion
2 eggs, beaten
3 tablespoons butter

Combine all ingredients in a buttered casserole. Set casserole in a pan of hot water and bake at 350° for about 1 hour.

BROCCOLI, HAM AND CHEESE BAKE

Ham slices or "scrids" of ham left over from a baked ham dinner? Make a broccoli, ham and cheese bake for another meal. If you have broccoli in your freezer, use that, in the amount enough to cover the bottom of a 2-quart casserole.

1 package frozen broccoli (10 oz.), or fresh
4 tablespoons butter or margarine
¼ cup finely chopped onion
4 tablespoons all-purpose flour
½ teaspoon salt
1½ cups skim milk
2 cups cooked ham (diced or chopped)
1 cup shredded Cheddar cheese (4 ounces)
2 tablespoons chopped pimiento
1 tablespoon chopped parsley
½ cup herb-flavored croutons

Cook broccoli in ½ cup water; drain and reserve ½ cup of cooking liquid. In a 2-quart saucepan, melt butter; saute onion. Stir in flour and salt until blended. Add a few grains of Cayenne pepper, if desired. Remove from heat; stir in milk and reserved cooking liquid. Heat to boiling, stirring constantly. Boil and stir for one minute. Remove from heat; stir in ham, cheese, pimiento and parsley. Place cooked broccoli in buttered casserole and cover with ham and cheese sauce. Sprinkle herb-flavored crumbs on top. Bake in a moderate oven, 350°, 20 to 25 minutes or until bubbly. Makes 6 servings.

BAKED HADDOCK CASSEROLE

2 pounds haddock fillets
2 tablespoons lemon juice
¼ cup butter or margarine, melted
3 or 4 slices American or Cheddar cheese
   Salt and pepper

Cut fish in serving-size pieces and sprinkle with salt and pepper, if desired. Melt butter and mix with lemon juice. Dip fish in butter and place in casserole. Pour remaining butter mixture over fish. Tear cheese in small portions and place on fish. Top with crisp cracker crumbs mixed with 3 tablespoons melted butter. Bake at 350° 25 to 30 minutes.

SALMON TORTELLINI WITH VEGETABLES

This one-dish casserole goes together fast and in large quantities. It combines a variety of different nutrients and can be served hot or cold, satisfying the cook as well as a hungry family. Serve it hot for dinner on Tuesday night, or mix up a batch on Friday to chill and take on a weekend picnic.

1 can (15½ oz.) salmon
2 cups cut fresh green beans
¾ cup julienne carrots
1 tablespoon vegetable oil
1 tablespoon butter or margarine
1 firm medium tomato, seeded, cut in strips
¼ cup water
1 teaspoon dried basil, crushed
1 teaspoon dried oregano, crushed
1 package (9 oz.) fresh cheese tortellini, cooked
¼ cup grated Parmesan cheese
   Salt to taste
   Pepper to taste

Drain the salmon, reserving 2 tablespoons liquid; break into bite-size pieces. Saute beans and carrots in oil about 5 to 7 minutes or until crisp-tender. Add tomato, water, reserved salmon liquid, basil and oregano. Cook until thoroughly heated. Add salmon, cooked tortellini, cheese, salt and pepper. Carefully toss to combine. Makes 4 servings.

ZUCCHINI-CARROT CASSEROLE

2 cups seasoned bread crumbs
½ stick butter, melted
6 cups sliced zucchini
1 can cream of chicken soup
1 cup sour cream
½ cup chopped onions
1 cup shredded carrots

Mix bread crumbs and butter. Set aside. Cook zucchini and onions in boiling water for 5 minutes. Drain. Mix vegetables with soup, sour cream and carrots. Put half of the bread crumbs in the bottom of a greased baking dish, add vegetable mixture, then top with remaining crumbs. Bake at 350° for 25-30 minutes.

SCALLOPED SCALLOPS

This is a seafood casserole that will go well with new potatoes, dressed with parsley butter, and green peas and needs only a dish of mixed fruit or a blueberry pie to complete the menu.

1½ pounds scallops
3 tablespoons butter
1 medium onion, finely chopped
1 cup mushrooms (or a 6-ounce can, drained)
¼ cup flour
1 cup liquid from cooking scallops
1 cup cream or half-and-half
   Salt and pepper
⅔ cup buttered bread or cracker crumbs

Parboil scallops in a small amount of water (just enough to prevent scallops from "catching on" to the pan) for about 6 or 8 minutes. Reserve the cooking liquid. Saute onions in butter until golden; add mushrooms and cook a few minutes longer. Blend in the flour. Add liquid from parboiling the scallops and, if desired, liquids from canned mushrooms to make 1 cup liquid. Add this liquid with the cream. Stir and cook until mixture is smooth and thickened. Add salt and pepper to season and the scallops. Spoon into a buttered casserole. Sprinkle with buttered crumbs or herb-seasoned stuffing crumbs. Bake in a moderate oven, 350°, for about 30 minutes, or until bubbly. Serves 6.

TILLIE'S BROCCOLI-ONION CASSEROLE

2 (10-ounce) packages frozen, cut up broccoli
2 cups frozen small onions
4 tablespoons butter
2 tablespoons flour
¼ teaspoon salt
  Dash of pepper
1 cup milk
1 (3-ounce) package cream cheese
1 cup soft bread crumbs
¼ cup grated Parmesan cheese

Cook broccoli and onions as directed on package; drain. In a saucepan, melt 2 tablespoons of the butter; blend in flour, salt and pepper. Add milk; cook and stir until thick and bubbly. Cut cream cheese in pieces and stir into hot mixture. Add vegetables. Spoon into buttered 1½-quart casserole. Bake at 350° for 20 minutes. Melt remaining butter; toss with bread crumbs and cheese. Sprinkle over casserole contents. Bake 15 to 20 minutes longer. Makes about 8 to 10 servings.

CHICKEN AND BROCCOLI CASSEROLE

Casseroles are not everyone's dish! Many people prefer a separation of meat or fish and rice or potatoes with other seasonings.

¾ cup chopped onion
¾ cup celery, thinly sliced
¼ cup peanut oil
⅛ (2½ to 3 lbs.) chicken, boiled and boned
¼ cup chopped roasted peanuts
1 small can mushrooms, drained
1 can (10½ oz.) cream of mushroom soup
1 cup shredded Cheddar cheese
1 box (10 oz.) frozen broccoli, cooked, drained

Saute onion and celery in the oil, being careful not to brown the onions. Add remaining ingredients; blend well. The cooked broccoli may be chopped before adding, or left in small pieces—do not overcook. Reserve a tablespoon of the peanuts to scatter on top of the casserole contents. Bake in a 2-quart buttered casserole for 30 minutes in a moderate, 350° oven. YIELD: 8 servings. If desired, two cups of coarsely chopped, cooked turkey or 1 large can of tuna, drained, can be substituted for the chicken.

AVIS'S SALMON CASSEROLE

This recipe comes from "The County." For the newcomers to Maine or the uninitiated, that is Aroostook County, where many of our recipes originated. This Mapleton homemaker usually made this salmon casserole to go with baked new potatoes.

1 can (1 pound) red salmon
3 eggs, slightly beaten
6 to 8 saltines, crumbled
1¼ cups milk
1 teaspoon salt
¼ teaspoon pepper
1 cup bread crumbs
⅓ cup butter or margarine

Break the salmon into small pieces; add the eggs, crackers, salt and pepper. Stir in the milk. Sprinkle the dry bread crumbs over all and pour the melted butter evenly over the crumbs. Bake in a hot oven, 375° to 400°, for about an hour, or until the casserole is puffy and a wooden pick indicates that the casserole is done all the way through. Serve at once with the potatoes, which have been in the oven baking at the same time. This is a quick dish to prepare.

MA'S SCALLOPED POTATOES

My mother always was asked to take a pan of scalloped potatoes to the church Ladies Aid dinner meeting. The long, slow cooking gave the potatoes a creamy color and a light brown, crusty look.

6 medium potatoes
3 medium onions
5 tablespoons flour
¼ teaspoon pepper
5 tablespoons butter or margarine
1½ to 2 cups milk or more

Pare potatoes and slice; peel onions and cut in ⅛-inch slices. In a buttered casserole layer the potato and onion slices. Sprinkle each layer with flour, salt and pepper. Dot with butter. Repeat until all vegetables are used. Add milk almost to top of potatoes. Cover and bake at 300° for 2 hours, or until potatoes are soft throughout. Remove cover during last half-hour of cooking. You may need to add more milk as the potatoes cook. A slow oven prevents milk from boiling over or curdling.

MARYELLEN'S BROCCOLI CASSEROLE

2 packages (8 ounces each) frozen chopped broccoli
2 tablespoons chopped onion
1 can cream of mushroom soup
1 cup mayonnaise
  Salt and pepper to taste
1 cup grated Cheddar cheese

Cook and drain broccoli. Combine drained broccoli, onion, mushroom soup, mayonnaise and salt and pepper. Place in buttered dish or casserole and top with cheese. Bake in a moderate oven, 350°, for 30 minutes or until done.

SAUERKRAUT AND FRANKFURTERS

One of the dishes suggested for a potluck supper is a casserole of sauerkraut and frankfurters. Simple to make and a favorite of many, it goes well with other casseroles that appear on the table.

1 large can sauerkraut
8 frankfurters
  A generous sprinkling of freshly ground black pepper

Pour the sauerkraut into a casserole and add the frankfurters, pushing them under the sauerkraut to prevent drying. Bake in a moderate oven, 350°, for 45 to 50 minutes.

MARGARET'S MACARONI AND CHEESE

1 package (8 oz.) elbow macaroni
2 cups cottage cheese, cream style
1 cup dairy sour cream
1 egg, slightly beaten
¾ teaspoon salt
⅛ teaspoon pepper
2 cups (½ pound) shredded Cheddar cheese
  Paprika

Cook macaroni according to package directions; drain. Combine cottage cheese, sour cream, egg, salt, pepper and Cheddar cheese. A dash of Cayenne pepper is also suggested. Mix well. Stir in drained macaroni. Spoon mixture into buttered 2-quart casserole; cover. Bake at 350° for 45 minutes. Uncover casserole; sprinkle contents with paprika; bake 5 minutes longer.

MAINE BAKED BEANS

Many homemakers still make Saturday night the baked bean night. Brown bread may be steamed or baked to go with the beans or whole-wheat and white rolls made to come from the oven, piping hot, to go with the beans. If the choice of the homemaker is to buy canned brown bread, then he or she can open the can and set the opened can in the oven to heat about a half hour while the beans finish baking. If you lived on a farm, you may have played "beano" every Friday night, picking over the required amount of dry beans to remove any debris left from winnowing the beans earlier in the day. The beans were then carefully washed and put to soak for parboiling and baking the next day. No method of baking can top the use of a stoneware bean pot. True, it takes a bit of watching and adding water to the baking beans, but the results are worth it for many homemakers.

2 pounds dry beans
¼ cup sugar
2 teaspoons dry mustard
1 tablespoon salt
½ pound salt pork
⅔ cup molasses
½ teaspoon pepper
1 medium onion or small apple

Pick over and wash the dry beans; soak in cold water overnight. In the morning, parboil the beans until the skins crack when blown upon. An onion or apple may be placed in the bottom of the bean pot, if desired. Either will be completely absorbed into beans, adding a bit of flavor. Fill the 3-quart bean pot to ¾ full with the parboiled beans. Cut the rind of the salt pork into a crisscross pattern, top the beans with it, then add remaining beans. Mix the molasses, sugar, salt, pepper and mustard with 2½ cups boiling water; pour this over the contents of the pot, then add boiling water to cover the beans and pork. Cover the pot and bake in a slow oven, 300°, for about 6 hours or longer. The cover of the pot may be removed during the last half hour to crisp the pork, which by now is probably on top of the beans. Add water as the beans cook to keep them covered. If there are leftover baked beans, use for another meal or freeze in meal-size containers. Or, plan on baking extra to send a few to a lone homemaker or neighbor with some of the rolls or brown bread. We have found that beans freeze very well for up to 2 months.

WELSH RABBIT

  2 tablespoons butter
2½ tablespoons flour
 ½ teaspoon salt
 ½ teaspoon dry mustard
   Few grains Cayenne pepper
  1 cup milk
  2 cups sharp shredded Cheddar cheese
  1 egg

In a saucepan, melt butter; stir in flour, salt, mustard and Cayenne. Add milk; cook and stir until sauce is thickened and smooth. Add cheese; stir until melted. Beat egg slightly; add two spoonsful of cheese mixture, mix and return to saucepan. Blend thoroughly. Serve over crisp crackers.

LAMB STEW

The wood stove is alive and well in many homes and makes an ideal place to cook this stew, or any stew for cold weather eating. This recipe calls for thickening the stew but it is not a hard and fast rule.

  2 to 2½ pounds boned shoulder of lamb
4½ cups water
  2 or 3 celery tops, cut
  2 teaspoons salt
  1 bay leaf (optional)
  3 or 4 sprigs parsley
  2 cups cubed yellow turnip
  2 medium carrots (optional)
  4 medium onions, peeled, sliced
  4 potatoes, pared, sliced
 ¼ teaspoon pepper
  2 tablespoons flour (optional)
  3 tablespoons water

Cut the lamb in cubes. In a heavy kettle with a cover, combine 4½ cups of water with meat, celery tops, bay leaf, parsley, salt and pepper; cover and cook for 2½ hours or until meat is tender. Add potatoes, onions, turnip and carrots. Cover and simmer for 30 minutes or until vegetables are tender. Combine flour and 3 tablespoons water; stir until smooth and add to stew, cooking and stirring until stew is slightly thickened. Taste for more seasoning. Remove bay leaf and serve stew. Makes 6 to 8 servings. Serve with crisp crackers or make corn bread.

QUICK SPAGHETTI SAUCE

1 pound ground beef
½ cup chopped onion
2 (15 oz.) cans tomato sauce
1 (4 oz.) can mushroom pieces and stems
½ teaspoon oregano leaves
½ teaspoon basil leaves
¼ teaspoon garlic powder
⅛ to ¼ teaspoon Cayenne pepper
⅛ teaspoon pepper

In large skillet or Dutch oven, brown ground beef and onion; drain. Drain and add mushrooms, herbs, garlic powder, Cayenne pepper and black pepper. Mix well. Simmer 15 minutes, stirring occasionally. Makes 10 (½-cup) servings.

LASAGNE

You may have your favorite lasagne recipe, or you may like this. Lasagne recipes, like spaghetti sauce, are well-held secrets in many families.

2 pounds lean ground beef
1 large clove garlic
½ cup chopped onion
½ cup chopped celery
1 tablespoon olive oil
2 cans (1 pound each) tomatoes
1 can (6 ounces) tomato paste
1 teaspoon salt
½ teaspoon allspice
½ teaspoon cinnamon
1 bay leaf
1 pound lasagne noodles, cooked
½ pound mozzarella cheese, sliced
  Parmesan cheese, grated

Saute garlic, onion and celery in oil. Add meat and let it cook a few minutes to lose red color. Add tomatoes, tomato paste, salt and spices. Let simmer for 2 to 2½ hours or until thickened, stirring frequently. Preheat oven to 375⁰. Grease a 9x13x2-inch baking dish. Layer cooked noodles alternately with sauce and mozzarella cheese until dish is filled, topping with Parmesan cheese. Bake at least 30 minutes or until cheese melts. Allow to stand for 5 to 10 minutes after removing from the oven before serving. This recipe has no cottage cheese in it, and if the celery is not your choosing, omit it.

NORWEGIAN CHEESE SOUFFLE

Add variety to the day's menu by serving a Norwegian cheese souffle. This recipe calls for Jarlsberg cheese, but if a sharp Cheddar is in your refrigerator that may be used. This is a good way to use leftover baked or boiled smoked ham.

2 tablespoons butter
3 tablespoons flour
1¼ cups milk
4 eggs, separated
2 teaspoons cornstarch
2 cups grated Jarlsberg cheese
1½ cups cooked, cured chopped ham

Make a thick white sauce with butter, flour and milk. Add egg yolks, cornstarch, cheese and ham. Beat egg whites and carefully fold them into sauce mixture. Bake in a buttered souffle dish at 325° for approximately 50 minutes. Serve immediately. Makes 4 servings.

ERDINE'S CRABMEAT SOUFFLE

4 slices bread, cubed
2 cups crabmeat
½ cup mayonnaise
1 medium onion, chopped
1 cup celery, chopped
1 medium-sized green pepper, chopped
4 to 6 slices of bread
4 eggs, beaten
3 cups milk
½ teaspoon salt
  Few grains pepper
1 can cream of mushroom soup (undiluted)
¾ cup shredded sharp Cheddar cheese

In an 11 x 7 x 2-inch buttered baking dish, arrange the cubed bread. Fold together the crabmeat, mayonnaise, onion, celery and green pepper and spoon the mixture over the bread cubes. Beat the eggs; beat in the milk, salt and papper; allow to sit while you trim the crusts from the 4 to 6 slices of bread. Put this bread over the crab mixture, fitting the slices as for a patchwork quilt. Pour the milk mixture over the contents of the pan. Spread the soup evenly over the top of the bread and then add the cheese. Cover with foil and refrigerate overnight. When time to bake, uncover and bake in a slow oven, about 1 hour at 325°.

DONNA'S NANA'S KIDNEY BEANS

Bits of smoked pork shoulder, left over from another meal, will find a home in this recipe. Sliced green tomato pickles from last fall's canning will go well with this menu, plus a pan of hot biscuits or a Johnny cake.

```
1 pound kidney beans
1 teaspoon salt
  Pieces of cooked smoked shoulder
6½ tablespoons white sugar
```

Parboil beans for one hour. Measure salt and sugar into bottom of beanpot. (The recipe read "a generous ⅓ cup of white sugar.) Drain parboiled beans and put into beanpot; with a long spoon, mix beans with sugar and salt in bottom of pot, adding pieces of the cooked pork shoulder. Place some of the smoked shoulder fat on top. Fill pot with boiling water. Cover and bake 3 hours at 300°. Uncover and bake one more hour. Check during baking time to see if more water is needed in the pot.

CHILI

There are some days when a bowl of chili is just the thing! This recipe has celery as an ingredient.

```
  2 pounds ground beef
  1 clove garlic, minced
  1 cup chopped onion
  1 cup chopped celery (optional)
  ½ cup chopped green pepper
  1 teaspoon salt
    Pepper
1½ tablespoons chili powder
  1 tablespoon paprika
  1 teaspoon ginger
  1 tablespoon sugar
  1 can ( 1 lb. 4 oz.) tomatoes
  1 can (6 oz.) tomato paste
  1 can (8 oz.) tomato sauce
  2 cans (1 lb. 4 oz. each) kidney beans
  2 tablespoons flour
  3 tablespoons water
```

Brown beef, garlic, onion, celery and green pepper in large saucepan. Add seasonings, tomatoes, paste and sauce; simmer gently one hour. Add kidney beans. Combine flour and water; stir into mixture and simmer 15 minutes longer. Makes 8 to 10 servings.

OVEN BEEF STEW

Let the oven do the cooking while you are engaged in other activities. This recipe will give you five hours of spare time. Add a salad and biscuits, reheated in the oven as you set the table and make the tea.

1½ pounds beef stew meat
1 can (16 oz.) tomatoes
1 cup chopped celery
4 or 5 potatoes, pared, cut in chunks
3 carrots, chopped
2 onions, diced
1 clove garlic, minced
1 tablespoon tapioca
1 teaspoon sugar
1 teaspoon salt
Pepper to taste

Combine all ingredients in a large casserole. Mix well. Cover tightly and bake at 250° for 5 hours.

PARMESAN PUFFY OMELET

4 eggs, separated
¼ cup water
1 teaspoon lemon juice
¼ cup finely chopped green onions with tops
¼ cup (1 oz.) grated Parmesan cheese
1 tablespoon butter

In a large mixing bowl, combine egg whites, water and lemon juice. Beat at high speed until stiff but not dry, just until whites no longer slip when bowl is tilted. In small mixing bowl, beat egg yolks at high speed until thick and lemon-colored. Gently but thoroughly, fold yolks, onion and cheese into whites. In 10-inch omelet pan or skillet with ovenproof handle, heat butter until just hot enough to sizzle a drop of water. Pour in egg mixture and gently smooth surface. Reduce heat to low. Cook until puffed and lightly browned on bottom, about 3 minutes. (Lift omelet at edge to judge color.) Bake in preheated 350° oven until knife inserted halfway between center and outer edge comes out clean, about 10 to 12 minutes. Loosen omelet edges with spatula. To serve folded, cut upper surface down center, but do not cut through to bottom. Tip skillet. With pancake turner, fold omelet in half and invert onto warmed plate or platter with a quick flip of the wrist. Serve immediately.

TUNABURGERS

These tunaburgers may be made on one slice of bread, half a hamburger roll or into sandwiches. A sour pickle or a dill pickle will go with this treat.

1 (7 oz.) can tuna, drained
1 cup chopped celery
½ cup shredded Mozzarella cheese
1 small onion, minced
¼ cup mayonnaise
¼ cup butter or margarine
4 slices bread or 2 hamburger rolls

In a bowl combine tuna, celery, cheese and onion; mix well. Add mayonnaise and season with salt and pepper and, if desired, a teaspoon of fresh lemon juice. Mix well and spoon onto slices of buttered bread or hamburger roll halves. Place on baking sheet and cover loosely with a piece of foil. Bake at 350° for 15 minutes. If the hamburger rolls are used whole with filling, you may have to cook a bit longer.

CRUSTLESS TUNA QUICHE

One can tuna, packed in water, will make six servings when mixed with other ingredients. There is no crust to this quiche, so fewer calories. Red cabbage slaw will make a good "go-with."

1 tablespoon butter
⅓ cup sliced green onion
¼ cup chopped red and/or green pepper
4 eggs
3 tablespoons flour
¼ teaspoon salt
¼ teaspoon dry mustard
⅛ teaspoon pepper
1½ cups skim milk
1½ cups (6 oz.) shredded Cheddar cheese
1 can (6½ oz.) tuna in water, drained, flaked
  Tomato cut in 6 wedges

Preheat oven to 350°. Melt butter in small skillet. Saute onion and pepper until tender, about three minutes. Combine eggs, flour and seasoning in medium-sized bowl, beat until well blended. Stir in milk; add cheese, tuna, and sauteed vegetables; mix well. Pour into well-buttered-9-inch pie plate. Bake 45 to 50 minutes or until knife inserted near center comes out clean. Let cool 10 minutes before serving. Garnish each serving with a tomato wedge. A Johnny cake could bake in the oven along with the quiche.

PORK CHOP SUEY

Oil or fat for browning
1 pound lean fresh pork, cut in strips
3 tablespoons soy sauce, divided
1 cup celery, sliced
1 cup sliced onions
1 can bean sprouts with liquid
1 tablespoon molasses
Corn starch to thicken
Cooked rice or Chinese fried noodles

Brown the pork in the oil with 1 tablespoon of the soy sauce. Prepare vegetables and add to browned meat with 2 more tablespoons soy sauce, molasses, and liquid from the can of sprouts. Cover and cook until crisp-tender, about 15 minutes. Add bean sprouts and cook 1 minute. Thicken mixture with cornstarch mixed with a bit of cold water. (Depending on liquid in the cooking pot, use 2 tablespoons corn starch to 3 tablespoons cold water.) Serve over hot cooked rice or fried canned Chinese noodles. Season with pepper, if needed.

PIZZA CUPS

Winter vacation is a time when basketball tournaments will keep many students busy. Others may enjoy the time at home, cooking a favorite food or trying new ones.

2 tablespoons margarine
⅓ cup chopped mushrooms
¼ cup chopped green pepper
¼ cup chopped onion
1 (6 oz.) can tomato paste
¼ cup water
½ teaspoon dried oregano leaves
1½ cups shredded mozzarella cheese (6 ounces)
1 (7½ oz.) can refrigerated buttermilk biscuits

Melt margarine over medium heat until bubbly. Add mushrooms, green peppers and onions to skillet. Cook, stirring frequently, until vegetables are tender. Add tomato paste, water and oregano to skillet, stirring to blend well. Cook over low heat 5 minutes, stirring occasionally. Add 1 cup of the shredded cheese, mixing well. Grease 10 medium-size muffin cups. Separate biscuit dough into 10 biscuits. Press each biscuit onto bottom and sides of muffin cups. Fill with vegetable mixture. Bake at 375° for 20 to 25 minutes or until biscuits are lightly browned. Remove from oven and sprinkle with remaining cheese. Serve warm.

CORNED BEEF AND CABBAGE

4 pounds corned beef brisket
1 small onion cut in wedges
1 carrot, cut in 1-inch pieces
1 head cabbage, cut in 8 wedges
¼ teaspoon pepper
1 bay leaf

Place corned beef in a kettle, cover with boiling water. Add carrot, onion, pepper and bay leaf. Reduce heat and simmer until meat is tender, about 4 hours. About 20 minutes before serving, add cabbage, then cook, uncovered, until cabbage is done. Do not overcook cabbage. If desired, potatoes may be added to the cooking meat 20 minutes before adding the cabbage. Mustard and horseradish are served with this menu for those who like extra with the corned beef. Corned beef hash may be another day's menu.

AMERICAN CHOP SUEY

There are probably more recipes for American chop suey than meat loaf! When I was a child, a neighbor taught me how to make her version. It was a new dish to our family of eight people (more during haying season) and made ground beef go farther for so many eaters. This is a dish that is quickly put together and seasonings may vary, according to what is on the spice shelf. Sometimes it was a "sloppy" dish spreading over the plate or sometimes a dish that was almost as spoonable as mashed potatoes. Green beans, fresh from the garden, were generally served with the dish.

1 pound ground beef
2 onions, sliced
2 tablespoons butter or margarine
2 cups canned tomatoes
3 cups macaroni, cooked
  Salt and pepper to taste

Melt butter in a kettle and brown the meat and onions, until the meat loses its pink color. Add the canned tomatoes and cooked macaroni and bring to simmering. Simmer for 20 minutes. Add salt and pepper to season. The new versions of the dish often add oregano or other selected herbs as seasoning. In the farm version, additional canned tomatoes were added to stretch the dish. It always tasted good to a hungry family.

MARGE'S PARMESAN SQUASH RING
CENTERED WITH CHICKEN

This is delicious served hot or cold with either chicken or turkey and is an excellent way to use leftover turkey.

Squash Ring:

½ cup chopped green onion
2 tablespoons butter or margarine
4 eggs
2 packages (12 ounces each) frozen squash, defrosted, or 4 cups fresh squash, cooked, mashed
¼ teaspoon salt
¼ teaspoon red pepper
1 cup Parmesan cheese

Chicken Mixture:

2 cups cooked chicken
2 cups celery, finely sliced
½ cup toasted almonds, chopped
½ teaspoon salt
1 cup mayonnaise
2 tablespoons lemon juice
½ cup Parmesan cheese, grated
2 teaspoons onion, grated

In skillet, cook onion in butter until tender. Set aside. Beat eggs in mixer until blended and add the squash, salt, pepper, Parmesan cheese and onion mixture. Pour into oiled baking ring. Bake at 350⁰ for 30 to 40 minutes or until set. Let stand 8 minutes. Loosen edges and turn onto serving dish. While squash is baking, combine chicken, celery, almonds, salt, mayonnaise and lemon juice. Grate the onion on top. If chicken is served cold, place in center of ring and top with cheese. If served hot, heat the mixture in a casserole about 10 minutes in a 450⁰ oven. Add to ring and add the cheese.

NANCY'S PORK CHOPS AND APPLES

6 pork chops, browned both sides
4 unpeeled apples, cored, sliced crosswise
¼ cup brown sugar
½ teaspoon cinnamon
2 tablespoons butter or margarine

Brown pork chops on both sides; set aside. In bottom of baking pan, arrange sliced apples; sprinkle with brown sugar and cinnamon and dot with butter. Add the browned chops on top of the apples. Cover pan with foil and bake in a moderate oven, 350°, for 1½ to 2 hours. The cover on the pan adds moisture to the baking chops, so the 2 hours is not too long.

PISTACHIO LAMB MEATBALLS IN INDIAN CURRY SAUCE

1 pound ground lamb
½ cup finely chopped shelled pistachios
1 egg
3 tablespoons bread crumbs
¾ teaspoon grated lemon peel
¼ teaspoon salt
¼ teaspoon pepper
¼ teaspoon ground cumin
2 tablespoons vegetable oil
2 tablespoons melted butter or margarine
1 cup chopped onions
2½ teaspoons curry powder
1½ teaspoons minced garlic
1 tablespoon sugar
1 tablespoon cornstarch
   Water
3 cups plain yogurt
   Hot cooked rice
   Chopped shelled pistachios
   Chopped, fresh coriander or parsley

Combine lamb, ½ cup chopped pistachios, egg, bread crumbs, lemon peel, salt, pepper, and cumin; mix well. Shape into 1-inch balls. Brown meatballs lightly in frypan on medium heat in oil; remove from heat and drain on paper towels while preparing the sauce. In same pan combine butter, onions, curry powder and garlic; cook until fragrant. In a separate bowl, combine sugar, cornstarch and enough water to make a smooth paste. Stir yogurt and sugar mixture into onions and heat slowly 10 minutes, stirring frequently. Pour sauce over meatballs. To serve, spoon meatballs and sauce over rice. Sprinkle with chopped pistachios and coriander. Makes 4 servings. The flat leaf Italian parsley or regular parsley may be used.

GOLDEN GLAZED HAM

1 (4 to 5 pound) boneless ham
1 (10 oz.) jar orange marmalade
½ cup orange juice
1 tablespoon prepared mustard
¼ teaspoon ground cloves
¼ to ½ teaspoon ground ginger
   Whole cloves
½ cup raisins

Place ham, fat side up, in shallow baking pan; score fat. Bake at 325°
for 1 hour and 15 minutes. Combine marmalade, juice, mustard,
ground cloves and ginger; simmer for 5 minutes. Spoon half of marmalade mixture over ham. Stud with whole cloves; continue baking
for 30 minutes. Combine remaining marmalade mixture with raisins;
serve with ham. Makes 10 to 12 servings.

BARBECUED PORK SPARERIBS

You'll not believe how delicious this is until you try it!

2½ pounds country-style pork spareribs
2 tablespoons cooking oil
½ cup flour
¼ cup vinegar
½ teaspoon salt
½ teaspoon dry mustard
2 teaspoons celery seed
1 tablespoon chili sauce
½ cup catsup
2 tablespoons sugar
2 tablespoons paprika
⅛ teaspoon pepper

Prepare barbecue sauce by combining vinegar, salt, mustard, celery
seed, chili sauce, catsup, sugar, paprika and pepper. Marinate pork
ribs, cut in serving portions, in sauce for three to four hours. Keep
refrigerated. This allows the meat to absorb flavors from the sauce.
Remove meat from marinade and roll it in the flour. Brown meat in oil
in a frying pan. Pour the marinade over the browned meat. Cover and
simmer over very low heat or in a 325° oven for about 2 hours. Serve
hot.

FRIED RABBIT

2 to 2½ pounds dressed rabbit
¼ cup cracker crumbs
1½ teaspoons salt
¼ teaspoon pepper
  Fat or oil for frying

Cut cleaned rabbit into serving-size pieces. Mix crumbs, salt and pepper in a paper bag; add pieces of meat and shake well to coat each piece thoroughly with the seasoned crumbs. Brown meat slowly in hot fat or oil in a heavy frying pan; cook slowly for 30 minutes longer or until tender.

MANDARIN PORK STIR-FRY

The fast-frying method, pioneered by the Chinese and symbolized by the wok, is a healthful low-fat and low-calorie way to cook. Vegetables, lean meats or fish are stir-fried in hot oil to achieve a light, crisp texture while retaining vitamins and minerals.

  Vegetable cooking spray
1 pound lean pork, cut in strips
¼ pound fresh mushrooms, halved or quartered
1 medium green pepper, cut in strips
1 small onion, chopped
1 cup water
2 teaspoons cornstarch
1 tablespoon soy sauce
1 chicken bouillon cube
½ teaspoon dry mustard
⅛ teaspoon garlic powder
1 can (8 ounces) water chestnuts
1 orange, sectioned
  Salt and pepper

Coat large skillet or wok with vegetable cooking spray. Heat over medium heat. Cook and stir half of pork at a time until lightly browned. Remove to a plate. Reduce heat to low; add mushrooms, green pepper and onion. Cook and stir 3 minutes. Stir together ¼ cup of water and cornstarch until smooth; mix in remaining water, soy sauce, bouillon cube, mustard and garlic powder. Add to skillet. Cook and stir until mixture thickens and boils. Add meat and water chestnuts (which have been drained and sliced); simmer 3 minutes. Gently stir in orange sections; heat to serving temperature; season to taste with salt and pepper.

BAKED PORK CHOPS WITH CREOLE SAUCE

4 pork chops
¼ cup chopped onions
1 small green pepper, chopped
2 teaspoons vegetable oil
1 cup canned tomatoes
¼ teaspoon salt
¼ teaspoon pepper
1 small bay leaf (optional)

Cook green pepper and onion in the oil until onion is clear. Add tomatoes, breaking up any large pieces. Add salt and pepper. Add bay leaf, if desired. Trim fat from pork chops and brown chops in a frypan. Place in baking pan or casserole; pour the sauce over the chops. You may wish to remove the bay leaf at this point. Cover and bake at 350° until chops are tender, about 1½ hours.

STIR-FRY PORK

For the stir-fry cooks, this recipe may be added to their long list of quick recipes, and it will be useful when roast pork, baked for Sunday dinner, needs using in a new way. Many stir-fry cooks have other ingredients on the shelf in preparation for anytime use.

12 ounces boneless cooked pork loin roast
1 tablespoon plus 1 teaspoon cornstarch
1 tablespoon water
1 cup water
1 tablespoon soy sauce
2 packets instant chicken broth and seasoning mix
2 ounces onion, chopped
2 small garlic cloves, minced
1 cup diagonally sliced celery
4 ounces Chinese pea pods
½ medium green pepper, seeded, cut into strips
1 cup drained, canned bean sprouts
½ cup drained, canned sliced mushrooms
½ cup drained, canned sliced bamboo shoots
1 cup cooked, enriched rice

Thinly slice pork and set aside. Mix cornstarch with 1 tablespoon water and set aside.

In large nonstick skillet or Chinese wok, bring water, soy sauce and broth mix to a boil. Add onion and garlic; cook until onion is tender. Add celery, pea pods and green pepper. Cook, stirring constantly, 3 to 5 minutes or until vegetables are crisp-tender. Stir in pork and remaining ingredients, except rice and cornstarch mixture, and heat. Add cornstarch mixture, stirring until sauce thickens. Serve over rice with additional soy sauce, if desired.

BOILED DINNER WITH DUMPLINGS

When a young man from Aroostook County moved to Augusta to join the State Department of Agriculture he said, "I like it fine, but no one in this area serves dumplings with boiled dinners." Inquiries confirmed that, indeed, it is an Aroostook custom. Cook extra vegetables for the red flannel hash that is as much a part of boiled dinners as the corned beef.

4½ pounds corned beef
 6 potatoes
 6 carrots
 4 parsnips
 6 slices turnip
 6 onions
 6 beets or 1 can
 1 medium cabbage, cut in wedges

You will need a large kettle. Cover corned beef with cold water; bring to simmering; cook at this temperature for 3½ to 4 hours or until meat is tender. At the end of 3½ hours, add pared potatoes, carrots, parsnips, turnips and peeled whole onions to meat in the kettle. Lay cabbage wedges over top of vegetables and meat. Cover; cook for about 25 minutes or until vegetables are tender. Cook beets separately. If fresh, cook until tender, depending on size. If canned, heat just to boiling. When all is cooked, remove meat and vegetables to a large platter; keep warm while the dumplings cook in the kettle juices.

AROOSTOOK FEATHER DUMPLINGS

 2 cups sifted all-purpose flour
 1 teaspoon salt
 4 teaspoons baking powder
 ¼ teaspoon pepper
 1 egg, beaten
 ⅔ cup milk (about)
 3 tablespoons melted butter

This needs to be a stiff, moist batter. Mix together and sift the flour, salt, baking powder and pepper. Combine egg and milk with melted butter; add to sifted dry ingredients. Have "pot likker" (liquid in which dinner was cooked) boiling. Spoon batter by tablespoonsful into boiling liquid. Cook, uncovered, until liquid boils again; cover kettle tightly and cook for 20 minutes. Do not lift cover during cooking. Serve on platter with dinner. Serve "pot likker" in a bowl.

ROAST LEG OF LAMB, SWEDISH STYLE

1 (5½ to 6-pound) leg of lamb
2 teaspoons salt
1 teaspoon dry mustard
1 clove garlic
½ cup water or bouillon
1 cup strong coffee
Cream and sugar as for drinking

Wipe meat with a damp cloth. Combine salt and mustard; rub meat with mixture. With point of a sharp knife, insert tiny slivers of garlic under suface of meat. Insert meat thermometer in thickest part of meat, taking care it does not touch bone. Pour water over meat. Bake in a 325° oven for 3 to 3½ hours. When meat is partly done, add cream and sugar to hot coffee and pour over leg of lamb; continue to cook meat until thermometer registers done. Allow meat to rest for 15 minutes before carving.

SAUERBRATEN

3 pounds bottom round of beef
1 cup vinegar
1 cup water
1 tablespoon mixed pickling spice
2 onions, sliced
1 tablespoon salt
1 tablespoon sugar
12 whole cloves
4 slices lemon
3 tablespoons shortening
8 to 10 gingersnaps
¾ cup flour, browned
1 cup cold water

Combine vinegar, 1 cup water, mixed spices, onions, salt, sugar, cloves and lemon slices. Place meat in a bowl and pour liquid and spice mixture over it. The bowl should be of such size that the meat is covered with the liquid. Refrigerate the meat in this marinade for 3 or 4 days; turn meat frequently to stir up marinade. Melt shortening in Dutch oven or heavy pan. Remove meat from marinade; drain. Brown meat in shortening, turning to brown all sides. Gradually add all marinade with spices to meat in Dutch oven. Add gingersnaps. Cover tightly and simmer for 3 to 3½ hours. Brown the flour in the oven (do not burn) or in a frying pan; add 1 cup cold water and mix well; then mix into the cooking liquid in the Dutch oven. Stir and cook for 10 minutes, or until gravy is thickened. Remove the meat. Strain the gravy and return it to pan with the meat to cook until thoroughly heated. If gravy is too thick, thin with cold water and cook until smooth.

ROAST BEEF

A roast of beef with potatoes browned in the pan, plus green beans or peas and a tossed salad is an easy meal to prepare.

Buy at least 4 pounds or at least 2 ribs if bone in. Allow ⅓ pound bone-in or ¼ pound boned roast per serving. Plan on leftovers. Place roast fat side up in a shallow open pan. The rib bones in a standing rib roast keep the meat off the bottom of the pan. Place the rolled roast on a rack in the pan. Wipe the meat with a damp cloth. Sprinkle with salt and pepper and garlic salt, if desired. A really good piece of beef needs little seasoning. Do not add water; do not cover. Check the roasting time to see when to start to cook the roast. Roast in a 325° oven until the meat thermometer indicates the doneness you desire: 140° rare, 160° medium, or 170° well-done. Remove the roast to a platter or a small pan. Keep the meat warm. Make gravy with pan juices. A standing rib roast will take from 1¾ to 2½ hours at 325°, depending on desired doneness. A rolled rib will take longer—2½ to 2¾ hours. Allow roast to sit for 10 minutes before slicing. These times are for a 4-pound roast.

SWISS STEAK

Swiss steak was often on the menu when we, as budding home economists, did our practice homemaking and teaching at North Hall on the University of Maine campus.

1½ pounds round steak, about 1 inch thick
 4 tablespoons flour
   Salt and pepper to taste
 3 tablespoons oil or shortening
 1 large onion cut in wedges
 1 or 2 sticks celery, sliced
 ⅓ pound mushrooms, fresh or canned
 1 clove garlic, finely chopped (optional)
 1 cup stewed tomatoes
 ¼ teaspoon dried basil
 ¼ teaspoon dried oregano or marjoram
 ¼ teaspoon dried thyme, crushed

Trim fat from meat. Mix flour, salt and pepper and, with the edge of a saucer or a meat mallet, pound the mixture into both sides of the meat. Heat oil or shortening in a large frypan. Brown the meat in the hot fat. Place browned meat in a baking dish. In fat remaining in pan, cook onion, celery, mushrooms and garlic (if used) until wilted and lightly browned. Stir in tomatoes and the herbs—basil, oregano and thyme. Pour this mixture over the steak; cover tightly with foil. Bake at 300° for about 1½ hours or until meat is tender. Serve the meat on a hot platter and pour the juices and seasonings from the baking pan over the meat.

PORK LOIN ROULADE

4 boneless center pork loin slices, about 1 pound
½ red bell pepper, cut in strips
½ green pepper, cut into strips
1 tablespoon cooking oil
⅔ cup orange juice
⅔ cup bottled barbecue sauce
1 tablespoon prepared Dijon-style mustard

Place cutlets between 2 pieces of clear plastic wrap. Pound with a mallet to about ¼" thickness. Place several red and green pepper strips crosswise on each pork portion; roll up jelly-roll style. Secure rolls with wooden toothpicks. In large, heavy skillet, brown the pork rolls in hot cooking oil. Drain fat from pan. Combine remaining ingredients and add to skillet. Bring mixture to boiling; reduce heat. Cover and simmer 10-12 minutes or until pork is tender. Remove toothpicks. Serves 4.

STUFFED MEAT LOAF

½ pound fresh mushrooms, finely chopped
2 tablespoons butter or margarine
¾ cup finely chopped onion
½ cup finely chopped celery
½ teaspoon crumbled dried thyme
¾ cup heavy cream
1 cup freshly ground bread crumbs
½ teaspoon salt
¼ teaspoon black pepper
2 pounds lean ground round or chuck
2 large eggs, slightly beaten

Clean and cook the mushrooms in butter over medium heat until about half of the liquid from the mushrooms has evaporated. Add onion, celery and thyme. Continue cooking until all liquid in the pan has evaporated and vegetables are tender. Add ½ cup of the cream and simmer for 5 minutes. Carefully mix in the bread crumbs and set aside. You may wish to add salt and pepper to this mixture. Mix eggs with salt and pepper and remaining cream. Carefully mix ground meat into this mixture. Line the bottom and sides of an 8-inch loaf pan with about ¾ of the meat mixture, leaving enough room for the stuffing. Add the mushroom mixture and top with remaining meat. Pat down, enclosing stuffing completely. Bake at 450⁰ for 20 minutes. Reduce heat to 350⁰ and bake 30 minutes longer. Allow to set for 10 minutes. Unmold and slice. Serves 8.

SWEET AND SOUR PORK

1½ pounds fresh pork shoulder
1 can (4 oz.) mushrooms
   Water
1 green pepper, cut in strips
1 medium onion, sliced
¼ cup molasses
2 teaspoons soy sauce
¼ cup vinegar
1 tablespoon cornstarch

Cut pork in 1-inch pieces; brown in skillet. Drain mushrooms; measure liquid and add enough water to liquid to make 1 cup. Add to meat and bring to boiling. Cover. Reduce heat and simmer 45 minutes. Add mushrooms, pepper and onion. Combine molasses, soy sauce and vinegar. Add to skillet and cook, stirring occasionally, 15 minutes longer. Blend cornstarch with a small amount of cold water; mix into hot liquid in skillet. Cook, stirring until slightly thickened. Serve with cooked rice. This makes 4 servings.

DRESSED-UP HAMBURGER

If hamburgers get to be old-hat with the family, dress up ground beef with a sauce spiced with oregano and Tabasco sauce, and pour the sauce over cooked egg noodles.

2 tablespoons olive oil or corn oil
1 onion, thinly sliced
3 pounds ground lean beef
2 (Number 2) cans tomatoes
1 can tomato puree
½ teaspoon salt (or more)
½ teaspoon oregano
¼ teaspoon pepper
⅛ teaspoon Tabasco sauce
1 pound egg noodles
2 or 3 tablespoons butter or margarine
   Parmesan cheese, as needed

Break up beef and cook in oil until lightly browned. Add sliced onions and simmer until tender. Add tomatoes, tomato puree, salt, oregano, pepper and Tabasco. Simmer slowly until thick. Cook noodles according to directions on box. Drain and add butter or margarine, then sprinkle with a liberal amount of Parmesan cheese. Just before serving, ladle sauce over noodles. You may have other spices you enjoy in this type of dish.

SMOKED SHOULDER

1 (6-pound) smoked pork shoulder
1 carrot, sliced
1 small onion, sliced
1 teaspoon salt
¼ cup brown sugar
¼ teaspoon clove
1 cup fruit juice or syrup
⅛ teaspoon pepper

Simmer meat in water nearly to cover. To cooking liquid, add carrot, onion, salt and pepper. Cover. Simmer until meat is tender, about 3½ hours; allow meat to cool in cooking liquid for 1 hour. Remove meat to baking pan and pull off the skin. Score the fat; sprinkle brown sugar and clove over the meat. Add fruit juice or syrup drained from pickled crabapples, canned fruits or maple syrup. Bake meat at 325° for 30 to 40 minutes. Serve hot or cold. The smoked shoulder may be cooked and used without the glazing.

SAVORY TURKEY MEATBALLS OR MEATLOAF

1 pound fresh ground turkey meat
1 egg, slightly beaten
½ cup chopped onions
2 tablespoons fine bread crumbs
1 clove garlic, peeled, chopped
1 tablespoon milk
Seasoned salt and pepper to taste
3 tablespoons oil or shortening
1½ tablespoons flour (optional)
1½ cups cold water (optional)
Few drops browning and seasoning sauce
1 tablespoon minced parsley, for garnish

In a bowl combine fresh ground turkey meat, egg, onion, bread crumbs, garlic and milk. Add seasoned salt and pepper to taste; mix well. Shape mixture into 1½- to 2-inch meatballs. In large heavy skillet thoroughly brown meatballs in oil over moderate heat 2 or 3 minutes; cover; simmer 10 to 15 minutes or until inside meat turns from pink to white. Remove meatballs with a slotted spoon; transfer to serving platter, cover and keep warm. Prepare gravy, if desired. Blend flour into remaining hot pan drippings until smooth. With a wire whisk, blend in cold water. Cook, stirring constantly, over moderate heat until bubbly and hot and slightly thickened. Add browning sauce, if desired. Serve with meatballs. Garnish with minced parsley. For a meatloaf, place mixture into a loaf pan lightly coated with vegetable oil spray. Bake, uncovered, 45 to 50 minutes in a 325° oven, until meatloaf is done. Omit parsley and gravy for meatloaf.

MEAT LOAF WITH APPLES

2½ pounds ground beef
3 tablespoons butter or margarine
1 large onion, finely chopped
1½ cups fresh bread crumbs
2 cups finely chopped apples, pared
3 eggs, beaten
½ teaspoon pepper
1 teaspoon salt
¼ teaspoon allspice
2 tablespoons chopped fresh parsley
1 tablespoon prepared mustard
¼ cup catsup

Pare and chop the apples. A crisp, tart apple is best. Saute the chopped onion in the butter until golden but not burned. Mix in the meat, bread crumbs, apples, eggs and seasonings, including mustard and catsup. Mix well. Pack into a 9 x 13-inch baking dish if you like to cut the loaf in squares, or into a large loaf pan if you prefer to slice the loaf. Bake at 350° for 1¼ hours or until cooked. Allow the loaf to rest for 10 minutes before slicing.

BEEF AND PORK MEAT LOAF

1 pound ground beef
1 pound ground fresh pork
2 shredded wheat biscuits
2 eggs
1 medium onion
½ teaspoon pepper
½ teaspoon salt
⅛ teaspoon basil
¼ teaspoon oregano
½ teaspoon garlic powder
1 (8 oz.) can tomato sauce
⅓ cup grated parmesan cheese
1 teaspoon prepared horseradish
1 teaspoon prepared mustard
1 tablespoon soy sauce
⅓ cup catsup

Set the catsup aside and combine all other ingredients in bowl; mix well. Shape into a loaf and place in bread pan; spread the catsup on the top of mixture. Bake for 1 hour at 375°.

POT ROAST

1 3-pound chuck roast (cut 2 inches thick)
¼ cup vegetable oil
2 large cloves garlic
1 large onion, cut in wedges
2 cups fresh mushrooms, halved
4 potatoes, halved
1 can (14 oz.) beef broth
1 pound carrots, cut in chunks
2 tablespoons cornstarch
3 tablespoons water
  Salt and pepper to taste

In a Dutch oven or heavy frypan, brown meat in oil on both sides. Add garlic, onion and mushrooms. Cook until onion is soft. Add beef broth; stir well, scraping the brown particles from the bottom of the cooking dish. Add carrots and potatoes. Cover and cook the pot roast in the oven at 350⁰ for one hour, or on low heat on stove top. Remove cover. Dissolve cornstarch in water, then stir into juices in the pan. Cover and cook 30 minutes longer in the oven, or on stove top, until the beef is tender. Add salt and pepper to taste. Serve with boiled or mashed turnip with the thickened meat juices.

SUMMERTIME MEATLOAF

¾ cup vegetable juice cocktail
¾ cup rolled oats
½ cup shredded carrots
1½ teaspoons beef-flavored instant boullion
1 egg, beaten
½ cup chopped onion
2 tablespoons chopped celery
2 tablespoons diced green peppers
2 tablespoons prepared horseradish
1½ pounds lean ground beef
  Horseradish cream

Preheat oven to 350⁰. In large bowl, combine all ingredients except meat and horseradish cream; mix well. Stir in meat. In shallow baking dish, shape into loaf. Bake 1 hour and 15 minutes. Chill. Slice and serve with horseradish cream. Refrigerate leftovers.

HORSERADISH CREAM: In small mixer bowl, combine 1 cup (½ pint) whipping cream and 1 tablespoon bottled lemon juice; beat until stiff. Fold in 2 teaspoons prepared horseradish and 2 teaspoons Dijon-style mustard. Refrigerate leftovers. (Makes about 2 cups.)

BAKED PORK CHOPS AND RICE

6 lean pork chops
  Salt and pepper
2 tablespoons vegetable oil
½ cup chopped onions
½ cup chopped celery
½ cup chopped green pepper
1 cup uncooked rice
½ teaspoon sage or thyme
2 cups boiling chicken broth

Season meat with salt and pepper. Using an oven-proof skillet, brown chops on each side in the oil; remove from skillet and drain off excess fat. Add onions, celery, green pepper and rice to skillet. Stir to loosen brown particles in skillet from cooking chops and cook until vegetables are tender and rice is golden. Stir in thyme and broth. Place browned chops on top of rice mixture. Cover and bake at 350° for 30 minutes or until chops and rice are tender and liquid is absorbed. Stir rice lightly with a fork. Makes 6 servings.

MEATBALL STROGANOFF

If it is a "quickie" you need for supper, try this meatball stroganoff. At least it will be a conversation piece as it is a far cry from the original stroganoff recipe!

1 pound ground beef
⅓ cup dry bread crumbs
⅓ cup milk
1 egg
½ teaspoon Worcestershire sauce
1 teaspoon salt
⅛ teaspoon pepper
¼ cup oil
2 tablespoons green onions, sliced
1 package (8 oz.) cream cheese, cubed
¾ cup water
1 (4 oz.) jar mushrooms, drained
4 cups (8 oz.) noodles, cooked, drained

Combine meat, bread crumbs, milk, egg, Worcestershire sauce, salt and pepper; mix lightly. Form into 24 meatballs; brown in oil. Cook 10 to 15 minutes or until done; remove from pan. Drain fat from pan, reserving 1 tablespoonful. Add green onions to fat; cook until tender. Add cream cheese, water and mushrooms. Cook over low heat; stir until smooth. Arrange meatballs over hot cooked noodles; cover with sauce. Makes 6 to 8 servings.

131

PORK CHOPS WITH SWEET POTATOES AND APPLES

If you were from the South, you would serve this pork chop and sweet potato dish with spoon bread. Make a pan of Johnny cake to go with the dish. Cook a green vegetable—broccoli or spinach. Cook the sweet potatoes early or use some leftover ones.

4 pork chops
2 tablespoons shortening
¼ teaspoon salt
2 large sweet potatoes, cooked, sliced
2 large cooking apples, pared, sliced
½ cup light brown sugar
¼ teaspoon cinnamon
¼ teaspoon nutmeg

In a large iron skillet, brown pork chops. Add salt. Move chops to one side of the pan to make room for the sweet potatoes. Place apples on top of sweet potato slices and top them with sugar and spices. Turn heat to low. Put a lid on the skillet and heat slowly until the apples are steamed tender and the sweet potatoes are glazed, about 30 minutes. Baste the sweet potatoes, apples and pork chops with syrup from bottom of skillet.

BAKED HAM

1 (12-14 pound) ham
½ cup vinegar
2 cups brown sugar
   Few grains pepper
2 tablespoons flour
2 tablespoons dry mustard
¼ cup pineapple juice

Bake the ham according to directions on the wrapper or can. This baking will take at least 3½ hours in a 325° oven. If you are using a meat thermometer, the internal temperature of the meat should register 150°. Baste the ham with pan juices as it cooks, or with pineapple juice. About 20 minutes before the ham is done, remove from the oven and score the fat with a knife. (If the skin is still on a portion of the meat, it may easily be removed at this time.) Combine sugar, pepper, flour and dry mustard. Mix in vinegar and pineapple juice. Spread this mixture over the scored ham. Return to oven and bake for 20 minutes longer to "set" the glaze. Canned cranberry sauce, orange marmalade or apricot preserves all make satisfactory and flavorful glazes for baked ham.

TOURTIERE OR PORK PIE

Tourtiere or pork pie is a regional French-Canadian dish usually served at Christmas. This recipe makes two pies, each pie makes 8 servings. There are many recipes for this pie, and this is called "Toochie" pie.

3 cups mashed potatoes
3 pounds lean pork, ground (or ground turkey)
1 cup water
¼ teaspoon nutmeg
¼ teaspoon allspice
1 tablespoon salt
¼ tablespoon pepper
½ cup chopped onion
   Pastry for 2 two-crust pies

In saucepan, combine ground pork or ground turkey with water, nutmeg, allspice, salt, pepper and onion. Cook over moderate heat for 30 minutes, stirring often to prevent sticking. Remove from heat; add mashed potatoes; mix well. Cool. Fill two pastry-lined plates; adjust top crusts, slashing pastry to allow for escape of steam as the pies bake. Bake at 425° for 40 minutes. Serve hot or cold.

ORIENTAL SHORT-RIB BARBECUE

When it's barbecue time, indoor and outdoor grills will be busy as folks entertain. This recipe won the Best of Beef Cook-Off at the 1988 National Beef Cook-Off.

⅔ cup thinly sliced green onions
½ soy sauce
½ cup soy sauce
¼ cup Oriental dark-roasted sesame oil
2½ tablespoons packed brown sugar
1½ tablespoons toasted sesame seeds, crushed
1 tablespoon minced garlic
1 tablespoon grated fresh ginger
½ teaspoon ground red pepper (Cayenne)
⅛ teaspoon crushed red-pepper pods
4 pounds well-trimmed beef short ribs

Combine green onions, soy sauce, water, sesame oil, brown sugar, sesame seeds, garlic, ginger, red pepper and red-pepper pods. Place beef short ribs in plastic bag; add marinade, turning to coat. Close bag securely and marinate in refrigerator 4 to 6 hours (or overnight if desired), turning occasionally. Remove ribs from marinade; reserve marinade. Place ribs on grill over medium coals. Cover. Grill 10 to 12 minutes, turning once and brushing with marinade before turning. Makes 12 servings.

ITALIAN MEAT LOAF

This meat loaf uses less meat. Ground lean round and natural whole wheat flakes cut the fat in the loaf.

2 egg whites, slightly beaten
1 cup natural whole wheat flakes
¼ cup chopped onion
2 tablespoons chopped parsley
½ teaspoon minced garlic
1 teaspoon basil leaves, crushed
1 teaspoon oregano leaves, crushed
¾ teaspoon salt
¼ teaspoon ground black pepper
3 tablespoons catsup
¾ pound ground lean round beef
1 tablespoon grated Parmesan cheese

In a medium bowl combine egg whites, cereal, onion, parsley, garlic, basil, oregano, salt, black pepper and catsup; mix well. Add beef and blend well. Shape meat into an oval loaf. Place in a baking dish coated with a non-stick vegetable spray. Bake in a preheated 350° oven for 40 minutes. Sprinkle with cheese and bake 5 minutes longer.

PEPPER STEAK

1½ pounds round steak
½ cup flour
1 teaspoon salt
¼ teaspoon pepper
⅓ cup salad oil
1 (8 oz.) can tomato sauce
1 cup water
½ cup chopped onion
1 small clove garlic, minced
1 beef bouillon cube
1½ teaspoons Worcestershire sauce
1 medium to large green pepper, cut in strips
Cooked rice for six servings

Combine flour, salt and pepper on a plate. Cut steak in ½-inch strips; coat thoroughly with the flour mixture and brown in the oil in a large skillet. When meat is browned, add tomato sauce, water, onion, garlic and bouillon cube. Cover and simmer for 1½ hours or until meat is tender. Uncover; stir in Worcestershire sauce and green pepper strips. Simmer for 10 to 15 minutes longer. Serve over the cooked rice.

LONDON BROIL

Apparently there are many ways for preparing London broil. One recipe says that it may be flank steak or round steak.

2 pounds round steak, cut ¾-inch thickness
1 clove garlic, mashed
½ teaspoon salt
2½ tablespoons soy sauce
1 tablespoon tomato paste
1 tablespoon cooking oil
½ teaspoon pepper
½ teaspoon oregano

Remove fat from the meat. Mash the garlic with the salt; add soy sauce, tomato paste, oil, pepper and oregano. Mix and rub into the meat on both sides. Place meat in a plastic bag with any marinating mixture left; seal bag and refrigerate for 6 to 7 hours or overnight. Broil 5 to 6 minutes on either side or until done. Slice crossways to the grain. Serve extra sauce from the marinating with the meat. Baked potatoes will go well with the meat, along with green beans, broccoli or corn.

ORIENTAL-STYLE BEEF STEAK

1 pound beef top sirloin steak that is 1¼ inches thick
1 tablespoon vegetable oil
1 teaspoon grated fresh ginger
1 clove garlic, minced
1 large carrot, coarsely grated
1 small onion chopped
1½ cups thinly sliced spinach leaves
½ cup thinly sliced Napa cabbage
½ cup fresh bean sprouts
3 tablespoons light soy sauce

Cook and stir ginger in oil in large frying pan over medium heat 1 minute. Stir in carrots and onion; continue cooking over medium-high heat 1 minute. Add spinach, cabbage, bean sprouts and soy sauce; cook and stir 2 to 3 minutes. Remove from heat. Cool slightly. Meanwhile, carefully make pockets in steak, cutting through the center (parallel to the surface of the meat) the length and width of the steak. Do not cut through the opposite side of the steak. Fill pockets of steak with vegetables and secure open sides with small wooden picks placed approximately 1 inch apart. Place steak on rack of broiler pan so surface of meat is 3 to 4 inches from heat. Broil 7 to 8 minutes, turn and broil second side of steak 7 to 8 minutes, to desired doneness. Remove picks and carve into 1½-inch slices. 4 servings.

BAKED HAM WITH FRUIT SAUCE

This 60-year-old recipe has never lost its followers. It has been used as a company main dish as well as a potluck dish. Serve with green beans and mashed potato. Corn scallop is also a suggested vegetable in place of green beans. Turkey ham was used recently and proved to be a good substitute for regular ham used for many years. Either ham may be used.

  2 pound slice of smoked ham or turkey ham
  1 cup pineapple juice
½ cup cherry juice from Maraschino cherries
  1 cup water
  2 tablespoons vinegar
  1 cup pineapple chunks, tidbits or crushed
½ teaspoon powdered cloves
½ cup brown sugar, packed
  1 cup Maraschino cherries
  1 cup seedless raisins
  2 tablespoons butter or margarine
  4 tablespoons cornstarch
½ teaspoon salt
⅓ cup cold water
  3 tablespoons cooking oil
  1 cup water

(If turkey ham is used, remove the outside covering of the meat edge.) Rub the meat on both sides with the cloves. Brown the meat on both sides in a frypan in the oil. Dissolve the brown sugar in 1 cup of water and pour over the meat and simmer for about 1 hour or until meat is tender. Turn the meat frequently and cook slowly. When the meat is tender, prepare the sauce. Combine pineapple juice, cherry juice, 1 cup water, vinegar, pineapple, cherries, raisins and salt. When hot and well-blended, add cornstarch mixed with ⅓ cup of cold water. Cook and stir until sauce is thickened and clear. Stir in butter. Cut meat in serving-size pieces and pour sauce over the meat or serve sauce in a separate bowl. A delicious addition to the sauce is the use of tarragon-flavored vinegar in place of the regular vinegar.

PEPPERED TURKEY LOAF

Black pepper is one spice that peps up more dishes than any other spice. To those limited on salt, black pepper adds a lift to any food. Ground fresh turkey meat is one meat that comes alive with black pepper.

 2 tablespoons instant minced onion
 2 tablespoons water
 2 slices firm-textured white bread
 2 large ribs celery, cut in chunks
 1 large carrot, cut in chunks
 ½ medium green bell pepper
 1 pound ground turkey
 1 egg, beaten
 1 can (8 oz.) tomato sauce
 1¼ teaspoons salt
 ½ to 1 teaspoon ground black pepper
   Apricot mustard sauce

Preheat oven to 400°. In a custard cup combine onion and water; set aside to soften, about 10 minutes. In a food processor fitted with a metal wing blade whirl bread until crumbs form; transfer to a medium bowl. Process celery until minced (makes about ⅔ cup); add to bread. Repeat with carrots and green pepper (makes about ⅓ cup of each). To mixture add ground turkey, egg, tomato sauce, minced onion, salt and black papper; toss lightly until just well mixed. Place mixture on a baking pan; form into a 10-inch long oval, or place in a loaf pan. Bake until cooked through, 50 to 60 minutes. Cool in pan for 5 minutes. Serve with apricot mustard sauce. Yield: 6 to 8 portions.

APRICOT MUSTARD SAUCE

 1 can (16 oz.) apricots in syrup, drained
 1 cup chicken broth
 2 tablespoons Dijon-style prepared mustard
 ½ teaspoon salt
 ¼ teaspoon ground black pepper
 ¼ teaspoon paprika

In a blender place apricots, chicken broth and mustard; whirl until smooth. Transfer to a saucepan. Add salt, black pepper and paprika; heat until hot, stirring occasionally. Yield: 2¼ cups.

CHICKEN WITH DUMPLINGS

Chicken with dumplings is a good dish for the cold weather. This recipe is modified to reduce saturated fat, cholesterol and sodium.

 2 tablespoons corn oil
 3 whole chicken breasts, halved, skin removed
 ½ cup thinly sliced carrots
 ½ cup thinly sliced celery
 ½ cup coarsely chopped onion
 2 chicken broth cubes (makes 2 cups broth)
 1 tablespoon lemon juice
 ⅛ teaspoon pepper
 1 bay leaf
   Parsley dumplings
 1 tablespoon corn starch
 ¼ cup skim milk

In 5-quart Dutch oven, heat corn oil over medium heat. Add the skinned chicken, a few pieces at a time. Cook 10 minutes or until lightly browned on all sides. Remove chicken. Pour off all excess chicken fat from Dutch oven. Add carrots, celery and onions. Cook 20 minutes, stirring frequently, or until onion is lightly browned. Stir in chicken broth, lemon juice, pepper and bay leaf. Bring to boil. Return chicken to Dutch oven. Cover and simmer 10 to 15 minutes or until chicken is almost tender. Drop dumpling mixture by tablespoonsful onto chicken. Cover and cook 10 minutes or until dumplings are cooked through. Remove chicken and dumplings to serving platter; keep warm. Discard bay leaf. In small bowl, stir together corn starch and skim milk until smooth. Stir into Dutch oven. Stirring constantly, bring to boil over medium heat and boil 1 minute. Serve over chicken and dumplings.

PARSLEY DUMPLINGS

 1 cup unsifted flour
 2 tablespoons chopped parsley
 2 teaspoons baking powder
 1 egg
 ¼ cup skim milk
 3 tablespoons corn oil

In medium bowl, stir together flour, parsley, and baking powder. In small bowl, beat together skim milk, egg and corn oil. Stir into flour just until well blended.

MARIE'S BAKED CHICKEN BREASTS

4 chicken breasts, halved and not boned
1 can of sauerkraut, drained
½ cup mayonnaise
¼ cup catsup

Wash chicken breast halves; pat dry with paper towel. Spread drained sauerkraut in baking dish; a large or small can may be used. (Some like to rinse the sauerkraut in cold water and then drain to lessen the amount of salt.) Place chicken, skin side up, over the kraut. Combine mayonnaise and catsup (or use 1 cup of Russian salad dressing) over the chicken. Bake, uncovered, in a moderate oven, 350° for about one hour or until chicken tests done. If the chicken browns too fast, place a piece of foil over it. You may like to add additional seasonings—herbs, salt or pepper—but this dish is great without additional seasoning.

QUICK CHICKEN AND HAM JAMBALAYA

Need a change in menu? This recipe pays homage to Cajun cooking. Ground red pepper and other authentic spices are used. Remember, red pepper is hot but very controllable.

¼ cup instant minced onion
¼ cup water
3 tablespoons butter or margarine
1 pound boned and skinned chicken breasts
¼ pound sliced boiled ham
1 cup sliced celery
1 cup coarsely chopped green peppers
1 teaspoon ground red pepper
1 teaspoon garlic powder
1 teaspoon thyme leaves
½ teaspoon ground black pepper
1 can (28 oz.) Italian plum tomatoes
½ cup chicken broth
1½ cups uncooked rice

Cut chicken breasts into 1-inch cubes; cut boiled ham into ½-inch squares. Crush the canned tomatoes. In a cup combine minced onion with water; let stand to soften, about 10 minutes. Melt butter in a large skillet. Add chicken, ham, celery, green pepper, ground red pepper, garlic, thyme, black pepper and reserved onion. Cook and stir until chicken is golden, about 3 minutes. Stir in tomatoes, chicken broth and rice; bring to a boil. Reduce heat and simmer, covered, until rice is tender, 15 to 18 minutes, stirring occasionally. Yields 4 to 6 portions or 8 cups.

CHICKEN ITALIANO

A dish that is quick to put together, chicken Italiano, cooks in the time that the table is set, the rice cooked and other little details that go with a meal. The rice can be cooked in a covered casserole to make full use of the oven. It takes about 25 minutes to an hour, depending upon the type of rice used. This makes 6 servings. Extra chicken may be reheated or removed from the bones to use in a sandwich.

12 choice chicken pieces (2½ to 3 pounds)
 1 envelope (1⅜ oz.) onion soup mix
 1 can (10¾ oz.) cream of mushroom soup
 ½ cup chicken broth
 1 cup drained canned tomatoes
 3 cups hot cooked rice

Drumsticks, thighs and/or breast halves may be used. Place chicken pieces in buttered shallow baking dish (about 9x13x2 inches). Sprinkle with onion soup mix. Blend mushroom soup and chicken broth and pour over chicken. Add tomatoes. Cover and bake at 375⁰ for 1 hour, or until chicken is tender. Serve over hot, fluffy rice. Makes 6 servings.

BARBECUED TERIYAKI CHICKEN MARINADE

Cold or hot, this barbecued teriyaki chicken will be popular for dinner or a picnic. It may be cooked in the oven or on the grill.

1¼ cups packed brown sugar
 1 cup soy sauce
 ½ teaspoon ground ginger
1½ to 2 cups canned crushed pineapple, undrained
 18 chicken legs, thighs or breast halves
 3 cloves garlic, crushed
 ½ teaspoon cooking oil

Preheat oven to 400⁰. Combine brown sugar, soy sauce, ginger, garlic cloves, and oil. Add pineapple, with juice. Place in 2 shallow glass or ceramic casseroles or baking pans. Place the chicken pieces in the dishes. Bake for 40 minutes in the hot oven. Remove casseroles from the oven, turn chicken pieces over, cover and refrigerate for 4 hours or overnight. When ready to serve, remove from refrigerator. Have a charcoal grill ready and cook over medium-hot coals for 6 to 7 minutes on each side, brushing frequently with the marinade. Allow more cooking time if using the grill.

ORANGE SAUCED CHICKEN

1 3-pound broiler-fryer, cut for serving
1 teaspoon salt
¼ cup butter or margarine
3 tablespoons flour
3 tablespoons sugar
¼ teaspoon dry mustard
½ teaspoon cinnamon
¼ teaspoon ginger
1½ cups orange juice

Sprinkle ½ teaspoon of salt over the chicken pieces. Brown chicken in butter or margarine in a frying pan. Remove chicken to baking dish. Mix flour, sugar, remaining salt and spices; add to drippings in frying pan, stirring to make a smooth paste. Gradually add orange juice and cook, stirring until mixture comes to a boil. Pour this sauce over the chicken and bake at 350° for 45 to 50 minutes or until the chicken is tender. Serve sauce with chicken.

OVEN-BARBECUED CHICKEN

Add spice to the main dish for supper and barbecue chicken to serve with mashed potatoes, green beans, cabbage slaw and lemon pudding.

1 cut-up chicken fryer (about 3½) pounds
1 stick butter or margarine
⅓ cup Worcestershire sauce
2 tablespoons lemon juice or vinegar
6 tablespoons catsup
2 tablespoons sugar
¼ teaspoon paprika
2 tablespoons A-1 sauce
¼ teaspoon Cayenne pepper (or less)

Place cut up chicken (may be halves or quarters or cut into serving-size pieces) in lightly greased baking dish or small roaster. In a bowl, combine butter, Worcestershire sauce, lemon juice, catsup, A-1 sauce, paprika, sugar (brown or white) and Cayenne pepper. Mix and pour over chicken. Cover and cook in a medium oven, 350°, for about 1¼ hours, or until tender. Uncover the last 15 minutes of cooking so that the chicken can brown. It may take a bit longer cooking time, depending on the meat.

CINDY'S EASY CHICKEN DIVAN

1 large bag frozen broccoli and cauliflower
1 large bag frozen carrots and broccoli
2 cups sliced cooked chicken
2 cans cream of chicken soup
¾ cup mayonnaise or salad dressing
1 teaspoon lemon juice
2 ounces shredded Cheddar cheese
1 cup soft bread crumbs
1 tablespoon margarine, melted

Cook vegetables; drain. Arrange in buttered 9x13x2-inch baking dish. Arrange cooked chicken on top of vegetables. Combine soup, mayonnaise and lemon juice and pour over chicken. Spread with bread crumbs and pour margarine over; sprinkle cheese over all and bake at 350° for 35 to 40 minutes.

BAKED CHICKEN

Baked chicken with a barbecue sauce is one way of preparing a meal for a visiting friend and family when they are a few miles away and the telephone announces the time of arrival. While the chicken cooks, a garden salad may be readied and a blueberry scone or muffins put into the oven to bake with the chicken. Or, yeast rolls from the freezer may be reheated.

1 broiler/fryer, cut in serving pieces
¾ cup chili sauce
2 tablespoons honey
2 tablespoons soy sauce
¼ teaspoon Cayenne pepper
1 teaspoon dry mustard
½ teaspoon prepared horseradish
¼ teaspoon garlic powder

Place chicken pieces, skin side up, in a shallow 9x13-inch baking pan. Combine chili sauce, honey, soy sauce, Cayenne pepper, dry mustard, horseradish and garlic powder; mix well and pour over chicken. Cover pan with foil and bake at 375° for 30 minutes. Uncover pan; spoon sauce from the baking pan over the chicken and bake 30 to 45 minutes longer or until chicken tests done. Several seasoned salts in the market are often used for this mixture of seasonings.

OVEN-FRIED CHICKEN

Preheat oven to 400⁰.

1 stick margarine
½ cup all-purpose flour
1 teaspoon salt
½ teaspoon paprika
¼ teaspoon pepper
6 to 8 cut-up chicken parts

Two breasts, halved, 4 thighs and 4 legs for 6 to 8 servings is suggested. Place butter in pan in oven to melt. Meanwhile, mix flour, salt, paprika and pepper in paper bag. Add chicken pieces, one at a time, and shake to coat evenly. Dip both sides of coated chicken in melted butter. Place in single layer, skin side down, in a 9x13x2-inch baking pan. Bake 30 minutes. Turn skin side up; bake another 20 to 30 minutes or until chicken is tender. The temperature for baking the biscuits is 450⁰, but you may find the 400⁰ oven with the chicken hot enough.

POTATO AND BACON STUFFING FOR SAVORY BIRDS

2½ pounds or 7 to 8 medium-sized potatoes, baked
½ pound bacon, diced
1½ cups chopped onion
1 cup sliced celery
1 tablespoon sage
1½ teaspoons thyme
¾ cup water
¼ cup butter or margarine, melted
1 package (7 ounces) seasoned bread cubes
¼ cup chopped parsley
Salt and pepper to taste

Scoop pulp from baked potatoes; break up and measure to make about a quart; set aside. Cook bacon in a broad skillet until crisp. Add onion and celery; cook 2 minutes longer. Add potato pulp, sage and thyme; toss to mix well. In a large bowl, pour water and butter over the bread cubes; toss to moisten evenly. Add potato mixture and parsley; season with salt and pepper. Use to stuff your holiday bird.
Suggestion: Save the skins from your baked potatoes for crisp and easy-to-prepare potato skins. Leave about ⅛ inch of pulp on the skins, slice into wedges, and brush with melted butter and soy sauce. Bake at 500⁰ until crisp, about 10 to 12 minutes. Salt and pepper to taste.

BROILED CHICKEN VON STURTZ

Use 2 to 2½-pound broilers. Wipe broilers with a damp cloth and place on broiler rack, skin side up. Do not separate meat at the breast until after the bird is cooked, thus keeping more juices in the meat. Dust the bird generously, inside and out, with celery salt. Lay slices of bacon over the bird. Broil the bird for 20 minutes, removing the bacon as it becomes crisp, but reserving the cooked bacon to serve with the chicken. Turn chicken and continue to cook, using fresh bacon, to desired doneness, about 45 minutes. Cut broiler in half to serve with crisp bacon as garnish. Some chefs suggest broiling the birds until brown on each side, then trasnferring to a shallow pan, adding 1 cup water, covering with foil and baking at a low temperature, 300°, for 40 minutes, or until done.

CREAMED FINNAN HADDIE

1½ pounds finnan haddie
2 tablespoons flour
⅛ teaspoon pepper
3 hard cooked eggs, chopped
2 tablespoons butter
1 small onion, minced
½ teaspoon salt
1¾ cup milk or cream

Put fish in pan, cover with cold water and bring to boil; drain and repeat once more. Flake fish. Melt butter and saute onions until golden. Stir in flour, salt and pepper and cream or milk. Cook until thickened, stirring constantly. Add fish and chopped eggs. Mix well. Serve over toast or boiled or mashed potatoes.

BAKED SWORDFISH WITH DILL SAUCE

4 (4-6 oz. each) swordfish steaks
  Salt
  White pepper
1 teaspoon oil
1 teaspoon lemon juice
  Dill sauce

Pat fish dry with paper towels. Season lightly with salt and white pepper. Combine oil and lemon juice; brush on both sides of steak. Place 1 inch apart on lightly oiled baking dish. Bake at 450°, allowing 10 minutes per inch thickness measured at its thickest part or just until fish flakes when tested with a fork. Transfer fish to warm plates. Spoon dill sauce over fish. Serve hot.

DILL SAUCE

½ cup dairy sour cream
1 teaspoon Dijon-style mustard
½ cup unflavored yogurt
2 tablespoons mayonnaise
2 tablespoons minced fresh dill (or ¾ teaspoon dry)
  Dash of bottled hot pepper sauce
  Salt and pepper

Combine sour cream, yogurt, mayonnaise, dill, mustard and pepper sauce. Add salt and pepper to taste. Blend well. Allow to stand at least ½ hour to blend flavors, or refrigerate up to 24 hours. Serve at room temperature. Makes about 1 cup.

FISH AND SEAFOOD

CLAM CAKES

2 cups shucked clams
2 eggs, beaten
2 tablespoons flour
1 teaspoon baking powder
1 teaspoon salt
⅛ teaspoon pepper
1 teaspoon sugar
½ cup rolled cracker crumbs
½ cup clam juice

Chop clams; drain and reserve juice to mix with eggs. Mix beaten eggs and clam juice. Mix and sift flour, baking powder, salt, pepper and sugar over cracker crumbs. Add clams, clam juice and egg mixture. Add more clam juice if mixture appears dry. Drop large spoonsful of batter into pan of hot fat—it does not need to be deep fat. Cook until golden brown; turn and brown other side. Fresh clams or canned minced clams may be used.

SALMON ROLL

⅓ cup diced onion
⅓ cup diced green pepper
⅓ cup diced celery
2 tablespoons butter or margarine
1 can (7 ounces) salmon, skin removed
½ can cream of mushroom soup
¼ cup stuffed olives, sliced
½ cup water (about)
2 cups biscuit mix
  Melted butter or margarine

Saute onion, green pepper and celery in butter or margarine. Drain and flake salmon, reserving liquid in can. Combine sauteed mixture with salmon, soup and olives. Add water to biscuit mix and mix to a soft dough. Turn dough onto floured board and knead 5 times. Roll to a ¼-inch-thick rectangle. Cover with salmon mixture to within an inch of edges. Roll up, jelly-roll style, starting at short end. Place on greased shallow baking pan. Be sure edges are well-sealed and the roll is on the baking pan seam side down. Brush with melted butter. Bake in a moderate oven, 350°, for about an hour. While roll is baking, combining remaining soup, 2 tablespoons lemon juice, ¼ cup juice from salmon can and ½ cup milk. Heat together to serve over the salmon loaf, which is cut into six slices for serving.

GOLDEN APPLE FISH KABOBS

1 green pepper cut in 1½-inch squares
1 large Golden Delicious apple
½ pound cod or halibut
6 cherry tomatoes
2 tablespoons lemon juice
1 tablespoon melted butter
¼ teaspoon salt
   Dash of pepper
   Dash of thyme

Core and cut apple into 8 slices. Cut fish into 1½-inch cubes. On six bamboo skewers, alternate green pepper, apple, fish, tomato, apple, fish and green pepper. Combine remaining ingredients; brush over all surfaces. Broil 3 to 4 inches from heat for 8 minutes total time, or until fish flakes when tested with fork; turn halfway through broiling time. Makes 3 servings.

ORIENTAL BAKED SEAFOOD

1 cup chopped almonds
1 cup long-grain white rice
2 cups water
½ teaspoon salt
1 tablespoon sesame oil
1 tablespoon grated ginger root
1 teaspoon grated lemon peel
1 pound halibut
½ pound large scallops
½ pound medium shrimp, shelled
1 clove garlic, minced
3 tablespoons lite soy sauce
½ cup slivered green onions

Spread almonds in shallow pan or on a cookie sheet. Toast at 350° for 10 minutes, stirring once or twice, until lightly browned; cool. Add rice to boiling salted water in saucepan. Stir in sesame oil, ginger root and lemon peel. Bring to boil. Cover, reduce heat and simmer 20-25 minutes. Remove from heat; stir in almonds; keep warm. Meanwhile, remove skin and bones from halibut; cut into large pieces. Cut 4 12-inch squares of foil and divide halibut, scallops, and shrimp among them. Sprinkle each square with garlic and soy sauce and seal tightly. Bake at 400° for 12 minutes or grill or broil 4 inches from the heat for 15 minutes, turning once. Pour fish and juices over rice to serve. Sprinkle with green onions.

BAKED FISH IN MILK

1½ pound haddock or other white fish
   Salt
   Pepper
4 tablespoons flour (about)
   Milk
4 tablespoons butter or margarine
2 onions, thinly sliced

Preheat the oven to 400°; put in potatoes to bake. Grease a shallow baking dish. Spread the sliced onions in the dish. Top with the fish fillets in a single layer. Sprinkle with salt, pepper and flour; dot with butter or margarine. Add milk to barely cover the fish and bake with the potatoes for the last 15 minutes of cooking time, or until the fish flakes easily.

STUFFED FISH FILLETS WITH CITRUS MUSTARD SAUCE

1½ tablespoons corn oil
½ cup chopped onion
¾ cup shredded carrots
1 cup natural bran flakes, lightly crushed
¾ teaspoon salt, divided
   Ground black pepper
4 large fish fillets (1½ pounds)
2 tablespoons Dijon-style mustard, divided
1½ cups orange juice
1 tablespoon cornstarch

Preheat oven to 400°. Coat a 9-inch square baking dish with non-stick vegetable spray; set aside. In a large skillet heat oil. Add onion; saute until almost tender, about 4 minutes. Mix in carrots; saute until tender, about 2 minutes. Measure out ½ cup of vegetable mixture and place in a medium bowl. Set skillet aside for later use. To vegetables in the bowl add cereal, ½ teaspoon of salt and ⅛ teaspoon black pepper; mix well. Place fillets, dark (skin) side up on flat work surface. Spread evenly with 1 tablespoon mustard. Spread cereal mixture evenly over mustard. Roll up each fillet from a narrow end. Place seam side down in prepared baking dish; cover tightly with foil. Bake until fish is opaque in the center, about 25 minutes. Five minutes before fish is done, stir orange juice, cornstarch, remaining 1 table-spoon mustard, ¼ teaspoon salt and a dash of black pepper into reserved vegetable mixture in skillet; bring to a boil; boil for 1 minute longer. Spoon over fish.

SCALLOPED OYSTERS

1 pint fresh oysters, drained, reserving liquid
½ cup butter, melted
2 cups cracker crumbs
1 teaspoon salt
⅛ teaspoon pepper
⅛ teaspoon nutmeg (optional)
¼ cup milk or cream
    Few grains Cayenne pepper

Crush about 40 saltines (lightly salted crackers) to make 2 cups of crumbs. Add pepper, salt and nutmeg, if desired. In a buttered, shallow baking dish, place a layer of the crumbs; add a layer of oysters, more crumbs, remaining oysters and top with remaining crumbs. Combine cream with liquid from the oysters and pour it over the contents of the dish. Add 4 strips of bacon, if desired. Bake at 425° for about 30 minutes. A few more tablespoons of milk may be added if the casserole seems dry, but it should not be sloppy. A teaspoon of Worcestershire sauce may be added and a few grains of Cayenne pepper.

CAJUN BARBECUED MACKEREL

Try any fish fillets with this Cajun seasoning mix. Broil, barbecue or bake the fish as you prefer.

2 to 3 pounds mackerel or other fish fillets
    Vegetable oil
    Cajun seasoning mix

Brush fish with a thin coat of vegetable oil. Dip each of the fillets in the seasoning mix, covering both sides completely. Using a well-oiled wire rack, barbecue both sides until cooked (approximately 4 minutes each side).

SEASONING MIX

1 tablespoon sweet paprika
2½ teaspoons salt
1 teaspoon onion powder
1 teaspoon garlic powder
1 teaspoon Cayenne pepper
¾ teaspoon white pepper
¾ teaspoon black pepper
½ teaspoon dried thyme leaves
½ teaspoon dried oregano leaves

Mix all seasonings together. This is a zesty mixture but good on fish.
NOTE: Try some of this mixture in your pot of chili.

BAKED SCALLOPS

A quick and easy to prepare dish is baked scallops. Serve broccoli and mashed potatoes to go with the fish. Add a cucumber and tomato salad if you wish a bigger menu.

1 pound fresh scallops
  Salt, to season
  Pepper, to season
  Fish blend herbs, if desired
  Butter or margarine
  Coffee cream or half-and-half
  Flour

The amounts of ingredients depend on amount of scallops used. Wash and drain scallops. Combine ¼ to ½ cup flour with ½ teaspoon salt and a few dashes of pepper. Roll drained scallops in flour mixture. (Fish blend herbs may be added to the flour mixture, if desired.) Place scallops in greased pie plate. Dot with butter. Pour about 1 cup cream around the scallops in the baking dish, so that it will come about half way up the sides of the scallops. Bake 30 to 40 minutes at 350⁰.

SALMON CAKES WITH CUCUMBER SAUCE

Salmon cakes with cucumber sauce will be a change from the usual fried or baked fish. The cucumber sauce is made and chilled to be served at the table with the salmon cakes.

½ cup plain lowfat yogurt
⅓ cup chopped tomato
⅓ cup chopped cucumber
2 tablespoons finely chopped onion, divided
2 tablespoons snipped, fresh dill, divided
1 (15½ oz.) can pink salmon
¾ cup rolled oats, uncooked
⅓ cup skim or lowfat milk
1 egg white or whole egg
¼ teaspoon salt
1 tablespoon margarine

For the sauce, combine the yogurt, tomato, cucumber, 1 tablespoon finely chopped onion and 1 tablespoon snipped, fresh dill; mix well. Chill. (NOTE: many markets have fresh dill on their vegetable displays; 1 teaspoon dried dill weed may be used.) For the cakes, combine the salmon, oats, milk, egg white, 1 tablespoon finely chopped onion, 1 tablespoon snipped, fresh dill or 1 teaspoon dry dill weed and salt; mix well. Form 5 oval patties; fry in margarine over medium heat 3 to 4 minutes on each side or until golden brown and heated through. Serve with sauce.

LEMON RICE-STUFFED SOLE

This recipe calls for sole fillets, but any white fish, such as haddock or hake, may be used.

¼ cup sliced celery
2 tablespoons butter or margarine
2 cups cooked brown rice
¼ teaspoon salt
¼ teaspoon thyme
⅛ teaspoon ground black pepper
2 teaspoons grated lemon peel
2 tablespoons fresh lemon juice
1 pound fresh or frozen sole fillets
1 tablespoon snipped fresh parsley

In medium skillet, cook celery and onion in 2 tablespoons butter until tender. Stir in rice, seasonings and lemon juice. Place fillets in buttered shallow baking dish. Spread rice mixture on lower portion of each fillet. Fold over to enclose rice mixture. Fasten with wooden picks. Brush with remaining 1 tablespoon butter, melted. Sprinkle with parsley. Bake at 350° for 20 to 30 minutes or until fish flakes easily with a fork. Makes 4 servings.

HERB-BASTED FISH FILLETS

Cod, pollock or haddock fillets, herb-basted, make the beginning of a menu for dinner. Parsley-buttered potatoes and steamed broccoli, with a shower of Parmesan cheese, may complete the menu.

1 pound cod, pollock or haddock fillets
2 tablespoons butter or margarine
2 tablespoons water or fish stock
1 tablespoon chopped green onion
1 tablespoon chopped parsley
  Dash of thyme, crushed
  Dash of marjoram, crushed
  Lemon slices

Cut fish into serving-size pieces. Thaw fish if necessary. Melt butter; add remaining ingredients, except lemon slices. Place fish on oiled broiler rack; baste generously with butter mixture. Arrange lemon slices on fish. Broil 4 to 5 inches from heat, allowing 10 minutes cooking time per inch of thickness, measured at the thickest part, or until fish flakes when tested with a fork. Baste once with butter mixture during broiling. Makes four or five servings.

SALMON LOAF

1 pound can salmon, flaked
½ cup milk
1½ cups bread crumbs
¼ cup melted butter or margarine
3 egg yolks, beaten
   Few grains pepper
1½ tablespoons lemon juice
2 tablespoons minced onion
½ cup minced green pepper
½ teaspoon salt
3 egg whites, stiffly beaten

Have all ingredients at room temperature. Drain and reserve liquid from canned salmon. Scald milk, add bread crumbs and butter and allow to sit for 5 minutes. Add salmon liquid or ½ cup water and heat gently until smooth. Combine with flaked fish, egg yolks, lemon juice, onion, green pepper, salt and pepper. Fold in egg whites. Line bottom of bread loaf pan with foil and grease foil. Spoon salmon mixture into pan, spreading into corners. Bake in a moderate oven, 350° for about 40 minutes.

FRIED HAKE SAUTE

Do you try different fish for your meals? Hake is one fish that is easy to prepare and has good flavor. We tried the recipe again with fresh catfish from the market, while cod is another fish that may be used.

2 pounds fresh hake fillets
   Flour
   Milk
   Dried bread crumbs
4 tablespoons butter or margarine
   Lemon slices for garnish
   Salt and pepper
   Shortening or oil
2 teaspoons lemon juice
   Parsley sprigs for garnish

Wipe fillets with a damp cloth. Cut into portions; roll fish in flour, dip in milk with salt and pepper added, then roll in dried bread crumbs. Sear fish in a sufficient quantity of shortening or hot oil to prevent the fillets from sticking to the pan. Brown on one side and then on the other. Melt butter in a saucepan, add the lemon juice, and while still bubbling, pour over fish. Garnish with slices of lemon and parsley. Serves 6.

STEAMED SALMON AND EGG SAUCE

A traditional Fourth of July dinner is fresh, new peas from the garden, with steamed salmon and egg sauce. Potatoes boiled and served with parsley butter go well, too. A strawberry shortcake or fresh strawberry ice cream will make a fine dessert. If you were a lucky fisherman, you may have already caught and frozen the salmon. Or you may want to order one early from the market. Cold leftover salmon is delicious in a salad.

2½ to 3 pounds fresh salmon
1 teaspoon salt

Wipe the salmon with a damp cloth. Tie the fish in a piece of cheesecloth for easy removal from the kettle. Place a rack on the bottom of the kettle with a small amount of water under the fish. Or, place a rack in a baking pan with water underneath the rack and cook in the oven. If a kettle is used, cover the kettle to keep the steam in. If the fish is cooked in the oven, a cover is not needed, and the cheesecloth is used as for kettle steaming. Steam for about 15 minutes to the pound of fish or until the fish flakes easily when tested with a fork. If it is a thick piece of fish, such as the tail piece, you may need to turn the fish once. When done, remove fish and remove skin. Place fish on a platter and keep it warm while you prepare the egg sauce.

EGG SAUCE

2½ tablespoons butter, softened
3 tablespoons flour
½ teaspoon salt
⅛ teaspoon pepper
   Few grains Cayenne pepper
1½ cups fish stock (water from steaming the fish)
2 teaspoons fresh lemon juice
2½ tablespoons butter, cut in small pieces
3 hard cooked eggs, sliced

Combine 2½ tablespoons butter, flour, salt, pepper and Cayenne pepper. Mix to combine and make a paste; slowly add the fish stock. Cook and stir until smooth and thickened. Stir in the lemon juice, then the remaining butter, bit by bit. Taste for further seasoning. When sauce is hot, carefully fold in the egg slices. This sauce is also good on boiled or mashed potatoes.

GINGER GLAZED CARROTS AND APPLES

4 large carrots
2 tart red apples
3 tablespoons butter or margarine
3 tablespoons honey
2 teaspoons prepared mustard
¾ teaspoon ground ginger

Pare carrots; cut into julienne strips. Cook in lightly salted water until tender-crisp, about 5 minutes. Drain. While carrots cook, core apples and cut into thick slices. Melt butter in large skillet. Stir in mustard, honey and ginger. Add apples and carrots; heat gently until apples are just tender, about 10 minutes. Makes 6 to 8 servings.

CAULIFLOWER AND CHEESE SAUCE

Covered dish or potluck suppers are fun meals. If you do not wish to sample all the dishes, a quick survey of the dishes as you stand in line allows you to pick a main dish, a vegetable, potato, salad and a dessert. Macaroni and cheese is one standby, but here is a suggestion for something a little different for your contribution to the pot luck supper. The cauliflower is cooked all in one piece.

1 head cauliflower
⅓ cup butter or margarine
½ cup flour
2 cups milk
¾ teaspoon salt
¼ teaspoon pepper
⅛ teaspoon Cayenne pepper
2 to 2½ cups shredded sharp Cheddar cheese

Wash cauliflower and remove leaves for a smooth base. Have a kettle of boiling water, about 2½ inches deep, with ½ teaspoon salt added. To easily place and take out the vegetable, set it in a piece of cheese cloth and have the ends extending 8 or 10 inches to both sides. Lower the cauliflower into the boiling water, cover and cook for about 25 minutes or until it tests done when tested with a fork. Do not overcook. In the meantime, prepare the cheese sauce. In a sauce pan melt the butter; stir in the flour and stir until it makes a paste. Add milk slowly, stirring and cooking all the while until the mixture is smooth and thick. Add the seasonings and the shredded cheese, stirring until it has melted into the sauce. Remove the vegetable to a warm serving dish, carefully slipping it from the cheesecloth to end top side up in the dish. Pour the hot sauce over the cauliflower. Dust with pimiento or chopped parsley.

BAKED APPLE AND CARROT CASSEROLE

6 or 7 apples, cored, pared, thinly sliced
2 cups carrot slices, cooked
⅓ cup brown sugar
2 tablespoons flour
½ teaspoon salt
¾ cup orange juice

Place half of the sliced apples in a buttered 2-quart casserole and cover with half the carrot slices. Combine the brown sugar, flour and salt and sprinkle half of the mixture over the carrots. Repeat layers and pour orange juice over the top. Bake at 350° for 45 minutes. Serves 6.

STUFFED ONION BERNESE

From Switzerland comes this recipe for stuffed onion bernese with this note, "a good-sized onion, bursting to fullness with a hearty ham and Swiss cheese stuffing, topped with a cap of melted cheese—it's as eye-catching as it is aromatic. If you like onions you will enjoy this recipe." It is suggested that it be served with green peas and slices of tomato; or as the Swiss do, with potato hash. This is another way to use our Maine potato crop.

1 large (1-pound) onion or 2 medium size
¼ cup chopped cooked ham
¼ cup grated Swiss (Emmentaler) cheese
¼ cup chopped onion
2 tablespoons Dijon-type mustard
 Water to moisten
1 slice Emmentaler cheese per onion
½ cup chicken broth or water

Peel onion; let simmer in boiling, lightly salted water. Drain. Let cool. Cut one-half inch off top; remove inside leaving one-half inch outer shell and base. Finely chop onion and saute in butter or margarine, briefly. Mix ham, cheese, sauteed onion with mustard. Stuff onion shell (or two medium) with this mixture. Pour enough water over to moisten well. Pour about ½-cup broth or water in a shallow casserole. Place onion in casserole. Bake in 350° oven for about 20 minutes. Cover with a slice of Emmentaler and continue baking until cheese is melty. If you have more chopped onion than necessary, reserve it for another use.

SUCCOTASH

Succotash, a combination of shell beans with corn, was eagerly looked forward to in the fall on the farm. Plump beans, just a shade under being fully ripe and hard, were cooked and mixed with cooked sweet corn, cut from the cob, and seasoned with butter, salt and pepper, and a small amount of cream. You may find these beans at a farm market or in the grocery stores—look for the red striped pods—or from your own garden.

Shell and wash whatever amount of beans you have on hand. Cook in salted water until tender. Add sweet corn, cooked and cut from the cob. Add pepper, salt and butter. Add 2 tablespoons butter or margarine and ½ cup or more of cream. Heat, but do not boil. Sometimes milk was added to make a soup from the mixture. Lima or butter beans also may be used.

TOMATO SCALLOP

Make a tomato scallop to go with sliced, cold pot roast or roast pork. This recipe uses canned tomatoes but 4 or 5 medium tomatoes, garden fresh, may be used.

1 tablespoon butter or margarine
1 small sliced onion
1 medium green pepper, diced
2 stalks celery, sliced
1 (1 lb.) can tomatoes or 4 or 5 ripe ones
½ teaspoon salt
⅛ teaspoon pepper
½ teaspoon dried basil or 1 small bay leaf
½ teaspoon brown sugar
1 slice bread, made into soft crumbs

Melt butter in a small skillet; cook the raw vegetables until tender. Put canned tomatoes into a buttered casserole; breaking up the large pieces. If fresh tomatoes, cut in narrow wedges. Season with salt and pepper; add dry basil or a small bay leaf. Add the brown sugar—a small amount, but it adds a bit of sweet to the tomatoes. With a slotted spoon add the onion, pepper and celery mixture. After removing the vegetables from the skillet, crumble the bread into the skillet and stir to absorb any juices left from cooking the vegetables. Stir the crumbs into the tomato/vegetable mixture. Bake at 350° for about 30 minutes, until thoroughly heated.

SAUTEED ONIONS

One of the finest additions to a barbecue is a nice nest of sauteed onions to put in a roll as a cushion for a hot dog or hamburger. While you are getting the go-withs of catsup, pickle relish and mustard together, prepare the onions and then carry them out to the barbecue to keep warm in their frypan.

9 or 10 medium-sized onions
¼ cup oil or margarine
   Salt and pepper

Peel and wash onions. Cut in narrow wedges. Heat oil or margarine (bacon fat is also good) in a heavy frypan. Dump the onions into the fat and stir to coat. Cook over low to medium heat, stirring frequently so the onions don't brown too much, but stay soft while cooking. When tender, cover to finish "steam cooking." Add salt and pepper to season.

VEGETABLE MEDLEY

This vegetable medley can be served hot from the stove or it is very good cold with meat. It is good with pasta and is made quickly and taste-tested for flavor. It is not quite a stir-fry as it is cooked slightly longer. The amounts of vegetables are changeable.

2 or 3 tablespoons olive or other oil
1 medium onion, cut in fine wedges
1 small eggplant, pared, diced
1 medium green pepper, sliced
5 or 6 mushrooms, optional
1 bay leaf, optional
1 pint (2 cups) canned tomatoes
½ to 1 teaspoon sweet basil
½ teaspoon salt
¼ teaspoon pepper
¼ teaspoon crushed oregano

In frypan, heat oil; add onion and cook until golden but not browned. Add eggplant, green pepper, mushrooms, if used, and tomatoes. Stir and cook, simmering until eggplant is soft. Add seasonings, tasting to determine flavor you like. Slow simmer the liquid down to desired thickness for purpose of use (thinner for a pasta sauce and thicker for a vegetable). Fresh tomatoes, skin removed and the tomatoes cut in pieces may replace the canned tomatoes.

SAVORY STUFFED POTATOES

4 medium potatoes, baked
½ cup milk
⅓ cup butter or margarine
1 (3 oz.) package cream cheese
¼ cup sour cream
1 teaspoon salt
⅛ teaspoon pepper
   Grated Parmesan cheese
   Chopped chives

Cut potatoes in half lengthwise; scoop out centers leaving ⅛-inch shell. Mash potato; add milk, butter, cream cheese, sour cream, salt and pepper; beat until fluffy. Spoon into shells; sprinkle with Parmesan cheese. Bake at 400° for 15 minutes. Sprinkle with chives, if desired, or mix the chives or a teaspoon finely chopped onion into the potato stuffing.

CUCUMBERS IN SOUR CREAM

One of the joys of gardening is to pick the first cucumber, having watched the plants from the first blossom. That joy dims somewhat when the crop begins to multiply and nearly daily pickings are necessary to fill jars of pickles for family, gifts and fairs. Cucumbers in sour cream make a good addition to any menu.

1 cucumber, thinly sliced, peeled or unpeeled
1 teaspoon salt
½ cup dairy sour cream
1 tablespoon vinegar
1 drop bottled hot pepper sauce
2 tablespoons chopped chives
1 teaspoon dill seed
   Few grains pepper

If there is fresh dill in the garden, chop a teaspoon of the leaves or foliage to use in the mixture. Sprinkle cucumber slices with the salt and let stand for 30 minutes; drain. Combine sour cream, vinegar, pepper sauce, chives, dill and a shake of pepper; pour over cucumber slices. Let stand 30 minutes. Try lemon pepper, found in the spice department at your market, in place of regular pepper.

CANDIED SWEET POTATOES

A good go-with for sweet potatoes is ham in any style. For baked ham try candied sweet potatoes. This makes good use of maple syrup, and paprika is a different spice to use in this recipe.

5 large sweet potatoes
Salt
Paprika
Butter or margarine
Maple syrup

Boil sweet potatoes until just tender; peel and slice lengthwise and place in buttered baking dish in layers. Sprinkle with salt and paprika and dot with butter or margarine. Pour maple syrup over the potatoes. (We used about ⅔ of a cup.) Bake in the oven with the ham at 325°, for the last ½ to ¾ hour. Remove the ham from the oven to sit for about 20 minutes before it is carved. This gives the potatoes time to slowly bake in the maple syrup. Paprika adds a good flavor to the potatoes.

STOVIES OR STOVE-TOP SCALLOPED POTATOES

After all these years we have learned that the real name of the potato dish that was a favorite supper dish was not stove-top scalloped potatoes, but a dish which the Scottish and English homemakers called stovies. By any name it is a good addition to the menu. Preparation time may take longer than opening a box of a similar dried product but the results are a bit different. Good with any meal or meat.

2 slices bacon or salt pork
5 or 6 potatoes, pared, sliced
1 large onion, sliced
1 to 1½ cups boiling water
Salt and pepper to season

In heavy frypan with a cover, cook bacon or salt pork until crisp. Pare and slice potatoes and put in pan in alternate layers with onion, using salt and pepper on each layer. Add boiling water; cover and cook slowly for about 1 hour or until tender. In the meantime, mix and bake a Johnny cake in the oven and slice meat to go with the meal. Cold sliced pot roast was the usual on the farm. Check the potatoes as more boiling water may be needed—not enough to make the potatoes mushy, but to keep them from sticking onto the pan.

BAKED STUFFED ZUCCHINI

Here is an opportunity to use zucchini which have grown a little large for other uses.

1 medium-size zucchini
  Salt and pepper to season
1 tablespoon butter or margarine
¼ cup chopped onion
½ cup chopped celery
1 cup ground beef or leftover cooked meat
1 slice of bread, cubed
1 can (8 oz.) tomato sauce
¼ cup grated Parmesan cheese

Wash and cook zucchini in boiling water for about 5 minutes. Cut in half lengthwise; scoop out pulp. Season the resulting zucchini shell with salt and pepper. In frypan, melt butter; add onion, celery and meat. Cook until lightly browned then add bread cubes, scooped-out pulp and tomato sauce. Stuff mixture in zucchini shells. Place in shallow baking pan. Sprinkle with cheese. Bake at 375° for 30 minutes or until vegetable is tender. Makes 6 servings.

SCALLOPED SWEET SPANISH ONIONS

These large, sweet onions are great in salads, fried, marinated or scalloped. This scallop will go with any meal.

4 cups thinly sliced sweet Spanish onions
6 tablespoons butter or margarine, divided
¼ cup flour
1 teaspoon salt
¼ teaspoon pepper
¼ teaspoon nutmeg
2 cups milk
½ cup buttered bread crumbs
1 cup grated Swiss cheese (optional)

Saute onions in 2 tablespoons butter until tender but not browned; set aside. Melt remaining butter in saucepan. Blend in flour, salt, pepper and nutmeg. Gradually add milk, stirring constantly until mixture boils and thickens. Place onions in 1½-quart casserole. Pour sauce over onions. Top with crumbs. Bake at 375° for 20 to 25 minutes or until crumbs are browned. One cup of grated Swiss cheese may be added to the sauce before pouring over onions. Makes 6 servings.

SAVORY SQUASH

When yellow summer squash or zucchini in your garden have you groping for more recipes for the vegetables, try this casserole to serve with ham, steak, chops, hot dogs or roast beef.

1½ pounds yellow summer squash or zucchini
½ cup chopped onions
3 cups cooked rice
2 cups grated Cheddar cheese
1 teaspoon seasoned pepper
½ teaspoon salt
3 eggs, slightly beaten
½ cup mayonnaise
1 cup soft bread crumbs
½ cup sliced almonds, optional

Cook squash and onions in small amount of water in covered saucepan until squash is tender but not soft. Drain well. Combine with rice, cheese and seasonings. Blend eggs and mayonnaise; stir into vegetable mixture. Turn into buttered, shallow 2-quart casserole. Top with bread crumbs and almonds. Bake at 350⁰ for 30 minutes. Serves 6.

RED CABBAGE

Red cabbage is not new but it makes a good supper dish to go with cold meat, corned beef or lamb patties. Frequently a chopped apple may be added to the cabbage for a good flavor.

1 medium-size red cabbage
2 tablespoons butter, bacon fat or oil
1 small onion, chopped
½ teaspoon salt
⅛ teaspoon Cayenne pepper
¼ teaspoon nutmeg
2 or 3 tablespoons vinegar
1½ teaspoons sugar

Shred cabbage. Melt butter in frying pan or saucepan and cook onions for 5 minutes. Add cabbage to pan with salt, nutmeg and pepper. Add the sugar mixing all well. Cover and cook over low heat until cabbage is tender. Then stir in the vinegar which adds flavor and brings the rosy glow back to the cabbage. Taste for further seasonings. A chopped apple may be added to the mixture just before covering the pan for cooking.

BAKED STUFFED TOMATOES

6 large tomatoes
¼ teaspoon salt
⅛ teaspoon pepper
½ cup finely minced onion or scallions
½ teaspoon garlic powder
2 tablespoons basil
¼ cup minced parsley
¼ teaspoon sugar
¼ teaspoon thyme
1 cup fresh bread crumbs
 Olive oil

Cut tomatoes in half crosswise leaving skin on. Squeeze the tomatoes to remove some of the seeds. Sprinkle lightly with pepper and salt; place in a buttered shallow pan. Mix together onion, spices, sugar, parsley and bread crumbs and fill cavity of each tomato. Drizzle with olive oil and bake in a 400° oven for 15 to 20 minutes until softened.

BAKED CORN WITH SOUR CREAM

Here is a good way to use up sour cream when you have purchased too much to use for a dip. This vegetable will go with sliced cold or hot ham, plus Johnny cake and mashed potatoes.

6 strips bacon
2 tablespoons chopped onion
2 tablespoons butter or margarine
2 tablespoons flour
¼ teaspoon salt
1 cup sour cream
2 (12 oz. each) cans whole kernel corn
 Few grains Cayenne pepper

Preheat oven to 350°. Cook and crumble bacon. Cook onions in butter until transparent but not burned; blend in the flour, salt and Cayenne pepper. Add sour cream gradually, stirring to keep smooth. Bring to boiling. Immediately reduce heat and add corn. Cook until heated through. Fold in half of the crumbled bacon; spoon into a greased casserole; add remaining crumbled bacon to top of dish. Bake 30 to 40 minutes.

SWEET AND TART GINGERED CARROTS

These carrots will go well with baked fish.

1 pound carrots, cut in ¼-inch slices
  Boiling water
2 tablespoons chopped green onions
2 tablespoons brown sugar
1 tablespoon butter or margarine
  Grated peel and juice of ½ fresh lemon
¼ teaspoon ground ginger
¼ teaspoon garlic powder

In covered saucepan, cook carrots in one inch boiling water until tender (about 10-12 minutes); drain water. Remove carrots. In same pan, combine remaining ingredients; simmer over low heat for two to three minutes to blend flavors. Add carrots and heat to serving. Makes four ½-cup servings.

RUTH'S BLUEBERRY NEWTONS

These blueberry newtons, made much like the familiar fig newtons, are good to tuck into the dinner pails and lunch boxes or with a glass of milk.

    5 tablespoons butter or margarine
    2 tablespoons sour cream
    ⅔ cup brown sugar, packed
    2 eggs
    1 teaspoon vanilla
    2 cups sifted all-purpose flour
    2 teaspoons baking powder
    ½ teaspoon soda
    ¼ teaspoon cinnamon
    ½ teaspoon salt

Beat butter and sour cream until light. Add brown sugar, eggs and vanilla, beating well after each addition. Mix and sift flour, baking powder, soda, salt and cinnamon and add to creamed mixture, mixing well. Wrap the dough in a sheet of floured plastic wrap or waxed paper and chill thoroughly. In the meantime, prepare the filling.

BLUEBERRY FILLING

    2 cups blueberries
    3 tablespoons flour
    ¼ cup water
    ⅓ cup sugar
    ¼ teaspoon salt
    2 teaspoons grated lemon rind
    ⅛ teaspoon lemon extract (optional)

Combine filling ingredients and cook very slowly at first to prevent sticking. Cook until mixture is very thick. Cool. Divide chilled dough into 4 parts; do same with filling. Roll one portion of dough into a rectangle, about 4 by 11 inches. Spread ¼ of filling on the center of the dough, leaving a ½-inch margin on all sides. Moisten edges of dough with water, and fold one side over the other and press down to seal. Transfer to lightly greased baking sheet. Repeat with remaining dough and filling. Bake at 350° for 25 minutes. Cool partially. Cut off ends and then slice crosswise, at a slant, about 1½ inches wide. These may be sliced all at once or stored and cut later.

NOTE: Date or fig filling may be used as substitutes.

MAUDIE'S FILLED COOKIES

A popular cookie for the brown bag, dinner pail or supper table is this filled cookie. The topping of the cookie drops down over the filling; no need to wet the edges of the dough or press the top down over the bottom round. Jam, raisin or date filling may be used. Makes about 40 cookies, depending on size.

  1 cup shortening or margarine
  2 cups sugar
  2 eggs
  6 cups sifted all-purpose flour
  2 teaspoons soda
  2 teaspoons cream of tartar
  1 teaspoon salt
1½ teaspoons vanilla
  1 cup sour milk or buttermilk

Cream shortening; add sugar and mix thoroughly. Beat in eggs. Mix and sift together flour, soda, cream of tartar and salt; add to creamed mixture alternately with sour milk or buttermilk. Stir in vanilla. Chill dough overnight. Roll dough on lightly floured board or pastry cloth to ⅛-inch thickness. Cut rounds with a 3-inch cookie cutter. Place rounds on a lightly greased cookie sheet, leaving two inches between rounds. Top each round with 1 dessert spoon of filling. Roll more dough and cut rounds, dropping a round over the filling on each cookie. Bake at 400° for 12 to 14 minutes. Remove cookies to cool on a rack.

DATE, RAISIN OR FIG FILLING
  1 pound dates, raisins or figs
  1 cup boiling water
½ teaspoon salt
  1 teaspoon grated lemon rind
  2 tablespoons lemon juice
  2 tablespoons flour or cornstarch
¼ cup cold water
⅔ cup sugar

Put dates, raisins or figs through medium blade of food chopper. In saucepan, combine ground fruit with sugar, 1 cup boiling water, salt, lemon rind and juice. Bring to simmer, stirring frequently. Combine cornstarch or flour and ¼ cup of cold water; mix well and stir into fruit mixture. Cook until mixture is thickened. If a thicker filling is desired, add 1 additional tablespoon flour or cornstarch, dissolved in cold water.

GROUNDHOG COOKIES

February 2 is hailed as Groundhog Day down Pennsylvania way. Maine people also take note of the tradition that says the groundhog or woodchuck is supposed to determine our winter weather from that date on. If he comes out of hibernation and sees his shadow, he returns to his hole for six weeks of winter weather. If, however, it's a cloudy day and he sees no shadow, it is a sign spring is on the way and he is happy to remain above ground. It is also Candlemas Day and as children our chant was, "If Candlemas Day be clear and bright, winter will take another flight." At least the tradition brightens the winter doldrums! So, make a batch of groundhog cookies to go with a cup of coffee while waiting for the groundhog's decision.

     2 cups sifted all-purpose flour
    ½ teaspoon salt
    ½ teaspoon soda
     1 teaspoon baking powder
     1 teaspoon ground ginger
     1 teaspoon ground cloves
    1½ teaspoons cinnamon
    ½ cup softened butter or margarine
     1 cup sugar
    ½ cup molasses
     1 egg yolk
     1 egg, slightly beaten
       Currants or raisins

Mix and sift together flour, salt, soda, baking powder and spices. Cream butter and sugar together until fluffy. Blend in molasses and egg yolk. (Reserve whole, slightly beaten egg for glaze.) Stir in flour mixture and mix well. Wrap in plastic or wax paper and chill for 24 hours or longer. Roll out a small amount at a time and cut in groundhog shape or in round cookies. If the former, use raisins or currants for eyes and nose. Place cookies on greased cookie sheets and brush with the slightly beaten egg. Bake 8 to 10 minutes in a moderate, 350° oven. Cool slightly before removing from the cookie sheets. The youngsters, always ready to help, may like to draw a picture of a groundhog on cardboard to cut out and trace around on the dough.

CRUNCHY COCONUT COOKIES

1 cup butter and margarine, mixed
1½ cups sugar
1 egg
1¼ cups quick-cooking rolled oats
1½ cups all-purpose flour
1 teaspoon cream of tartar
½ teaspoon soda
½ teaspoon salt
1 cup coconut

Cream shortenings and sugar; add egg and mix in remaining ingredients. Roll in balls and flatten with fork. Bake at 375° until lightly browned — about 15 minutes.

TILLIE'S CRISP MOLASSES COOKIES

1 cup molasses
1 cup sugar
1 cup melted shortening
4 teaspoons soda
⅔ cup boiling water
2 teaspoons cream of tartar
1 teaspoon salt
2 teaspoons vanilla
1 teaspoon ginger
7 cups sifted all-purpose flour

Mix and sift together flour, cream of tartar, ginger and salt. In a mixing bowl, combine sugar and molasses; mix well and mix in the melted shortening. (A mixture of lard, butter, margarine and shortening is suggested for the old-fashioned flavor.) Add boiling water in which the soda has been dissolved. Stir in vanilla. Add sifted dry ingredients all at once and stir to thoroughly mix. Let the mixture rest for 15 minutes, then divide into four or five portions and knead each portion until smooth and shiny. Wrap each portion in waxed paper or plastic wrap and refrigerate. When ready to bake, roll a portion of the dough very thin, and for an old-fashioned mark of distinction, draw a table fork crosswise on the dough, first in one direction and then another, for a plaid pattern. Cut cookies with a 3-inch cutter and bake on lightly greased cookie sheets in a moderately hot oven, 375°, for 6 to 8 minutes, depending on thickness. Molasses cookies burn easily; watch baking closely. One suggestion is to fill several cookie sheets before starting to bake. Remove cookies at once from the tin to cool on a rack.

HELEN'S APPLE BROWNIES

½ cup butter or margarine
1 cup sugar
1 egg
2 medium apples, cored, pared and chopped in small pieces
1 cup all-purpose flour
½ teaspoon soda
½ teaspoon baking powder
¼ teaspoon salt
½ teaspoon cinnamon

Cream the butter and sugar; beat in the egg until all is well-blended. Add the apples. Mix and sift flour, soda, baking powder, cinnamon and salt and stir into the apple mixture. Spoon into a greased 7x9x2-inch baking pan and bake at 350° for about 40 minutes or until the brownies test done. Cool and cut in squares.

EASY-FILL COOKIES

FILLING
2 cups chopped raisins or dates
¾ cup sugar
¼ teaspoon salt
¾ cup water
½ cup chopped nut meats
½ teaspoon grated lemon rind (optional)

In a saucepan, combine raisins, sugar, salt and water, and lemon rind if used. Cook until thickened. Cool and stir in nut meats.

COOKIES
3½ cups all-purpose flour
1 teaspoon salt
1 teaspoon soda
1 cup margarine or shortening
2 cups brown sugar, packed
2 eggs, beaten
½ cup sour milk or buttermilk
1½ teaspoons vanilla

Mix and sift together flour, salt and soda. Cream margarine or shortening with brown sugar; beat in eggs, buttermilk and vanilla. Stir in sifted dry ingredients and mix well. Drop dough by spoonsful on greased cookie sheets. Flatten slightly with a spoon and add a teaspoon of filling to top of cookie; partially cover with another bit of the dough. Bake at 350° for 10 to 12 minutes or until done. Remove at once from pan to cool on rack.

RUSSIAN TEA CAKES

These tea cakes or cookies go by several names, including pecan puffs, Mexican wedding cakes and snow drops.

1 cup butter or margarine
½ cup confectioners' sugar
1 teaspoon vanilla
2¼ cups sifted all-purpose flour
¼ teaspoon salt
¾ cup chopped pecan or walnut meats

Cream butter and sugar. Add vanilla. Mix flour with salt and add to creamed mixture. Stir in nuts. Chill. Shape teaspoons of dough in a round, finger-like or crescent cookie. Place on ungreased cookie sheets and bake in a 400° oven, for 6 to 8 minutes. (Since these cookies contain butter they burn easily.) When baked, roll in confectioners' sugar. Store in tight tins.

SOFT MOLASSES COOKIES

1 cup molasses
1 cup sugar
1 cup melted shortening
1 egg
4 teaspoons soda
2 teaspoons vanilla
5¾ cups sifted all-purpose flour
1½ teaspoons cream of tartar
1½ teaspoons ginger
1½ teaspoons cinnamon
½ teaspoon cloves
¾ teaspoon salt
⅔ cup boiling water

Mix sugar and melted shortening. (Use a mixture of margarine, butter and lard for the shortening to capture the old-fashioned flavor.) Stir in molasses and vanilla. Beat in egg. Mix and sift together flour, cream of tartar, salt and spices; set aside. Dissolve soda in boiling water; add to molasses mixture; stir to mix. Add sifted dry ingredients all at once. Mix well to make a smooth dough. Chill overnight. On floured board or pastry cloth, roll dough to ¼-inch thickness. Cut with 3-inch cutter or with a gingerbread man cutter. If candies or raisins are used for decorating the cookies, add them before baking. Place on lightly greased cookie sheets, leaving 2½ inches between each cookie. Bake at 400° for about 10 minutes; Watch baking carefully—molasses cookies burn easily.

PRISCILLA'S PINEAPPLE CHEESECAKE TARTS

These cheesecake tarts are especially good on a tray with bars and cookies.

1 package (3 ounces) cream cheese
1¼ cups flour
3 tablespoons sugar
1 stick (½ cup) margarine

Mix all together to form a dough; roll into a ball and chill. When ready to use, divide dough into thirds and shape into logs. Divide each log into 12 segments. Flatten each segment into a circle and press into small cupcake tins, making sure dough comes up to top of sides. Prepare filling. In small mixing bowl, cream together 8 ounces of cream cheese with ⅔ cup of sugar. Beat in 1 egg and 1 teaspoon vanilla with ⅔ cup crushed pineapple, drained. Fill pastry cups and bake at 350° 30 to 40 minutes or until golden brown on top. These freeze well.

CARROT COOKIES WITH ORANGE ICING

1 cup shortening or margarine
¾ cup sugar
2 eggs, beaten
⅔ cup coconut
2 cups all-purpose flour
2 teaspoons baking powder
1 cup cooked, mashed carrots
½ teaspoon salt

Cream shortening and sugar in mixing bowl; add eggs and beat until fluffy. Add mashed carrots. Mix and sift flour, baking powder and salt together and add to creamed mixture. Stir in coconut. If desired, ⅓ cup raisins may be added with the coconut. Drop by teaspoons on greased baking sheets and bake in a hot oven, 400°, for 8 to 10 minutes. This is a high temperature, so watch cookies carefully so as not to burn them. Remove from tin at once to cool on a wire rack. When cold, frost with orange icing.

ORANGE ICING

1 cup confectioners' sugar
2 tablespoons softened butter or margarine
¼ teaspoon salt
1 tablespoon orange juice, or more
2 teaspoons grated orange rind

Combine all ingredients; mix well and ice cookies.

PECAN BARS OR STICKS

2 cups packed brown sugar, divided
1 cup butter
2 eggs
2 cups sifted all-purpose flour
½ teaspoon salt
1 cup finely chopped pecan meats

In mixing bowl, combine butter, 1 cup, packed, of brown sugar, 1 of the eggs, flour and salt. Mix until smooth. Spread evenly in wax paper-lined and greased jelly roll pan or 15½ x 10½-inch broiler pan. Spread the other egg (beaten) over the dough. Sift or sprinkle ½ cup brown sugar over this layer, followed by the nut meats and the remaining sugar. Bake at 350° for 25 minutes. Do not overbake. Cut in squares or sticks.

JULIE'S WHOOPSIE PIES

½ cup shortening
1 cup sugar
2 egg yolks, beaten
5 tablespoons cocoa
2 cups sifted all-purpose flour
1 teaspoon baking powder
1 teaspoon soda
1 teaspoon salt
1 cup milk
1 teaspoon vanilla

Cream shortening and sugar; beat egg yolks into creamed mixture. Mix and sift together flour, cocoa, baking powder, soda and salt; add to creamed mixture alternately with milk. Stir in vanilla. Drop from dessert spoon onto ungreased cookie sheets, leaving about three inches between each cookie. Bake at 375° for 8 to 10 minutes. Remove at once from cookie sheets to cool on a rack. Put two cookies together with filling.

FILLING FOR WHOOPSIE PIES

¾ cup shortening
¾ cup confectioners' sugar
1 cup marshmallow fluff
¼ teaspoon salt
1 teaspoon vanilla

Cream shortening and sugar with marshmallow fluff; stir in salt and vanilla. Wrap each "pie" individually in plastic or wax paper. Store in tins or freezer. These "pies" are delicious eaten directly from the freezer.

COCONUT COOKIES

2 cups sifted all-purpose flour
3 teaspoons baking powder
1 teaspoon soda
½ teaspoon salt
1 cup margarine or shortening
1 cup granulated sugar
1 cup packed brown sugar
2 eggs
1 teaspoon vanilla
2 cups quick rolled oats, uncooked
1 cup coconut
1 cup cornflakes

Sift together flour, baking powder, soda and salt. Cream shortening and sugars; beat in eggs. Add dry ingredients and mix well. Add vanilla, oats, coconut and cornflakes. Drop on greased baking tins. Bake at 375°, 8 to 10 minutes. Cool on rack.

CHOCOLATE-NUT PINWHEEL COOKIES

½ cup butter or margarine, softened
¾ cup sugar
1 egg
1 teaspoon vanilla extract
1¾ cups all-purpose flour
½ teaspoon baking powder
¼ teaspoon salt
⅓ cup sliced almonds, ground
⅛ teaspoon almond extract (optional)
¼ cup cocoa powder
1½ tablespoons butter or margarine, melted

In large mixer bowl, cream butter and sugar. Add egg and vanilla; beat well. Combine flour, baking powder and salt; add to creamed mixture, blending well. Divide dough in half. Blend ground almonds and almond extract (if used), into one part of dough. Add cocoa and melted butter to remaining dough; blend well. Chill, if necessary, for easier handling. Between 2 pieces of wax paper evenly roll out light dough to a 16" x 8" rectangle. Repeat procedure with chocolate dough. Peel off top sheets of wax paper. Invert light layer onto chocolate layer; peel off top sheet of wax paper. Roll up jellyroll-fashion, starting with 16-inch side. Wrap roll in wax paper or plastic wrap; chill 4 to 5 hours. Cut roll into ¼-inch slices. Place slices on ungreased cookie sheet. Bake 9 to 12 minutes or until set. Remove to wire rack. Cool completely. Makes 5 dozen cookies.

CHIPPER OATMEAL COOKIES

1 cup margarine
½ cup packed brown sugar
½ cup granulated sugar
2 eggs
1 teaspoon vanilla
1¼ cups all-purpose flour
1 teaspoon soda
1½ cup rolled oats, uncooked
1 12-oz. package semi-sweet chocolate pieces
1 cup chopped nut meats

Beat margarine and sugars until light and fluffy. Blend in eggs and vanilla. Sift soda with flour and add to egg mixture. Stir in rolled oats, chocolate pieces and nuts. Drop rounded teaspoonsful of dough onto ungreased cookie sheet and bake at 375° for 10 to 12 minutes or until golden brown. Remove cookies to wire rack to cool. Makes about 50-60 cookies. If there is a limit on your time, spread the dough in a well-greased 13x9-inch baking pan. Bake at 375°, 25 to 30 minutes or until golden brown. Cool and cut into bars.

OATMEAL COOKIES FOR THE FREEZER

1½ cups all-purpose flour
1 teaspoon baking powder
½ teaspoon salt
⅔ teaspoon allspice
1 cup butter or margarine
1 cup sugar
2 eggs, lightly beaten
1 teaspoon vanilla
3 cups rolled oats, uncooked
1 cup raisins or chocolate bits

In a bowl, sift flour, baking powder, salt and allspice. Set aside. In mixer bowl, cream butter and sugar; beat in eggs and vanilla. Stir in dry ingredients. Add oats and raisins which have been chopped. One-half cup chopped nut meats may also be added or ¾ cup chocolate bits and ½ cup nut meats—try a different addition each time. Divide dough into 4 portions and shape each into a log, 6 inches by 1½ inches in diameter. Wrap in wax paper, then foil, and freeze. Be sure the package is air-tight. When ready to bake, cut in 1½ inch- thick slices and place on very lightly greased baking cookie sheet. Bake in moderate oven, 350°, for about 12 minutes. Keep checking as time varies in individual ovens. Remove at once from the tin when taken from the oven.

174

CRUNCH TOP APPLESAUCE BARS

1 cup sugar
1 cup unsweetened applesauce
½ cup shortening, melted
2 cups sifted all-purpose flour
1 teaspoon soda
1½ teaspoons cinnamon
1 teaspoon nutmeg
¼ teaspoon cloves
½ teaspoon salt
1 cup seedless raisins
¼ cup chopped nut meats
1 teaspoon vanilla

Combine sugar and applesauce; add shortening and blend. Mix together and sift flour, soda, spices and salt; add to applesauce mixture and stir until smooth. Add raisins, nuts and vanilla. Spread mixture evenly in a greased jelly roll pan. Sprinkle topping over batter. Bake at 350° for 30 minutes, or until done. Cool; cut into bars. These bars freeze well. Store in foil or covered tin.

FLO'S MOLASSES COOKIE SANDWICH

½ cup butter or margarine
¾ cup sugar
2 eggs
2¾ cups sifted all-purpose flour
1 teaspoon soda
½ teaspoon salt
1¼ teaspoons cinnamon
½ teaspoon ginger
½ cup milk
⅔ cup molasses

Cream butter; add sugar and cream until light. Add eggs and beat well. Mix and sift together flour, soda, salt, cinnamon and ginger; set aside. Mix molasses into the creamed mixture, then add sifted dry ingredients alternately with the milk. Chill for an hour. Drop by tablespoons on greased baking sheets and bake in a moderately hot oven, 375°, for 8 to 10 minutes or until done. Remove to a rack to cool. Put two cookies together with this filling: Cream ½ cup butter or margarine with 3 cups confectioners' sugar, 1¼ teaspoons ginger, ¼ cup molasses and 2 or 3 tablespoons milk to make a frosting or a filling for the cookies. The filling should be light and fluffy, so it may take a bit more milk.

HONEY BROWNIES

⅓ cup butter or margarine, softened
½ cup sugar
2 teaspoons vanilla
2 eggs
⅓ cup honey
½ cup all-purpose flour
⅓ cup cocoa powder
½ teaspoon salt
⅔ cup chopped nuts

Heat oven to 350⁰. Grease a 9-inch square pan. In small mixer bowl, cream butter and sugar; blend in honey and vanilla. Add eggs and beat well. Combine flour, cocoa and salt; gradually add to creamed mixture. Stir in nuts. Spread mixture into prepared pan. Bake 25 to 30 minutes or until brownies begin to pull away from sides of pan. Cool in pan. If desired, the brownies may be frosted.

FAVORITE DROP COOKIES

Poultry fat is one of the finest fats for cooking and may be used in biscuits, some cakes, gingerbread, cookies and for sauteing potatoes. Try out the fat from a fowl or roasting chicken by putting the pieces of fat in a pan in a very low oven, 300⁰. Cook until fat has been rendered; pour off clear fat. Store in refrigerator. This cookie recipe was developed during a shortage of fats and sugar. Butter or margarine may be substituted for poultry fat.

¾ cup poultry fat or drippings
¾ cup sugar
2 eggs
¾ cup thick sour cream
¾ cup molasses
2 cups raisins
4 cups sifted all-purpose flour
3 teaspoons soda
1 teaspoon cinnamon
1 teaspoon ginger
1 teaspoon cloves
1 teaspoon nutmeg
1½ teaspoons salt
1 cup nut meats, chopped

Mix and sift together flour, soda, spices and salt. Beat chicken fat, sugar and eggs together. Add sour cream, molasses, raisins and nut meats. Stir in sifted dry ingredients. Drop by teaspoonsful on greased cookie sheets and bake at 375⁰ for 10 to 12 minutes. Remove at once from the tins to cool on a rack.

APRICOT BARS

⅔ cup dried apricots
½ cup butter or margarine, softened
¼ cup sugar
1⅓ cups sifted all-purpose flour
½ teaspoon baking powder
¼ teaspoon salt
1 cup brown sugar, firmly packed
2 eggs, well beaten
½ teaspoon vanilla
½ cup chopped nut meats

Rinse apricots; cover with water, boil for 10 minutes. Drain, cool and chop. Mix together ¼ cup sugar, butter and 1 cup flour. Pack into greased 7x11x1-inch pan; bake in 350° oven for 25 minutes. Sift together remaining ⅓ cup flour, baking powder and salt. Gradually beat brown sugar into eggs; mix in sifted dry ingredients; add vanilla, nuts and apricots. Spread over baked layer. Bake for 30 minutes, or until done. Cool in pan. Cut in bars or squares. Sprinkle with confectioners' sugar, if desired.

SPICY FRUIT BARS

1 cup sugar
½ cup butter or margarine
1½ teaspoons soda
2 eggs, beaten
3 cups sifted all-purpose flour
¾ teaspoon cinnamon
¾ teaspoon ginger
¾ teaspoon allspice
1 teaspoon salt
¼ cup water
¼ cup molasses
1½ cups seeded raisins, chopped or ground
1 cup nut meats, coarsely chopped

Grease a cookie sheet and set aside. Cream butter or margarine. Add sugar and soda and blend well. Add eggs, water, raisins and molasses. Mix and sift together flour, salt and spices; add to creamed mixture. Stir in nut meats. Chill dough for several hours or overnight. Roll dough on floured board or pastry cloth, keeping dough two to two and one-half inches wide and about one- quarter inch thick, the length of the cookie sheet. When bars are ready to bake, brush each strip with a wash made of 2 tablespoons beaten egg and 2 tablespoons molasses. Bake in at 350° for about 20 minutes. Cut into 3-inch lengths as you remove bars from cookie sheets to cool on a rack.

177

MOLASSES THINSIES

1 cup butter (no substitute)
1 cup sugar
1 cup molasses
¼ cup milk
4¾ cups sifted all-purpose flour
½ teaspoon salt
2 teaspoons soda

Cream butter until soft and waxy; gradually beat in sugar. Add molasses and 2 tablespoons of milk. Mix well. Mix and sift flour, soda and salt and add to creamed mixture with remaining 2 tablespoons milk. This is a stiff dough. Shape in two wax paper-lined ice cube trays. Wrap well. Chill. For baking, slice the dough very thin. (A half hour or longer in the freezer makes the dough easy to slice.) Cut each tray of dough in four even sections; slice from narrower end of each. Place on greased cookie sheets. Bake at 375° for 6 to 8 minutes. Remove at once from the tin. This recipe makes 240 small tea cookies.

MYRTLE'S HERMITS

My neighbor calls these cookies "benders" because they are soft and "bendy." These cookies were put into our dinner pails before we trudged the mile to our country schoolhouse.

1 cup butter or margarine
1½ cups sugar
3 eggs
4 cups sifted all-purpose flour
½ teaspoon salt
1½ teaspoons soda
1 teaspoon cinnamon
½ teaspoon nutmeg
1 package (15 ounce) seeded raisins
1 teaspoon vanilla (optional)
1 teaspoon lemon extract (optional)
2 tablespoons sour milk or buttermilk

Cream butter and sugar; beat in eggs. Mix and sift together flour, salt and spices. Dissolve soda in sour milk and add to creamed mixture. Mix in sifted dry ingredients. Chop or grind raisins; add to dough. If lemon or vanilla flavoring is added, do so at this time. Roll dough on lightly floured board or pastry cloth; cut with 3-inch cutter. Place on greased cookie sheets and bake at 375° for 8 to 10 minutes. Do not overbake. These cookies bear watching as raisins burn easily. Makes 3 dozen cookies.

DATE AND NUT COOKIES

1¼ cups sifted all-purpose flour
¼ teaspoon baking powder
½ teaspoon soda
½ teaspoon salt
 1 egg
¾ cup packed brown sugar
¼ cup butter or margarine
¼ cup sour cream
 1 teaspoon vanilla
½ cup cut up dates
½ cup chopped walnuts or pecan meats
  Confectioners' sugar butter frosting

Cream butter and sugar; beat in the egg and vanilla. Mix and sift flour, baking powder, soda and salt and add to the creamed mixture alternately with the sour cream. Mix in dates and nuts. Drop by spoonsful onto greased cookie sheets. Bake at 350° for 10 to 12 minutes or until done. Frost, if desired, with a frosting of 2 tablespoons butter or margarine mixed with 1½ cups confectioners' sugar and just enough hot water to mix to spreading consistency.

CHOCOLATE TURTLE COOKIES

¾ cup all-purpose flour
½ teaspoon baking powder
¼ teaspoon salt
 1 6 oz. package semi-sweet chocolate morsels, divided
⅓ cup butter, softened
½ cup sugar
 1 egg
 8 dozen pecan halves

Preheat the oven to 350°. In small bowl, combine flour, baking powder and salt; set aside. Combine over hot (not boiling) water, ½ cup semi-sweet chocolate morsels and butter. Stir until morsels are melted and mixture is smooth. Transfer chocolate mixture to a small bowl. Stir in sugar and egg; beat with wooden spoon. Stir in flour mixture; mix well. For each cookie, place 3 pecan halves (with ends touching at center) on cookie sheet. Drop rounded teaspoonfuls batter in center of pecans. Bake 8 to 9 minutes. Remove cookies from tins and cool completely. Spoon glaze on top.

GLAZE

Melt remaining morsels over hot, not boiling water; stir until smooth. Place ¼ teaspoon in center of each cookie.

RAISIN NUT DROP COOKIES

1 cup raisins, packed
½ cup water
½ cup shortening
1 cup sugar
2 eggs, well beaten
1 teaspoon vanilla
½ cup chopped nut meats
2 cups plus 2 tablespoons flour
½ teaspoon soda
1 teaspoon baking powder
½ teaspoon salt
1 teaspoon cinnamon
½ teaspoon nutmeg

Boil raisins in water for three minutes. Allow to cool. Mix together shortening, sugar, eggs, vanilla and nut meats; add cooled raisin-water mixture. Mix and sift together flour, soda, baking powder, cinnamon and nutmeg; add to raisin mixture, mixing well. Drop by rounded teaspoons on greased cookie sheets. Bake at 375° for 10 to 12 minutes. Makes about 50 cookies.

PEACH OATMEAL COOKIES

These will be a new taste treat for the snackers. To help you decide how many peaches to purchase for the recipe you wish to make, this peach arithmetic may be of use. One pound of fresh peaches equals 2 large or 3 medium-sized peaches or 2 cups peeled and sliced or 1⅔ cups peeled and diced or 1½ cups peeled and pureed.

2 eggs
1½ teaspoons vanilla extract
¾ cup shortening or margarine
¾ cup sugar
¾ cup brown sugar, packed
1½ cups whole wheat flour
1 teaspoon salt
2 teaspoons baking powder
2½ cups rolled oats
1½ cups fresh peaches, diced
1 cup raisins

In mixing bowl, beat together eggs, vanilla, shortening and sugars. In separate bowl combine whole wheat flour, salt and baking powder; add to egg mixture and beat at low speed 2 or 3 minutes or until smooth. Stir in oats, peaches and raisins; chill. Drop by heaping tablespoons onto greased baking sheets and bake at 350°, 10 to 15 minutes or until golden. Makes 2 to 2½ dozen large cookies.

CHEWY BROWNIES

¼ cup butter
4 squares chocolate
1 cup sugar
2 eggs, beaten
1½ teaspoons vanilla
1 cup flour
¼ teaspoon salt
½ cup sour cream
1 cup coarsely broken pecans

Melt the chocolate and butter in a saucepan or double boiler. In a mixing bowl, beat the sugar and eggs together. Slowly add the chocolate mixture. Gradually add the flour and salt, 2 tablespoons at a time, beating well after each addition. Stir in the sour cream and pecans. For a different accent, add a sprinkle of ground cinnamon to the batter. Spoon batter into a lightly greased 8-inch square pan. Bake in a moderate oven, 350°, for 25 minutes. Do not overcook; these should be slightly moist and chewy.

SOUTHERN PECAN BARS

CRUST
1 cup butter
¾ cup firmly packed light brown sugar
2¼ cups all-purpose flour
½ teaspoon vanilla extract
1 egg white, slightly beaten

Cream butter. Beat in sugar until light and fluffy. Gradually add flour, then vanilla; beat until well combined. Press dough on bottom of 9x13-inch baking pan. Brush with egg white. Bake 15 minutes at 350°. Cool 5 minutes before spreading filling.

FILLING
4 eggs
1 cup light corn syrup
⅓ cup firmly packed light brown sugar
¼ cup butter, melted
3 tablespoons flour
1 teaspoon vanilla extract
2 cups coarsely chopped pecans

Beat eggs until thick and lemon-colored. Stir in corn syrup, brown sugar, butter, flour and vanilla until smooth. Stir in pecans. Spread filling on cookie crust. Bake 25 to 30 minutes, or until knife inserted near center comes out clean. Remove from oven. Cool completely on wire rack. Store in airtight container in refrigerator.

MRS. DAIGLE'S HONEY DROPS

This cookie, from Aroostook County, adds a not-too-sweet cookie to the tea tray.

      1 cup shortening, part butter
      1 cup packed brown sugar
      2 eggs
      6 tablespoons honey
      1 teaspoon vanilla
   3½ cups sifted all-purpose flour
      2 teaspoons soda
    ½ teaspoon salt
      Apricot jam or preserves

Cream the shortening and brown sugar; beat in eggs, honey and vanilla. Mix and sift together flour, soda and salt and add to creamed mixture. Chill dough overnight, or until firm. Form balls, about 1 inch in diameter, and place on ungreased cookie sheets. Bake in a 350° oven for 10 to 12 minutes, or until cookies test done. When slightly cooled, put two cookies together with apricot jam or rpreserves. Raspberry is also suggested as a filling. For the lunchbox, make balls of dough larger.

TILLIE'S PECAN ICEBOX COOKIES

This pecan icebox cookie has been to many parties. It may be kept refrigerated, after mixing, or all the cookies may be cut and baked at one time and packaged in tightly covered boxes and frozen to have ready at any time.

      1 cup butter
      2 cups light brown sugar, packed
      2 eggs
    ½ teaspoon salt
   3½ cups all-purpose flour
      1 teaspoon soda
    ¼ teaspoon nutmeg (optional)
      1 cup pecans, coarsely chopped

Cream the butter and sugar and beat in the eggs. Mix and sift together flour, salt, soda and nutmeg. Add to creamed mixture to make a firm dough. Form into rolls or use a wax-paper-lined ice-cube tray to form the dough. Chill for several hours or overnight. When ready to bake, slice the dough crossways, about ⅛ inch in thickness. Place on lightly greased cookie tins and bake in a moderately hot oven, 375°, for 6 to 8 minutes. Remove at once from tins and cool on wire rack. Store in tightly covered tins. Depending on width cut, there will be 80 or 90 cookies.

MARBLE SQUARES

1 8-oz. package cream cheese
⅓ cup sugar
1 egg
½ cup margarine
¾ cup water
1½ 1-oz. squares unsweetened chocolate
2 cups flour
2 cups sugar
2 eggs
½ cup dairy sour cream
½ teaspoon salt
1 teaspoon soda
1 6-oz. package semi-sweet chocolate bits

Combine softened cream cheese and sugar, mix well. Add 1 egg, mix well and set aside. Combine margarine, water and chocolate in a saucepan. Bring to boil. Remove from heat. Stir in combined sugar and flour. Add eggs, sour cream, soda and salt. Mix well. Pour into greased and floured 15½ x 10½-inch pan. Spoon cream cheese mixture over the top. Run a knife through. Sprinkle with chocolate bits. Bake at 375⁰ for 25 to 30 minutes or until done.

DOUBLE CHOCOLATE CHIP COOKIES

1¾ cups flour
¼ teaspoon soda
1 cup butter or margarine, softened
1 teaspoon vanilla extract
1 cup granulated sugar
½ cup dark brown sugar, firmly packed
1 egg
⅓ cup unsweetened cocoa
2 tablespoons milk
1 cup chopped pecans or walnuts
6 ounces (1 cup) semisweet chocolate chips

Combine flour and soda; set aside. Use an electric mixer to cream butter. Add vanilla and sugars and beat until fluffy. Beat in egg. At low speed beat in cocoa, then milk. With a wooden spoon mix in dry ingredients just until blended. Stir in nuts and chocolate chips. Drop by rounded teaspoonsful onto non-stick or foil-lined baking sheets. Bake at 350⁰, 12 to 13 minutes. Remove from oven and cool slightly before removing from tin. Makes about 36 cookies.

ANNE'S BROWNIES

This "oldie but goodie" recipe for brownies provided some students a means of making a few pennies in college toward books or sorority dues. It is more of a cake-like bar than the brownie recipes of today.

¼ cup butter
1 cup sugar
1 egg
2 squares melted chocolate
1 teaspoon vanilla extract
½ cup milk
1 cup sifted all-purpose flour
½ teaspoon baking powder
½ teaspoon salt
½ cup chopped nut meats

Cream butter and sugar; beat in egg. Add melted and slightly cooled chocolate. Sift flour with salt and baking powder and add to chocolate mixture alternately with the milk. Stir in vanilla and nut meats. Bake in a greased 8- or 9-inch square pan at 350º for 25 minutes. Cut into squares or bars.

BANANA PECAN BARS

When the bananas get soft-ripe, mash them and make banana pecan bars. Walnuts or peanuts may be used if pecans are not available.
⅔ cup shortening
1½ cups sugar
2 egg yolks
1 cup mashed bananas
1½ cups sifted all-purpose flour
1 teaspoon soda
¼ teaspoon salt
¼ cup sour cream
½ teaspoon vanilla
2 egg whites, stiffly beaten
¼ cup chopped pecans
Confectioners' sugar

Cream together shortening and sugar; beat in egg yolks. Stir in banana. Mix and sift together flour, soda and salt and add to creamed mixture alternately with sour cream. Mix well. Add vanilla and fold in stiffly beaten egg whites. Fold in nut meats. Pour into a greased and wax paper-lined (bottom only) 9x13x2-inch baking pan, spreading evenly. Bake at 325º for about 45 minutes. When cool, cut into strips and roll in confectioners' sugar.

SALTED PEANUT COOKIES

2 eggs, beaten
2 cups packed brown sugar
1½ cups butter or margarine, melted
2½ cups sifted all-purpose flour
1 teaspoon baking powder
1 teaspoon soda
½ teaspoon salt
3 cups rolled oats, uncooked
1 cup corn flakes
2 cups small salted Spanish peanuts, with skins

Combine beaten eggs and brown sugar and mix well. Add melted butter. Carefully stir in salted peanuts. Mix and sift together flour, soda, baking powder and salt. Add rolled oats and cornflakes, and add to the peanut mixture, mixing well. Drop dough by teaspoons on slightly greased cookie sheets. Bake at 400° for 8 to 10 minutes. Remove cookies at once from baking sheets; cool on rack. This cookie freezes well. The recipe makes about 6 dozen cookies.

CHOCOLATE FRUIT STICKS

1 package (6 ounces) chocolate bits
1½ cups sifted all-purpose flour
1 teaspoon baking powder
1½ teaspoons cinnamon
½ teaspoon cloves
½ teaspoon salt
2 tablespoons butter
¾ cup sugar
4 eggs
½ cup molasses
1 cup mixed candied fruit
1 cup pecan meats

Cream butter and sugar together. Beat in eggs, one at a time. Melt chocolate bits over warm, not hot, water; combine with molasses; add to creamed mixture. Mix and sift flour, baking powder, spices and salt together; stir into molasses mixture. Put fruit and nuts through medium blade of food chopper; stir into batter. Bake in greased and wax paper-lined jelly roll pan at 350° for 25 minutes. Do not overbake. When cool, frost with 2 cups confectioners' sugar, 1 tablespoon butter, 1½ teaspoons vanilla and enough hot milk to make frosting of spreading consistency. Cut butter into sugar; the hot milk will soften butter as it is mixed into sugar. Spread at once. Chopped nuts may be sprinkled on top or the nut meats may be mixed into frosting. Cut into bars. To freeze, wrap in plastic wrap, then foil.

PEANUT BUTTER CHOCO-NUT COOKIES

⅔ cup shortening
½ cup sugar
½ cup packed brown sugar
1 egg
½ cup plain peanut butter (if chunky peanut butter is used, omit chopped nuts)
1½ cups sifted all-purpose flour
½ teaspoon soda
½ teaspoon salt
½ teaspoon vanilla
1 cup chocolate morsels (6 oz. bag)
½ cup chopped nuts

In a mixing bowl cream shortening with granulated and brown sugars until light and fluffy. Add egg, then peanut butter and vanilla, beat until smooth and creamy. Sift together the flour, soda and salt and add to creamed mixture. Stir in the nut meats and chocolate morsels. Drop by rounded tablespoons onto ungreased cookie sheets. Bake at 375⁰ for 8 to 10 minutes or until lightly browned. Cool on cookie sheet for 5 minutes; remove to wire rack to cool completely. Makes about 3 dozen cookies.

OATMEAL DROP COOKIES

2¼ cups sifted all-purpose flour
2 teaspoons baking powder
1 teaspoon cinnamon
½ teaspoon nutmeg
½ teaspoon salt
1 cup butter or margarine, softened
1 cup granulated sugar
1 cup brown sugar, packed
2 eggs
⅓ cup milk
2 cups uncooked oats, quick or old-fashioned
1 cup raisins
⅔ cup chopped nuts

Preheat oven to 375⁰. Combine flour, baking powder, cinnamon, nutmeg and salt; set aside. Cream butter or margarine and sugars. Beat in eggs until light and fluffy. Add flour mixture alternately with milk and beat well after each addition. Stir in oats, raisins and nuts and mix thoroughly. Drop by heaping teaspoon onto ungreased baking sheets. Bake 12 to 15 minutes.

HONEY PINEAPPLE OATMEAL COOKIES

1 can (20 oz.) crushed pineapple
4 cups old-fashioned rolled oats
2 cups raisins
1 cup butter, softened
1 cup honey
1 egg
1 teaspoon vanilla extract
2 cups flour
1 teaspoon baking powder
1 teaspoon ground cinnamon
½ teaspoon salt
½ teaspoon ground nutmeg

Combine undrained pineapple, oats and raisins. Cream butter and honey for 5 minutes. Beat in egg and vanilla, then pineapple-oat mixture. Combine remaining ingredients. Beat into pineapple mixture until well-blended. Drop by 2 tablespoons onto greased cookie sheets. Bake at 350⁰ for 20 minutes until golden. Makes about 4 dozen.

TIGER EYE COOKIES

If there is no pumpkin on hand to cook to make these cookies, canned pumpkin may come to the rescue.

½ cup butter or margarine
1¼ cups brown sugar, packed
2 eggs
1½ cups cooked, mashed pumpkin
½ teaspoon salt
½ teaspoon ginger
½ teaspoon nutmeg
½ teaspoon cinnamon
2¼ cups flour
4 teaspoons baking powder
1 cup raisins or walnut meats, chopped
1 cup (6 ounces) chocolate morsels
1 teaspoon vanilla

Cream shortening and brown sugar; beat in eggs, one at a time; add pumpkin and salt. Mix and sift together spices, flour and baking powder and add to creamed mixture. Stir in vanilla, raisins or nut meats and chocolate morsels. Drop by teaspoons on greased baking sheets and bake in a moderately hot oven, 375⁰, for 10 to 15 minutes. Ovens vary, so watch the baking time in your oven.

VIRGINIA'S MOLASSES PEANUT BUTTER COOKIES

This molasses peanut butter cookie offered to us at lunchbreak time at Bangor Fair tasted so good that we thought you might like it to help fill the empty holes in the ever-hungry youngsters any time of day. (No, it was not an entry in the food division which we were judging later.)

½ cup shortening or margarine
½ cup sugar
½ cup light molasses
½ cup chunk-style peanut butter
1 egg
2 cups sifted all-purpose flour
¼ teaspoon baking powder
¼ teaspoon soda
¼ teaspoon salt

Cream shortening and sugar; beat in molasses, peanut butter and egg. Mix and sift together flour, baking powder, soda and salt and stir into peanut butter mixture. Drop by rounded teaspoons onto ungreased cookie sheet, leaving cookies two inches apart. Flatten cookies slightly with a fork and bake in a 375° oven for 8 to 10 minutes. Makes about 48 cookies. Store in tightly covered cookie jar or tin.

AMY'S CEREAL COOKIES

½ cup butter or margarine
½ cup brown sugar, packed
½ cup granulated sugar
1 egg
1 cup all-purpose flour
½ teaspoon soda
¼ teaspoon baking powder
½ teaspoon salt
1 cup crisp rice cereal
1 cup rolled oats
1 cup coconut
1 teaspoon vanilla

Cream together butter, granulated and brown sugar until light. Beat in the egg. Mix and sift flour with baking powder, soda and salt; add to creamed mixture. Stir in vanilla, rice cereal, rolled oats and coconut. Mix well. This is a firm dough. Dip by teaspoons and roll into balls; place on lightly greased cookie sheets and flatten with a fork as for peanut butter cookies. Bake at 350° for 8 to 10 minutes or until brown. Remove from tins to cool on a rack. Makes 60 cookies, depending on size. Store in tight tin to keep crisp.

CRISP SUGAR COOKIES

This plain, crisp sugar cookie is a special treat with a cup of tea. Stored in a tin, tightly covered, the cookie remains crisp. Vanilla, nutmeg or lemon may be used as the flavoring.

½ cup butter
1 cup sugar
1 egg
2½ cups sifted all-purpose flour
1 teaspoon cream of tartar
½ teaspoon soda
½ teaspoon salt
¾ teaspoon nutmeg
⅓ cup milk
Sugar for topping

Cream butter and sugar; beat in egg. Mix and sift together flour, cream of tartar, soda, salt and nutmeg; add to creamed mixture alternately with the milk. Chill. Roll dough to ⅛-inch thickness and cut with your favorite cookie cutter. Place on lightly greased cookie sheets. Sprinkle with sugar, colored sugar or small candies. Bake at 375⁰ for 8 to 10 minutes, or until cookies are browned at the edges. Remove at once from the cookie sheets.

GWEN'S LEMON SLICES

2 cups all-purpose flour
1 cup butter
½ cup confectioners' sugar

4 tablespoons all-purpose flour
2 tablespoons confectioners' sugar
4 eggs, beaten
2 cups granulated sugar
½ teaspoon salt
6 tablespoons fresh lemon juice
1 tablespoon grated lemon rind

Combine the 2 cups all-purpose flour with the ½ cup confectioners' sugar and the butter. Mix well and press, as a crust, in an even layer in a greased 9x13x2-inch baking pan. Bake in a moderate 350⁰ oven, for 15 minutes or until light brown. Remove from the oven and sprinkle with 4 tablespoons flour and 2 tablespoons confectioners' sugar. In a bowl, beat eggs well; beat in granulated sugar, salt, lemon juice and grated lemon rind. Pour over crust and continue to bake for 30 minutes. Remove from the oven and sprinkle with confectioners' sugar. Cool. Cut in bars. These bars freeze well.

DOTTIE'S BROWNIES

½ cup butter or margarine
2 cups sugar
4 eggs
3½ squares baking chocolate, melted
1 cup sifted all-purpose flour
½ teaspoon salt
¾ cup nut meats, coarsely broken
2 teaspoons vanilla

Cream butter and sugar. Beat in eggs. Mix and sift together flour and salt and add to creamed mixture. Stir in melted chocolate, nut meats and vanilla. Bake in greased and wax paper-lined 9x13x2-inch pan at 350° for 25 to 30 minutes. Cool. Remove wax paper from bottom of brownies.

VARIATIONS:

Leave one-half of brownies unfrosted and frost other half with vanilla or chocolate butter icing. Or, add a few drops of peppermint or wintergreen oil or extract to butter frosting. Color peppermint light green; wintergreen light pink. Melt 2 squares baking chocolate and drizzle over frosting, spreading it with a light touch of the back of a spoon.

MINCEMEAT OATMEAL DROPS

A gift of mincemeat, your own product or the supermarket's offering may be used in this drop cookie for the menu, school lunch or brown bag. This cookie is great for snacking—unless you are working on a slimmer you!

¾ cup soft margarine
½ cup packed brown sugar
½ cup granulated sugar
1 egg
1 cup-ready-to-use mincemeat
1 teaspoon vanilla
1½ cups flour
1 teaspoon baking powder
½ teaspoon salt
2 cups old-fashioned/or quick oats, uncooked

Beat margarine and sugars until light and fluffy. Blend in egg, mincemeat and vanilla. Add combined flour, baking powder and salt; mix well. Stir in oats. Drop rounded teaspoons of dough onto ungreased cookie sheet. Bake at 375°, 10 to 12 minutes or until golden brown. Approximately 4½ dozen. Substitute stick margarine for soft margarine.

AMY'S PEANUT BUTTER BARS

½ cup peanut butter
¼ cup shortening
½ teaspoon vanilla
 1 cup firmly packed brown sugar
 2 eggs
½ cup sifted all-purpose flour
¼ teaspoon salt
 1 cup chopped salted peanuts

Blend peanut butter, shortening and vanilla. Gradually add brown sugar, creaming well. Beat in eggs, one at a time. Mix and sift together flour and salt (there is no baking powder); blend into creamed mixture. Add chopped peanuts. Spread batter in greased 8-inch square pan. Bake at 350° for 25 minutes.

JEAN'S APPLE SLICES

 4 cups sifted all-purpose flour
 1 teaspoon salt
1½ cups shortening
 6 tablespoons cold water
 3 tablespoons lemon juice
 2 eggs, beaten
12 tart apples
1½ cups sugar
 3 cups confectioners' sugar
 6 tablespoons hot milk

One-half hour before preparing this recipe, pare, core and slice apples in thin slices. Sprinkle apple slices with 1½ cups sugar as you slice them into a bowl. Allow to set for 30 minutes. Sift flour and salt into a bowl; cut in shortening as for pie crust. Add water, lemon juice and eggs. Mix. Roll half of dough to fit a jelly roll pan, or a cookie sheet with sides. Because of richness, this pastry does not handle as easily as pie pastry, but the breaks and tears are easily patched. Spoon apple slices from bowl, leaving juice which collects in bowl. Arrange apple slices evenly over crust. Roll and add top crust. (Rolling the crust over a rolling pin and unrolling over apples is suggested.) Bake at 450° for 15 minutes; reduce heat to 350° and bake 30 minutes longer. When cool, frost with confectioners' sugar mixed with hot milk.

SOFT SUGAR COOKIES

This is a soft sugar cookie recipe that makes about 40 large cookies. The dough rolls best when chilled overnight. Not only is this a family favorite, but a ready seller at food sales and fairs, especially for ones who like the old-time flavor of the cookies. This is very popular with children.

    1 cup shortening
    1 teaspoon nutmeg
    ½ teaspoon salt
    1 teaspoon vanilla
 1½ cups sugar
    2 eggs
    4 cups sifted all-purpose flour
    1 teaspoon soda
    1 teaspoon baking powder
    1 cup sour cream

A mixture of butter, lard, margarine and/or vegetable shortening is suggested for the cup of shortening. Cream shortening with nutmeg, salt and vanilla; beat in sugar. Beat in eggs, one at a time. Mix and sift together flour, soda and baking powder; add to creamed mixture alternately with sour cream. Chill dough thoroughly. Roll dough to ¼-inch thickness and cut with a 3½-inch cutter; place cookies on lightly greased cookie sheet about 3 inches apart. Sprinkle cookies with granulated sugar and bake in a 400⁰ oven for 8 to 10 minutes. This is a high temperature but it makes a soft cookie.

PEGGY'S HUNGARIAN APPLE NUT CAKE

3 cups all-purpose flour
1½ teaspoons soda
¾ teaspoon nutmeg
1 teaspoon salt (optional)
1 cup plus 2 tablespoons vegetable oil
¾ teaspoon cinnamon
2 cups sugar
3 eggs
3 cups chopped apples with skins
1 cup chopped walnuts

Mix all ingredients together in a large bowl. Bake in a greased 10-inch tube pan for 70 minutes, at 350°. Let cool in the pan on a rack 2 to 3 hours. This is a firm cake and keeps well.

JANE'S PUMPKIN ROLL

3 eggs, beaten
1 cup sugar
⅔ cup mashed cooked pumpkin
1 teaspoon lemon juice
¾ cup sifted all-purpose flour
1 teaspoon baking powder
1 teaspoon cinnamon
1 teaspoon ginger
¼ teaspoon nutmeg
½ teaspoon salt
2 packages (3 ounces each) cream cheese
1 cup powdered sugar
¼ cup butter or margarine
½ teaspoon vanilla
⅓ cup chopped nut meats

In a mixing bowl, beat the eggs at high speed for 5 minutes. Gradually beat in the 1 cup sugar. Stir in the mashed pumpkin and lemon juice. Mix and sift together flour, baking powder, spices and salt. Fold into the pumpkin mixture. Grease and line a jelly-roll pan with waxed paper. Grease the paper. Pour the mixture into the pan, spreading evenly. Sprinkle with the nut meats. Bake in a moderately hot oven, 375°, for 15 minutes. Remove from the oven and turn onto a towel sprinkled with powdered sugar. Remove waxed paper and roll the cake, beginning from the narrow end, in the towel. Cool. Beat the cream cheese, powdered sugar, butter and vanilla together. Unroll the cake and spread with the cheese mixture. Remove towel; roll cake again and store in refrigerator. Slice into 10 slices and serve with whipped cream on top.

AMY'S MOCHA POUND CAKE

This mocha pound cake is baked in a long loaf pan and is moist and fine-grained. It stands by itself with no frosting necessary.

⅔ cup butter or margarine
2 cups sifted cake flour
1¼ cups sugar
1 tablespoon (3 teaspoons) instant coffee
1 teaspoon salt
½ teaspoon cream of tartar
¼ teaspoon soda
½ cup cold water
1½ teaspoons vanilla
3 eggs
2 squares chocolate, melted
Confectioners' sugar (optional)

In the bowl of the electric mixer, put butter, flour, sugar, instant coffee powder, salt, cream of tartar and soda. Add cold water and vanilla. Mix slowly to dampen, then beat for two minutes, scraping the bowl frequently. Add the eggs and melted chocolate and beat for one minute. Pour the batter into a long, broad pan, 9½x5x3-inch. Bake in a slow oven, 325°, for 65 to 70 minutes. Test for doneness with a cake tester. Cool for 10 minutes in the pan before removing to a rack to cool. If desired, sprinkle with confectioners' sugar before slicing to serve.

GAYLE'S BLACK MIDNIGHT CAKE

¾ cup salad oil
2½ cups sugar
4 large eggs
1 cup cocoa
2 cups boiling water
3 cups sifted all-purpose flour
1 teaspoon soda
1 teaspoon baking powder
1 teaspoon salt
1 teaspoon vanilla

Combine all ingredients in a large bowl. Beat until thoroughly mixed and pour into a greased and floured 9x13-inch baking pan. Bake in a moderate oven, 350°, 45 to 50 minutes or until center tests done. Cool in the pan for 10 minutes or longer, before removing from the pan to cool on a rack. Frost, if desired, when thoroughly cooled. A quick frosting is made by cutting 3 tablespoons butter or margarine into 3 cups confectioners' sugar. Add 1 teaspoon vanilla and hot milk, hot cream or hot black coffee to make a frosting of spreading consistency. The hot liquid melts and distributes the butter. Spread the frosting quickly.

CHOCOLATE DATE CAKE

8 egg yolks
1 egg
⅔ cup sugar
⅔ cup butter (1 stick plus 2 tablespoons)
8 ounces German sweet chocolate or semi-sweet chocolate
1 cup chopped walnuts or pecans
8 egg whites
1 teaspoon cream of tartar
   Date cream filling
   Walnut or pecan halves (optional)

Stir together yolks and one egg until thoroughly blended. (Do not beat.) Add sugar and stir until sugar is dissolved. Set aside. In small saucepan over low heat, stirring occasionally, melt butter and chocolate. Stir into reserved yolk mixture, blending thoroughly. Return one cup of the chocolate mixture to saucepan and refrigerate. Stir walnuts into remaining chocolate mixture. Set aside.

In large mixing bowl, beat egg whites with cream of tartar at high speed until stiff but not dry, just until whites do not slip when bowl is tilted. Gently fold one cup of the beaten whites into reserved chocolate-walnut mixture. Gently, but thoroughly, fold chocolate-walnut mixture into remaining beaten whites. Pour into greased 9x3-inch spring-form pan. Bake in preheated 350º oven until top springs back when lightly touched with finger, about 45 minutes. Cool on wire rack 5 minutes. (Cake will fall while cooling.) With a spatula, gently loosen cake from pan at side. When completely cool, remove pan side. Cut horizontally into 2 equal layers. Carefully remove top layer and set aside. Spread bottom layer with date cream filling. Replace top layer. Over very low heat, stir reserved chilled chocolate mixture until pourable, just a few seconds. Pour over top of cake. Garnish with walnut halves, if desired. Refrigerate at least an hour before serving. Refrigerate any leftovers.

DATE CREAM FILLING

¼ cup sugar
1 tablespoon flour
1 cup milk
1 egg, well beaten
1 cup chopped walnuts or pecans
⅔ cup chopped dates
1 teaspoon vanilla

In small saucepan, stir together sugar and flour until well blended. Stir in milk. Cook over medium heat, stirring constantly, until mixture comes to boiling. Stir about half of the mixture into beaten egg. Return warmed egg mixture to saucepan and stir until blended. Stir in walnuts, dates and vanilla. Chill.

CARROT CAKE

The traditional white cake for the wedding luncheon or dinner has been replaced by chiffon, chocolate or carrot cake. Today's brides have chosen to replace the old with the new on that happy day. A carrot cake has flavor and retains its moistness for several days and it freezes well. Cream cheese frosting is another choice. If you like carrot cake just whip up some for supper or to take on a picnic; you do not have to wait for a wedding. This recipe makes a 9x13-inch cake.

1 cup salad oil
2 cups sugar
4 eggs
2 cups sifted all-purpose flour
2 teaspoons soda
2 teaspoons cinnamon
¼ teaspoon salt
3 cups shredded fresh carrots
1 cup chopped walnut meats

Grease a 9x12x2-inch pan and fit wax paper into the bottom. In mixing bowl, combine oil and sugar; beat well. Add eggs, one at a time, beating well after each addition. Mix and sift together the flour, soda, salt and cinnamon; add to egg mixture and beat for one minute. Fold in the nut meats and shredded carrots. (It takes about 3 good-sized carrots, shredded, to make 3 cups.) Pour into prepared pan and bake at 350° for about 1 hour. Cool. Frost with cream cheese frosting.

CREAM CHEESE FROSTING

2 (3 oz. each) packages cream cheese
4 tablespoons butter or margarine
1 pound package confectioners' sugar
2 teaspoons vanilla

In beater bowl combine cream cheese and butter; cream well and beat in the confectioners' sugar and vanilla. You may wish to add a teaspoon of water, but beat the sugar, cream cheese and butter well before doing so. Spread on the cooled cake. This frosting forms a thin crust. We spread the cake with apricot preserves or jam 10 minutes before frosting the cake to "lay the crumbs." This very thin bit of jam also adds flavor to the cake.

SPRING FRUIT PIE

1 Ready-Crust pie crust, butter-flavored
1½ cups fresh pineapple
1½ cups fresh chopped rhubarb
¾ cup sugar
3 tablespoons minute tapioca
2 tablespoons orange juice
1½ cups strawberries

Cut rhubarb and pineapple into small pieces and mix with sugar, tapioca and orange juice. Let stand for 15 minutes. Cook over medium heat until tapioca dissolves and mixture thickens. Stir in strawberries cut into small pieces. Fill pie crust. Chill for 4 hours. Serve with whipped topping.

AUDREY'S WHITE CHRISTMAS PIE

This recipe is called a White Christmas Pie but it is welcome anytime by the family who sent this recipe. The homemaker wrote, "I usually make the pie for special holidays and for the two oldest boys' birthdays. They prefer this to a birthday cake." You will need a baked 9-inch pie shell for the pie.

¼ cup flour
½ cup sugar
1 envelope (1 tablespoon) unflavored gelatin
½ teaspoon salt
1¾ cups milk
¾ teaspoon vanilla
¼ teaspoon almond flavoring
3 egg whites
¼ teaspoon cream of tartar
½ cup sugar
½ cup cream, whipped
1 cup moist, shredded coconut

Blend flour, ½ cup sugar, gelatin and salt thoroughly in a saucepan. Gradually stir in the milk. Cook over medium heat until mixture boils, stirring constantly. Boil one minute. Remove pan from heat and set in dish of cold water. Cool until mixture mounds slightly when dropped from spoon. Blend in vanilla and almond flavorings. Make a meringue with beaten egg whites, cream of tarter and ½ cup sugar. Fold into cooled mixture. Fold in the whipped cream and coconut. Fill pie shell. Sprinkle with additional coconut. Chill pie for several hours until set. Serve cold. Delicious topped with crushed strawberries or raspberries. No cream of tartar? Use one teaspoon fresh lemon juice.

RASPBERRY PIE

1 quart fresh raspberries
1 cup minus 2 tablespoons sugar
¼ teaspoon salt
2 tablespoons flour
2 tablespoons butter or margarine
   Pastry for 2-crust pie

Prepare pastry for two-crust pie. Wash and drain raspberries and spoon into the pastry-lined pan. Combine sugar, salt and flour and spread over the berries. Dot with butter. Add top crust after making slits to allow for steam to escape as the pie bakes. Tuck upper crust under lower crust and press to seal pie. At this stage the pie crust may be brushed with a bit of cream or milk. Bake at 400° for about 40 minutes or until the juices bubble from the slashes in the crust, and the crust appears to be done. Cool. Serve plain or with ice cream. An open-face pie may be made by cutting pastry in strips and weaving it onto the top of the fruit. More sugar may be added if the berries are on the tart side.

STRAWBERRY AND RHUBARB PIE

When it's rhubarb time, rhubarb desserts always are welcomed in many homes. Coffee cakes, pies, puddings and jams will be in order. Rhubarb pies are delicious, as is a strawberry and rhubarb pie and sauce. The combination of the rhubarb and strawberries may vary with the amounts of each available, so using this recipe as a starter, make your own combination.

   Pastry for 2-crust pie
2 cups sliced rhubarb
1½ cups sliced strawberries
2 tablespoons flour
1 cup sugar
½ teaspoon salt
2 tablespoons butter

Prepare rhubarb. Many homemakers wash and slice the rhubarb and use; others pour boiling water over the rhubarb, leave for 2 or 3 minutes and drain, claiming that the sharpness or acidity of the rhubarb is lessened. Combine the rhubarb with the strawberries and spoon into the crust-lined plate. Combine sugar, flour and salt and pour over contents of the pie; top with pieces of butter. Add the top crust after making slits in it for the steam to escape as the pie bakes. Bake in a hot oven, 425°, for 40 minutes or until the juices bubble through the slits.

PAT'S BLUEBERRY GLAZE PIE

¼ cup (heaping) brown sugar
¼ cup (heaping) granulated sugar
1 tablespoon flour
¼ teaspoon salt
1 tablespoon fresh lemon juice
1 tablespoon butter
4 cups blueberries, divided
   Baked 8 or 9-inch pie shell
   Flavored whipped cream

In a heavy saucepan, mix together brown sugar, granulated sugar, flour and salt. Add lemon juice, butter and 2 cups of blueberries. Cook over low to medium heat without additional liquid, stirring until thickened, about 2 to 4 minutes. Cool. Add 2 cups of raw blueberries; mix well and fill a baked pie shell. Top with flavored whipped cream. NOTE: You may use a graham cracker crust if you wish.

LEMON SPONGE PIE

Lemon sponge pie is a change from the lemon meringue pie so often served. This goes with any menu. It also may be made into a pudding by baking the mixture in custard cups in a pan of water or in a casserole set in a pan of water in the oven.

   Juice of 1 lemon
   Rind of 1 lemon, grated
1 cup sugar
3 tablespoons flour
3 eggs, separated
½ teaspoon salt
2 tablespoons butter
1½ cups hot water or milk
   Pastry for 9-inch, single-crust pie

Line a pie plate with pastry, crimping the top edge of the pastry at the rim of the plate. Cream the butter, add sugar and egg yolks and beat well. Add milk or water mixed with lemon rind, lemon juice, salt and flour. Mix well. Fold in stiffly beaten egg whites. Pour into unbaked, prepared crust. Bake in a moderate oven, 350°, for 45 to 50 minutes. When the pie is done, there is a pudding-like layer topped with a foam-like layer.

JOYCE'S APPLE CAKE PIE

If you want to make an apple pie but do not like to make a crust, try this apple cake pie.

1 egg, beaten
¼ teaspoon salt
1 teaspoon vanilla
½ cup all-purpose flour
½ cup plus 2 tablespoons sugar
¼ to ½ teaspoon cinnamon
½ teaspoon baking powder
1 cup chopped raw apples
½ raisins or nut meats

Beat the egg with the salt and vanilla added. Mix in the sugar. Mix and sift flour with baking powder and cinnamon and add to egg mixture. Stir in apples and raisins or nuts. Grease a 9-inch pie plate; spoon batter into plate and bake in a moderate oven, 350º, for about ½ hour. Cut in wedges to serve.

RHUBARB PIE

This is the old-fashioned way of making a rhubarb pie. Another choice is a strawberry and rhubarb pie.

4 cups rhubarb sliced in ½-inch pieces
   Boiling water
1½ cups sugar
¼ teaspoon salt
¼ to ½ cup raisins
1 egg, beaten
2 tablespoons flour
2 tablespoons butter or margarine
   Pastry for two-crust pie

Wash and slice rhubarb into a bowl. Pour boiling water over the rhubarb and allow to sit for 5 minutes; drain. To the rhubarb add sugar, salt, raisins, beaten egg and flour. Mix well and pour into a pastry-lined pie plate. Top with the butter cut into pieces. Add the top crust after making slits to allow for the escape of steam as the pie bakes. Seal the edges. Bake at 425º for about 45 minutes or until the juices boil up through the slits in the crust. As an added bonus, serve with a small scoop of ice cream, if desired.

BLUEBERRY PIE

What tastes more like Maine than blueberry pie made from freshly picked berries and still warm from the oven? Nothing, unless it is blueberry pie with ice cream on top!

1 quart fresh blueberries
¾ cup sugar
¼ teaspoon salt
2 tablespoons flour
2 tablespoons butter or margarine
¼ teaspoon cinnamon, optional
    Pastry for 2-crust pie

Line a pie plate with half the pastry. Wash and pat berries dry with paper towel and dump into pastry-lined pan. Combine sugar, flour, salt and cinnamon if the latter is used. Spread mixture over the fruit. Dot with butter. Add top crust which has been slashed to allow for the escape of steam as the pie bakes. Tuck top crust under bottom crust to make a tight seal. Bake in a 425° oven for about 40 minutes, or until the fruit bubbles in the slashes and the crust is browned. As the pie cools the juice from the berries thickens slightly.

BARBARA'S CHERRY AND PINEAPPLE PIE

This two-crust pie has a mixture of canned cherries (or substitute frozen cherries) and crushed pineapple. A bit of food coloring can be added to enhance the color of the filling.

    Pastry for 2-crust pie
2 cups cherries, drained; reserve juice
1 (8 oz.) can crushed pineapple
1 cup sugar
3 tablespoons cornstarch
2 tablespoons honey
1 tablespoon butter or margarine
    Red food coloring, optional
¼ teaspoon salt

Line a pie plate with pastry. In saucepan, combine crushed pineapple and juice, sugar, cornstarch, salt, honey and butter. Add juice from cherries; mix and cook over medium heat until thickened. Fold in cherries and pour mixture into prepared crust. Add top crust after slashing to allow for escape of steam as the pie bakes. Bake at 425° for about 40 minutes, or until the pie filling bubbles, and the crust is brown.

THELMA'S VENISON MINCEMEAT

If you have frozen some of the venison that the family hunter brought home, you may like to use the neck meat or some of the other cuts for your yearly supply of mincemeat. There are many recipes for mincemeat. This is one person's old-time recipe in which the ingredients are measured by the bowlful. A quart bowl was used in this case. The recipe makes 9 quarts of mincemeat. This recipe also offers an opportunity to clean out all your leftover jams and jellies you may have canned in the past. In this recipe the cook melted the suet in a Dutch oven over low heat and added it in liquid form—suet is hard to grind in a hand meat grinder.

3 (1 quart) bowls cooked, chopped meat
   Grape juice and/or apple juice
5 bowls pared, chopped apples
1 bowl vinegar
1 bowl suet
3 bowls sugar
1 bowl liquid from cooking meat
2 bowls raisins
1 bowl molasses
2 tablespoons cinnamon
2 tablespoons ground clove
2 tablespoons nutmeg
1 tablespoon black pepper
3 or 4 jars jams or jelly

Cook the meat in a mixture of grape juice and apple juice; reserve the liquid. Apple cider can be used as part of the cooking liquid. (Remember, this recipe was used when "make do" was the motto.) Combine all of the ingredients in a large, heavy kettle. (Some homemakers use the bottom half of their roasting pan and cook the mincemeat in the oven.) Stir frequently, adding more liquid if needed, for two or three hours, until the flavor suits your taste. Spoon the mincemeat into hot, sterilized jars; seal according to manufacturer's directions. Process in a pressure cooker at 10 pounds pressure for 20 minutes or in a boiling water bath for 1½ hours.

PRISCILLA'S APPLE OATMEAL CRISP

1½ pounds tart cooking apples
 ½ cup (1 stick) butter or margarine
 ¾ cup firmly packed brown sugar
 ¾ cup quick cooking rolled oats, uncooked
 ½ cup flour
 1 teaspoon cinnamon

Pare and slice apples. Arrange in a buttered 6-cup baking dish. Melt butter in a saucepan; stir in the brown sugar, rolled oats, flour and cinnamon; mix. Sprinkle over apples. Bake at 350° for 35 minutes or until crumbs are golden brown and apples are soft. Serve warm with vanilla ice cream, whipped cream or cool whip.

BLUEBERRY COBBLER

 4 cups blueberries, fresh or frozen
 ¼ cup melted butter
 1 cup, less 2 tablespoons, sifted all-purpose flour
 ¼ teaspoon salt
 ¼ milk
 3 tablespoons shortening
 1 cup sugar
1½ tablespoons lemon juice
 3 teaspoons baking powder
 ¼ teaspoon nutmeg
 1 egg

Stir together berries, sugar, melted butter and lemon juice. Spoon into a 9-inch square baking pan. Mix and sift together flour (one cup cake flour may be used in place of the sifted all-purpose flour), salt, baking powder and nutmeg. Cut in the shortening as for biscuits. Beat egg and milk together and stir into this mixture. Mix and spoon over the blueberries. Bake at 350° for about 40 minutes. Cut in squares and serve with the following sauce, if desired, or with ice cream.

PUDDING SAUCE

 3 egg yolks
 3 egg whites
 2 teaspoons vanilla
 ½ cup sugar
 2 cups whipping cream

Beat egg yolks with ¼ cup sugar. Beat whites until stiff, adding ¼ cup of sugar while beating. Beat cream until stiff; add yolks, whites and vanilla.

JUNE'S COFFEE TAPIOCA

3 cups brewed coffee
½ cup sugar
½ cup tapioca
⅛ teaspoon salt

Heat the brewed coffee in the top of a double boiler. Combine the sugar, tapioca, and salt; mix and stir into the hot coffee. Cover and cook until thickened, stirring occasionally.

STRAWBERRY SHORTCAKE

This recipe is similar to the one my mother made with the wild strawberries we children had picked in nearby fields.

1 quart strawberries, sliced
¼ to ½ cup sugar
½ cup butter or margarine, softened, divided
2 cups all-purpose flour
¼ cup sugar
4 teaspoons baking powder
¼ teaspoon salt
   Dash of ground nutmeg
½ cup milk
2 eggs, separated
¼ cup sugar
1 cup whipping cream or whipped topping
¼ cup powdered sugar

Combine strawberries and ¼ to ½ cup sugar; stir gently and chill 2 to 3 hours. Butter two 9-inch cake pans with ½ tablespoon butter each; set aside. Combine flour, ¼ cup sugar, baking powder, salt and nutmeg in large bowl. Cut in remaining butter with pastry blender until mixture resembles coarse meal. Combine milk and egg yolks; beat well. Add to flour mixture; stir with a fork until soft dough forms. Pat dough out evenly into cake pans. (Dough will be sticky; moisten fingers with egg whites, if necessary.) Beat egg whites until stiff, but not dry. Brush surface of dough with beaten egg whites; sprinkle evenly with ¼ cup sugar. Bake at 450° for 10 to 12 minutes or until layers are golden brown. Cool on wire racks. Beat whipping cream until foamy; gradually add powdered sugar, beating until soft peaks form. (You may use whipped topping.) Place one cake layer on serving plate. Spoon on half of whipped cream, and arrange half of sliced strawberries on top. Repeat procedure with remaining cake, more whipped cream and strawberries. Garnish top of cake with remaining whipped cream and whole berries.

CRANBERRY SURPRISE

2½ cups cranberries
1½ cups sugar, divided
½ cup chopped nuts
2 eggs
1 cup flour
½ cup butter, melted
¼ cup shortening

Spread cranberries over the bottom of a buttered 10" pan. Sprinkle with ½ cup of the sugar and the nuts. Beat eggs well; gradually add the remaining cup of sugar and beat thoroughly. Add flour and melted butter and beat well. Pour batter over berries; dot with shortening. Bake at 325° for 50 minutes or until golden brown. Cut in wedges and serve warm with vanilla ice cream or plain thickened sauce.

COZY CARAMEL CUSTARDS

1¾ cups granulated sugar, divided
3 whole eggs
3 egg yolks
2 cups milk
1 cup whipping cream
1 teaspoon vanilla extract

Preheat oven to 350°. Place one cup of the sugar in a small, heavy saucepan. Cook the sugar over low heat until it begins to melt. Continue heating, stirring constantly, until the sugar is light brown and caramelized, about 5 to 7 minutes. (Sugar may form lumps at first, but will melt as it continues to cook.) Immediately divide the caramel evenly among eight custard cups. Carefully and quickly tilt the cups, coating the sides. (Caution—caramel is very hot.) Whisk the eggs, egg yolks and remaining ¾ cup of sugar in a medium-sized bowl until thick and lemon-colored. Bring the milk and cream to simmer in a small saucepan. Whisking constantly, gradually add the hot milk mixture to the eggs. Stir in the vanilla. Pour custard mixture into the caramel-lined cups. Place the filled cups into a 9x13-inch baking pan. Add hot water to the pan to a depth of 1 inch. Cover the top of the custards with a sheet of lightly-buttered wax paper. Bake for 40 to 45 minutes, or until knife inserted near center comes out clean. Remove from water, cool at least 30 minutes on wire rack. To serve, gently run spatula around edges of custard cup. Invert onto serving plate. Serve warm or cold. Makes 8 servings.

PRUNE WHIP

1 pound prunes, cooked
½ cup sugar
1 teaspoon grated lemon rind
¼ teaspoon lemon juice
5 egg whites
½ cup nuts (optional)

Put cooked prunes through ricer to make 1 cup pulp. In mixer, combine prune pulp and sugar. In a separate bowl, beat 5 egg whites for 3 minutes; add to prune mixture gradually and beat until light and fluffy, about 5 minutes. Chill before serving.

BLACK FOREST PUDDING CAKE

This is another version of an old-time pudding which was enjoyed as a dessert. This Black Forest pudding cake is easy to assemble as ingredients are layered in a square pan and baked. Emerging from the oven is a cake-type dessert on the top and a pudding sauce on the bottom.

1¼ cups granulated sugar, divided
1 cup all-purpose flour
3 tablespoons unsweetened cocoa
2 teaspoons baking powder
¼ teaspoon salt
½ cup milk
⅓ cup butter or margarine, melted
1½ teaspoons vanilla extract
½ cup packed light brown sugar
¼ cup unsweetened cocoa
1¼ cups hot water
2 tablespoons cold water
½ teaspoon almond extract
   Cherry pie filling

Heat oven to 350°. In medium mixing bowl combine ¾ cup granulated sugar, flour, 3 tablespoons cocoa, baking powder and salt. Blend in milk, melted butter and vanilla; beat until smooth. Spread in 8- or 9-inch square pan. In small bowl combine remaining ½ cup granulated sugar, brown sugar and ¼ cup cocoa; sprinkle mixture evenly over batter. Combine hot water and cold water mixed with almond extract; pour over batter; do not stir. Bake 40 minutes or until center is almost set. Let stand 15 minutes; spoon into dessert dishes, spooning sauce from bottom of pan over cake. Serve with cherry pie filling. Makes 8 to 10 servings.

BENTLY'S QUICK APPLE COBBLER

¼ pound (½ stick) margarine
1 cup flour
1 cup sugar
1 cup milk
1 teaspoon baking powder
½ teaspoon salt
¼ to ½ teaspoon nutmeg (optional)
½ teaspoon cinnamon (optional)

Heat oven to 350°. Melt the margarine in a baking dish. Mix together until smooth the flour, sugar, milk, baking powder, salt and spices (if used). Pour the flour mixture into the baking dish but do not stir. Pare 4 cups of apples and cut in slices or chunks. Add to baking dish but do not stir. Bake until top has crusted over and browned, about 1 hour. This same recipe may be used with peaches, blackberries, pears and the like. Serve plain or with cream or ice cream.

STRAWBERRY ICE CREAM

Fresh Maine strawberries from the market or from the pick-them-yourself plots can be used in many pleasing dishes—shortcake, bread, pie and ice cream to mention a few. Then there is jam and freezing the berries for later use. We have used the wild strawberries in ice cream as well as the cultivated ones. The wild berries also make a delicious pie. Use either in this recipe.

2 quarts strawberries
½ cup sugar
5 eggs
1¾ cup sugar
½ teaspoon salt
1 tablespoon vanilla
1 quart heavy cream
3 cups all-purpose cream or half and half
About 3 cups milk to fill can of freezer

Wash, hull and mash the berries with ½ cup sugar. Set aside for 2 hours to blend. Beat eggs well, then beat with the 1¾ cups sugar. Stir in salt, vanilla and cream. Stir in prepared strawberries. Pour into the freezer can and add milk to fill three-fourths of the can. Add dasher and cover and pack the can with ice and salt as needed, and freeze until the handle will no longer turn. Remove cover and dasher, scraping the frozen cream back into the can. Cover can with wax paper and top with the cover. Place a cup over the top after placing a cork or stopper in the opening. Repack ice and allow the ice cream to "ripen" for a few hours.

FRUIT FILLED TARTS

For a different dessert make fruit filled tarts and serve with a tablespoon of whipped cream on each serving. A simple but tasty dessert.

  1 (3 oz.) package raspberry gelatin
  1 cup boiling water
  1 cup apple juice
  6 prepared tart shells (5-inch)
  ½ cup apple slices
  ½ cup fresh or frozen blueberries
    Whipped cream for topping

Dissolve gelatin in boiling water; stir in apple juice. Chill until slightly thickened. Arrange prepared fruit in tart shells; spoon thickened gelatin over the fruit and chill until firm. Serve with whipped cream or whipped topping. If desired, thinly sliced banana may be added to the apple and blueberry mixture.

NANCY'S BLUEBERRY DESSERT

While some recipes will be "old hat," or "just like mine-except," they will be new to others. If you are a berry picker you may like to try this blueberry dessert. Your own wild blueberries may be used, thickened with cornstarch and sugar added, or canned pie filling may be used.

  1 cup (2 sticks) margarine
1½ cups sugar
  4 eggs
  1 teaspoon vanilla
  3 cups sifted all-purpose flour
1½ teaspoon baking powder
  ¼ teaspoon salt
  1 can (21 oz. or larger) blueberry pie filling
    Nutmeg
    Glaze for dessert

Cream margarine and sugar; beat in eggs and vanilla, beating well. Mix and sift together flour, baking powder and salt and add to creamed mixture, mixing well. Beat to thoroughly mix. Spread one-half of dough in an ungreased jelly roll pan. Spoon pie filling evenly over the dough. Sprinkle with nutmeg. Drop remaining dough by spoonsful over filling; do not spread (baking will do this). Bake in a 350° oven for 35 to 40 minutes. Remove pan from oven, cool slightly.

GLAZE

Combine 1¼ cups confectioners' sugar with 1 tablespoon melted margarine and 2 tablespoons fresh lemon juice, mix and drizzle over baked dessert.

ORANGE CREAM SOUFFLE

2 3-oz. packages orange gelatin
2 cups boiling water
1 8-oz. package cream cheese
¼ cup sugar
¾ cup cold water
½ cup orange juice
1 cup heavy cream, whipped
   Orange slices
   Grated orange rind

Dissolve orange gelatin in boiling water. Combine softened cream cheese and sugar, mixing well until blended. Gradually add gelatin, cold water and orange juice. Chill until slightly thickened; fold in whipped cream. Wrap a 3" collar of aluminum foil around top of a 1-quart souffle dish; secure with tape. Pour mixture into dish. Chill until firm. Remove collar before serving; garnish with orange slices and rind. Makes 6 servings.

EMMA'S BLACKBERRY SHORTCAKE

Do certain foods trigger your memory as to where and when? Ripe blackberries, fat and juicy, bring to mind blackberry shortcakes served years ago at a summer boarding home in Maine. (We were on the dishwashing crew!) Raspberries and blueberries were also used in the same way, but the blackberries were special. The recipe doesn't call for cream to be served, but thick cream was always on the table for those who wished it.

2 cups all-purpose flour
½ teaspoon salt
4 teaspoons baking powder
½ teaspoon cream of tartar
2 tablespoons sugar
½ cup butter or shortening
⅔ cup milk
1 egg (optional)
   Meringue

Mix and sift together flour, salt, baking powder, cream of tartar and sugar. Cut in shortening as for biscuits. Add milk to make a soft dough. (An egg may be beaten in with the milk.) Roll dough on a greased and floured cookie sheet, to ½ inch-thickness. Bake in a hot oven, 450°, for 15 to 20 minutes, depending on thickness of dough. Remove from the oven and apply butter generously to the surface. Cover with crushed and sweetened (to taste) blackberries. Top with meringue and return to oven until meringue is golden.

MOUSSE AU CHOCOLAT

Check carefully when buying chocolate. Semi-sweet chocolate is often mistaken for bitter chocolate squares.

6 squares semi-sweet chocolate
¼ cup cream or milk
1 teaspoon vanilla
⅛ teaspoon salt
4 egg yolks
4 egg whites
¼ cup sugar

Melt chocolate in saucepan over very low heat, stirring constantly. Remove from heat; blend in cream, vanilla and salt. Gradually add to beaten egg yolks, beating with wire whisk until thick and creamy. egg whites until foamy throughout. Gradually beat in sugar and continue beating until mixture will form stiff peaks. Gently but thoroughly fold into chocolate mixture. Spoon into individual dishes or serving bowl. Chill at least 2 hours. Makes 4 cups or 8 to 10 servings.

MERINGUE SHELLS

Meringue shells for a party may be made ahead and stored in a closely covered tin. Place wax paper between each layer of shells. Left white, the shells will look festive with vanilla ice cream with mashed strawberries on top, or the shells may be colored when mixing for holding vanilla or strawberry ice cream.

3 egg whites
½ teaspoon cream of tartar
1 cup sifted sugar
1 teaspoon vinegar
½ teaspoon vanilla
8 to 10 drops vegetable food coloring (optional)

Combine egg whites, at room temperature, with cream of tartar and beat until soft peaks form. Add sugar gradually. Add vinegar and vanilla. Beat for 12 minutes or until stiff peaks form. (This is very important.) For pastel shells, add food coloring at this point, beating to blend evenly. For each meringue shell pile 2 large rounded tablespoons of the meringue in a solid heap on brown paper or aluminum foil, or fill in heart-shaped outlines on the foil. With rounded side of spoon make a hole in the meringue, pushing down quickly but lightly to make a well in the meringue. A pastry bag with a star tip is also excellent for shaping the meringue. Bake in a very slow oven (300°) for 1½ hours. Turn off heat and let shells cool in the oven until oven is cold. Gently peel meringues from the foil and store.

LEMON CHIFFON PUDDING

This pudding is one of the most refreshing of desserts, nice to serve ice cold in the spring or summer, with or without a topping.

```
5 tablespoons flour
1 cup sugar
3 tablespoons butter
3 egg yolks, beaten
¼ cup lemon juice
  Grated rind of 1 lemon
1 cup milk
3 egg whites, stiffly beaten
```

Cream together flour, sugar and butter. Add egg yolks, lemon juice and rind, and milk. Mix thoroughly. Fold beaten egg whites into mixture and pour into buttered casserole or custard cups. Set in a pan and add warm water halfway up sides of casserole. Bake at 350° for 35 to 40 minutes. As this bakes, a "crust" is formed with a clear lemon layer below.

APPLE BROWN BETTY

In some communities during the fall days, oyster stew suppers were in style. With these suppers, the dessert nearly always was apple brown betty, a really old-fashioned and delicious dessert.

```
⅓ cup melted butter or margarine
6 slices day-old bread, lightly buttered
6 cups apples, pared, cored, sliced
½ cup brown or granulated sugar
½ teaspoon nutmeg
¼ teaspoon cinnamon
  Grated rind of 1 lemon
2 tablespoons fresh lemon juice
¼ cup water
```

Butter the slices of bread and cut into ½-inch cubes. Butter a 1½-quart casserole, then pour in the melted butter. Put in a third of the bread cubes and half of the sliced apples; add half of the combined cinnamon, nutmeg, sugar and lemon rind. Add another third of the diced, buttered bread cubes. Add remaining apples. Sprinkle with remaining sugar mixture. Mix lemon juice and water and pour over contents of casserole. Top with remaining cubes. Cover and bake in a moderately hot oven, 375°, for about 30 minutes. Remove cover and bake another half hour or until apples are done. May be served with cream or ice cream.

BLUEBERRY BUCKLE

This may be used as a coffee cake or as a dessert.

½ cup shortening
½ cup sugar
1 egg, beaten
2 cups sifted all-purpose flour
½ teaspoon salt
2½ teaspoons baking powder
½ cup milk
2½ cups fresh or frozen blueberries

Cream shortening and sugar; add beaten egg and mix well. Mix together and sift flour, salt and baking powder; add to creamed mixture alternately with milk. Spread dough in greased 8x8x2-inch pan. Spread blueberries over dough. Mix and sift together ½ cup sugar, ½ cup flour and ¾ teaspoon cinnamon; cut in ⅓ cup margarine or butter until a crumbly mixture results. Spread this mixture over the blueberries. Bake in a 375⁰ oven 1 to 1¼ hours. Serve warm from the oven.

BLUEBERRY CLAFOUTI

Nearly every family has its own special blueberry recipe. Like to try another? There's a delicious and simple French dessert called Clafouti. It's not a fancy dessert; it came from the French countryside, not from the Paris cafes. In France, clafoutis are always served warm. Sometimes confectioners' sugar is sprinkled over them. Could this be a relative of the blueberry pancake?

1¼ cups all-purpose flour
3 large eggs, beaten
¾ cup sugar
¼ teaspoon salt
1 teaspoon baking powder
1¼ cups warm milk
1 tablespoon butter
3 cups blueberries, rinsed, drained

Preheat oven to 375⁰. Mix flour, sugar, eggs, salt and baking powder in a large bowl. Stir in milk until smooth. Butter a 9-inch cake pan with removable bottom. Pour batter to a ¼-inch thickness in prepared pan. Bake for 7 to 8 minutes or until batter has set. Spread 2 cups blueberries over set batter. Pour remaining batter over blueberries. Continue baking for 30 to 40 minutes until puffed and golden. Cool on wire rack. Remove rim of cake pan. Top with remaining berries. Reheat before serving. Yield: 8 servings.

ORANGE CHIFFON DESSERT

Make a light, flavorful orange chiffon dessert to serve with a soft custard sauce. Skim milk is used to reduce calories, but whole milk may be used.

2 tablespoons unflavored gelatin (2 envelopes)
½ cup sugar
1 cup water
2 cups vanilla yogurt
1 can (6 oz.) concentrated orange juice
2 egg whites
4 tablespoons sugar
1 teaspoon vanilla extract

In a 1-quart saucepan combine gelatin and ½ cup sugar; add water. Heat over low heat, stirring occasionally until gelatin is dissolved. In a bowl gradually add thawed orange juice to yogurt; stir in gelatin mixture. Chill until partially set. Beat egg whites until frothy; gradually add 4 tablespoons sugar, two tablespoons at a time, and beat until stiff. Fold into orange mixture. Chill until mixture is firm. Layer into parfait glasses with custard sauce. Makes six ⅔-cup servings.

CUSTARD SAUCE

2 cups low-fat milk
2 eggs (or 2 egg yolks and 1 whole egg)
½ cup sugar
¼ teaspoon salt
1 teaspoon vanilla extract
½ teaspoon grated orange peel
½ teaspoon nutmeg

Scald milk in 1½-quart saucepan. Lightly beat eggs in a bowl. Stir in sugar and salt. Blend a small amount of milk into egg mixture; return mixture to a double boiler. Cook, stirring occasionally, until mixture thickens enough to coat a metal or silver spoon. Remove from heat, add vanilla, orange peel and nutmeg. Chill. Makes 2½ cups custard sauce.

RHUBARB CRISP OR BETTY

4 cups rhubarb cut in ½-inch slices
1 cup sifted all-purpose flour
¾ cup rolled oats, uncooked
1 cup brown sugar, packed
½ cup melted butter or margarine
1 teaspoon cinnamon
1 cup sugar
2 tablespoons cornstarch
1 cup water
1 teaspoon vanilla

Prepare the rhubarb. Combine the butter, brown sugar, rolled oats, flour and cinnamon and mix until crumbly. Press half of the mixture into a buttered 9-inch square baking pan in an even layer; add diced or sliced rhubarb. In a saucepan, combine sugar, cornstarch, water and vanilla. Mix well. Cook, stirring constantly until mixture is thick and clear. Pour over the rhubarb. Top with remaining crumb mixture. Bake at 350° for about 40 minutes or bubbly. Cut in squares and serve warm, with or without plain cream or whipped topping. This is also good served cold.

PENUCHI

1 pound package light brown sugar
1 cup thin cream
1 tablespoon butter or margarine
1½ teaspoons vanilla
¼ teaspoon salt
⅔ cup walnut or pecan meats

In a saucepan, combine sugar and cream. Cook, stirring constantly, until 236° on candy thermometer, or soft ball stage. Remove from heat; add butter; set aside to cool without stirring. When the mixture is lukewarm (110°), remove thermometer; add vanilla and salt and beat until thick and creamy and the candy loses its gloss. Add nut meats, coarsely broken, and mix thoroughly. Pour at once into a buttered pan. Vary the recipe by the addition of ¼ cup finely cut candied ginger (sugar removed from ginger).

FUDGE ORLEANS

It's a change from the usual fudge, but this Fudge Orleans is much more than just a candy. This innovative recipe boasts a buttery-tasting pecan cookie base and a rich and creamy topping of chocolate fudge. The easy-to-prepare, two-layer treat sports real New Orleans praline flavor. It's worth a try.

1 cup margarine
1 cup packed brown sugar
1 egg
2 cups flour
1 cup chopped pecans
3 cups granulated sugar
¾ cup margarine
⅔ cup (5-ounce can) evaporated milk
1 package (12 ounces) semisweet chocolate pieces
1 jar (7 ounces) marshmallow creme
1 teaspoon vanilla

Beat 1 cup margarine and brown sugar until light and fluffy. Blend in egg; add flour and mix well. Stir in pecans. Spread dough into 15x10x1-inch jelly-roll pan. Bake at 350° for 20 to 30 minutes or until edges are lightly browned. Combine granulated sugar, margarine and milk in heavy 3-quart saucepan; bring to full rolling boil, stirring constantly. Continue boiling 5 minutes over medium heat or until candy thermometer reaches 234°, stirring constantly to prevent scorching. Remove from heat; stir in chocolate pieces until melted. Add marshmallow creme and vanilla; beat until well-blended. Spread over crust. Cool at room temperature. Cut into squares. Makes 5 pounds.

CANDY

HONEY-BUTTER POPCORN

When school vacation arrives and the weather is keeping the young-sters indoors, make some honey-butter popcorn to keep them busy.

10 cups freshly popped corn
 1 cup coarsely chopped peanuts
⅓ cup butter
⅓ cup honey

Preheat oven to 325°. Combine popcorn and nuts in a large mixing bowl. Heat butter and honey in small saucepan, stirring frequently, until butter is melted. Gradually pour over popcorn mixture. Mix until well combined. Spread mixture evenly in an unbuttered jelly roll pan, 15x10x1-inch. Bake about 20 minutes, stirring two or three times, until mixture is golden. Cool in pan on wire rack. Break into small pieces. Store in airtight container at room temperature.

RUTH'S DIVINITY FUDGE

Divinity fudge is a good addition to a box of mixed candy, but be sure to put each piece in an individual paper or foil cup to keep it from coming in contact with other candies in the box. All fudges and soft candies benefit from this treatment in a box of mixed sweets.

4½ cups sugar
 ¾ cup white Karo syrup
 1 cup minus 2 tablespoons cold water
1½ teaspoons pure vanilla
 ⅛ teaspoon salt
 ½ cup egg whites (at room temperature)
 1 to 1½ cups chopped walnut or pecan meats

In saucepan, combine sugar, syrup, water and salt; stir over heat until syrup boils, then cook without stirring until the thermometer reaches 234° (soft ball stage). When syrup begins to boil cease stir-ring; wipe down sides of the pan with a wet cloth to remove sugar crystals that form. Beat egg whites until stiff with mixer at high speed. Slowly pour in half of the boiling syrup with mixer at high speed, beating until thoroughly mixed. Boil remaining syrup until candy thermometer reaches 280° (hard ball). Pour syrup slowly in thin stream over egg white mixture, beating at high speed. Add vanilla and beat until thoroughly mixed. Remove beater. Add chopped nut meats. Beat with spoon until candy loses its gloss and holds shape when dropped from a spoon. Pour quickly into 9x13x2-inch pan to cool.

MOLASSES POPCORN BALLS

These popcorn balls may be made a day or two ahead and kept at room temperature, each in a sandwich bag. They are a great treat for Halloween, or a good item for a church fair food table.

10 quarts of popped corn
1 cup molasses
¼ teaspoon salt
1 cup sugar
2 tablespoons butter or margarine

In a saucepan combine the sugar, salt, molasses and butter or margarine. Cook slowly while popping the corn. Pop the corn, turn onto a large pan and pick out the unpopped kernels; measure the corn into a large pan or 16-quart kettle. When the molasses mixture becomes brittle when tested in a cup of cold water, pour it over the popped corn, stirring all the while to coat the corn. (It's much easier when two people are working together.) Work quickly to form into balls as the syrup cools rapidly. Makes 28 large or 36 medium popcorn balls.

CHOCOLATE FUDGE

A pan of chocolate fudge will add to the dessert tray. The candy can be made a week ahead and "ripened" in a closed tin box. Wrap the candy, uncut, in aluminum foil and keep in covered tin until needed.

2 cups sugar
2 squares baking chocolate
2 tablespoons light corn syrup
⅔ cup milk
2 tablespoons butter
1 teaspoon vanilla
¾ to 1 cup broken walnut meats

In saucepan combine sugar, chocolate, milk and corn syrup. If the chocolate is cut into coarse pieces it will melt easily in the mixture. Cook slowly at first to melt chocolate; increase heat and cook, stirring constantly, until the candy thermometer reaches 236°, or when a bit of the candy forms a soft ball when dropped into cold water. Remove from the heat and add butter, without stirring. Allow candy to sit until thermometer reads 110°. Remove thermometer; add vanilla and beat until candy begins to hold shape and loses its glossy look. Add nut meats and mix. Pour into a lightly buttered 8 x 8-inch pan. Cool and cut in squares.

CHOCOLATE PRALINES

1½ cups sugar
1½ cups packed light brown sugar
 6 tablespoons unsweetened cocoa
 1 cup light cream
 6 tablespoons butter
 1 teaspoon vanilla extract
 2 cups coarsely broken pecans

Line two cookie sheets with wax paper; set aside. In heavy 3-quart saucepan combine sugar, brown sugar, cocoa and light cream. Cook over medium heat, stirring constantly, until mixture boils. Reduce heat to low; cook, stirring occasionally, to 234⁰ (soft ball stage) or until syrup, when dropped into very cold water, forms soft ball which flattens when removed from water. Remove from heat. Add butter and vanilla. Do not stir. Cool at room temperature to 160⁰. Add pecans. Beat with wooden spoon just until mixture begins to thicken (about 1 to 2 minutes), but is still glossy. Quickly drop by teaspoonsful onto prepared cookie sheets. Cool. Store tightly covered or wrap individually in plastic wrap. Makes about 3 dozen candies.

ALMOND BUTTER CRUNCH

Before starting to make this candy, have all ingredients ready. This candy cooks and cools rapidly.

½ cup butter (1 stick) NO SUBSTITUTE!
 1 cup chopped, toasted almonds
 1 cup sugar
 2 cups (12 oz. package) chocolate bits, melted
   Chopped almonds for topping

Lightly toast almonds, blanched or unblanched, in a slow oven, 250⁰. Cool. Put through medium blade of food chopper. Measure ½ cup of almonds; set aside. In saucepan, mix sugar and butter. Stir and cook over high heat until mixture melts and becomes a brown liquid; do not burn. Stir constantly. When mixture is liquid and "smokes" it is nearly ready to remove from heat. Add ½ cup chopped almonds. Stir quickly and pour onto buttered marble or cookie sheet; spread to ⅛-inch thickness. Mark in squares. Have ready in double boiler the chocolate which has been melted over warm, not hot, water. Spread chocolate over candy and sprinkle with chopped almonds. Cool until chocolate hardens; with a spatula, flop candy over and repeat with chocolate and nuts. Break candy into pieces when cold. Makes about 1¼ pounds.

ZELMA'S CHOCOLATE CARAMELS

½ pound (8 squares) baking chocolate
3 cups brown sugar (1 pound box)
3cups granulated sugar
1 bottle light Karo syrup (1 pound)
½ pound butter
1 pint cream
4 tablespoons vanilla
1½ cups nut meats, coarsely chopped

In a heavy kettle, combine chocolate, sugars, syrup, butter and cream. Mix well. Cook, stirring constantly, until the temperature of 248° is reached on the candy thermometer. Remove thermometer. Stir in vanilla. Add nut meats or sprinkle nut meats in a buttered pan and pour caramel over them. As this makes a large batch of caramels, pecan meats may be sprinkled in one pan, walnuts in another. Toasted almonds may be used. This makes a 17x7x1-9nch pan, plus a bread tin of candy, or two 8-inch square pans plus a bread tin. Cool until very firm. Cut in ¾-inch squares. Wrap in wax paper.

CARAMELS

Close attention and about 1½ hours of cooking time result in one of the finest candies. Nuts may be omitted.

3 cups sugar
4 cups heavy cream
½ cup milk
1 bottle (1 pound) light corn syrup
1½ cups walnut or pecan meats
1 tablespoon vanilla

In a heavy kettle, combine sugar, corn syrup and 1½ cups cream. Cook to 232° on candy thermometer. Remove thermometer and stir in 1½ cups cream and milk mixed; replace thermometer and again cook to 232°. Remove from heat; remove thermometer and add remaining 1½ cups of cream and milk mixture. Replace thermometer and cook to 242°, stirring constantly. Remove from heat, remove thermometer, stir in vanilla and nut meats. Pour into buttered pans. A pan 17x7x1-inch will take one batch of caramels, or two 8-inch square pans. Cool until very firm. Remove from pan. Cut with a sharp knife. Wrap individually in wax paper.

MARCIA'S SUGARED PECANS

1 stick (½ cup) butter or margarine
1 pound pecan halves, unsalted
1 cup sugar
2 unbeaten egg whites
¼ teaspoon salt

Melt butter in a 10x15-inch jelly roll pan in an oven preheated to 325°. In mixing bowl, stir together egg whites, sugar and salt. Stir in pecans until well-coated. Spread pecans evenly in melted butter. Bake about 45 minutes, stirring every 10 minutes. Remove nuts to cool on a brown paper bag or paper towels, spreading nuts with two forks. Store in refrigerator in airtight container.

FONDANT

2 cups sugar
⅛ teaspoon cream of tartar
1 cup water

Combine sugar, cream of tartar and water in a saucepan. Stir until mixture starts to boil, then do not stir, but wipe sides of pan with a wet cloth to keep free of sugar crystals. Cook to soft ball stage or 236° on the candy thermometer. Pour onto a water-rinsed platter. (Do not scrape pan.) When cool to the touch, beat with a fondant paddle or spatula until mixture is creamy and holds shape. Shape into forms for dipping in chocolate or for stuffing dates. If flavoring is added, add just before beating.

MAINE POTATO CANDY

¾ cup mashed potatoes
4 cups confectioners' sugar
4 cups shredded coconut
1½ teaspoons vanilla
½ teaspoon salt
4 squares baking chocolate

Mix mashed potatoes (plain mashed, no seasonings or milk) and confectioners' sugar. Stir in coconut, vanilla and salt; blend well. Press into buttered pan so that candy is about ½-inch in depth. Melt chocolate over warm, not hot, water. (Too hot water causes melted chocolate to have white streaks when it hardens.) Pour chocolate over candy. Cool and cut in squares. For variation, make haystacks by forming coconut mixture into cones about 1-inch high. Allow to stand for 20 minutes. Dip base of each cone in melted chocolate, to cover cone up to ¼ inch. Place on wax paper until candy hardens.

DORIS LADD'S WHITE CANDY KISSES

4 cups sugar
1 cup hot water
¼ cup vinegar
¼ teaspoon cream of tartar
¼ cup butter
½ teaspoon vanilla

Combine sugar, water, vinegar and cream of tartar in a saucepan. Cover and cook for 3 minutes without stirring. Remove cover and cook, without stirring, to 286° on candy thermometer. Add butter; do not stir; pour candy onto buttered platter. Add vanilla. As candy cools, turn edges of candy to center, working in vanilla. Pick up cooled candy and pull until very white and stiff. Cut in 1-inch pieces. Wrap each piece in wax paper. Flavors suggested in place of vanilla: oil of cinnamon, oil of clove, oil of wintergreen or peppermint. A few drops of food coloring may be added.

Index

225

Sandwiches and Fillings

Soups and Chowders

T

V

Vegetables

and Cheese Sauce, 155; Cucumbers in Sour Cream, 159; Ginger Glazed Carrots and Apples, 155; Red Cabbage, 162; Sauteed Onions, 158; Savory Squash, 162; Savory Stuffed Potatoes, 159; Scalloped Sweet Spanish Onions, 161; Stovies, 160; Stuffed Onion Bernese, 156; Succotash, 157; Sweet and Tart Gingered Carrots, 164; Tomato Scallop, 157; Vegetable Medley, 158.
Virginia's Molasses Peanut Butter Cookies, 188

W
Walnut Crunch Bread, 70
Walnut Rhubarb Bread, 78
Welsh Rabbit, 110
Winter Salad, 27

Y
Yeast Breads
All-Bran Refrigerator Rolls, 58; Anadama Bread, 60; Basic White Bread, 57; Brioches, 64; Burlap Bread, 58; Butterhorn Rolls, 65; Cherry Cinnamon Swirl Bread, 63; Cinnamon Rolls, 57; Danish Pastry, 54; Doris's Yeast Rolls, 62; Fifty-Five-Minute Rolls, 62; Fruit-Filled Twists, 55; Garlic-Buttered French Bread, 59; Holiday Fruit Bread, 66; Horseshoe Rolls, 55; Mildred's Oatmeal Bread, 65; Oat Bran Loaf, 60; Pecan Nut Rolls, 56; Pineapple Upside-Down Rolls, 61; Shredded Wheat Bread, 61; Sour Dough Bread, 53; Sour Dough Starter, 53; Squash Yeast Bread, 59; Sweet Rolls, 56.

Z
Zelma's Chocolate Caramels, 219
Zippy Lemon Chili Dip for Fish, 44
Zucchini Bread, 71
Zucchini-Carrot Casserole, 105

HELPFUL HINTS FROM BROWNIE'S KITCHEN

Many Mainers would call these hints "string savers," an old term for this and that. You, too, may know many ideas or hints that mean a saving when you are cooking.

● When preparing chicken, crabmeat, tuna or lobster for a salad or sandwich filling, cut the cooked food into sizes for the purpose and add about one tablespoon of fresh lemon juice per cup of mixture. Mix, cover and refrigerate overnight. When ready to use, add mayonnaise, salt and pepper to season.

● If you're squeezing a lemon for just a small amount of juice, squeeze all the juice out of the lemon and freeze what you don't use. Lemons don't keep well once they are cut, and this will eliminate waste.

● A few drops of fresh onion juice will brighten up many foods, such as sandwich fillings. To get the juice of the onion without any of the pulp, peel and cut the onion crossways, and scrape the cut surface with a sharp knife. A second or third cut may be needed. Reserve the slices of onion to use in salads, soups, stews or other food.

● For easy removal of quick breads or cake from the baking pan, lightly grease the bottom of the pan, then insert a piece of wax paper cut to fit in the bottom. Lightly grease the paper. After baking cool for ten minutes, turn the food out of the pan and peel off the paper.

● When removing quick breads, cake or yeast breads from the freezer, leave them fully wrapped until completely thawed, to prevent moisture loss.

● Before doubling a recipe read the directions; some foods do not take to this treatment. This is especially true of jams and jellies when using liquid or powdered pectin. Instead, make the recipe twice—you may save time and ingredients, and will have more predictable results.

● Small sprigs of parsley placed on a tray of sandwiches will do a lot to dress up the table at any function.

● After stuffing your roasting chicken, lace up the bird with unwaxed dental floss. The floss is equally good for tying the legs together.

● Many homemakers use the foil wrap from margarine quarters to grease their baking pans.

● Smoked turkey ham, ground with onion and green pepper and seasoned with Dijon-style mustard and pickle relish, makes a sandwich filling with less fat and a fine flavor.

● Toasted, coarsely chopped pecan meats added to chicken salad gives an extra touch to sandwich filling, when combined with mayonnaise and black pepper.

● When making coffee in quantity in 35- or 45-cup percolators, and the red light indicates the coffee is ready, draw a pitcher of the coffee and pour it back into the top of the pot; repeat this step. This blends the coffee. Taste the coffee and if it's too strong, another quart or two of boiling water may be added. It does make a difference.

● When baking, have all ingredients at room temperature for best results. Egg whites whip to a larger volume at room temperature than if taken directly from the refrigerator.

● When baking a cake, if you do not have the exact size pan called for, use your grade school math. Multiply the length and width of the pan called for to determine the number of square inches you need to fill. Then find the pan you have that is closest to size, even though it may not be the same shape.